DATE			

**Business/Science/Technology
Division**

CHILTON'S REPAIR & TUNE-UP GUIDE FOR SNOWMOBILES 1976-80

Walter J. Niesen

Arctic Cat ● John Deere ● Polaris ● Ski-Doo ● Yamaha

Managing Editor KERRY A. FREEMAN, S.A.E.
Senior Editor RICHARD J. RIVELE, S.A.E.

President WILLIAM A. BARBOUR
Executive Vice President JAMES A. MIADES
Vice President and General Manager JOHN P. KUSHNERICK

CHILTON BOOK COMPANY
Radnor, Pennsylvania
19089

SAFETY NOTICE

Proper service and repair procedures are vital to the safe, reliable operation of all motor vehicles, as well as the personal safety of those performing repairs. This book outlines procedures for servicing and repairing vehicles using safe, effective methods. The procedures contain many NOTES, CAUTIONS and WARNINGS which should be followed along with standard safety procedures to eliminate the possibility of personal injury or improper service which could damage the vehicle or compromise its safety.

It is important to note that repair procedures and techniques, tools and parts for servicing motor vehicles, as well as the skill and experience of the individual performing the work vary widely. It is not possible to anticipate all of the conceivable ways or conditions under which vehicles may be serviced, or to provide cautions as to all of the possible hazards that may result. Standard and accepted safety precautions and equipment should be used when handling toxic or flammable fluids, and safety goggles or other protection should be used during cutting, grinding, chiseling, prying, or any other process that can cause material removal or projectiles.

Some procedures require the use of tools specially designed for a specific purpose. Before substituting another tool or procedure, you must be completely satisfied that neither your personal safety, nor the performance of the vehicle will be endangered.

Although information in this guide is based on industry sources and is as complete as possible at the time of publication, the possibility exists that the manufacturer made later changes which could not be included here. While striving for total accuracy, Chilton Book Company cannot assume responsibility for any errors, changes, or omissions that may occur in the compilation of this data.

PART NUMBERS

Part numbers listed in this reference are not recommendations by Chilton for any product by brand name. They are references that can be used with interchange manuals and aftermarket supplier catalogs to locate each brand supplier's discrete part number.

Copyright © 1980 by Walter J. Niesen
All Rights Reserved
Published in Radnor, Pa. by Chilton Book Company
and simultaneously in Ontario, Canada
by Nelson Canada, Limited

Manufactured in the United States of America
1234567890   9876543210

Chilton's Repair & Tune-Up Guide: Snowmobiles 1976–80
Walter J. Niesen
ISBN 0-8019-6978-6 pbk.
Library of Congress Catalog Card No. 80-66510

Contents

1

General Information and Maintenance

INTRODUCTION

Snowmobiles are generally considered to be recreational vehicles even though a number of owners rely on them for transportation during the winter months. Whether sport or transportation, however, the snowmobile must be a reliable machine to ensure that you can drive back, rather then walk, from wherever the machine may carry you. The subjects of maintenance and repair, then, are far more important when applied to a snowmobile than to most other recreational vehicles—your very life may well depend on the machine's performance.

The snowmobile engineers and designers have done a thorough job of simplifying the machinery to help reduce the number of potential mechanical problems. The engines in all of the machines in this book, for example, are either two-strokes or Wankel rotary engines. There are no camshafts, tappets, or valves like those in most automobiles to complicate the maintenance and repair. The simplified automatic transmission systems, the suspension and the steering are equally as simple and effective in design. All of these components, however, are engineered to operate within certain tolerances and, when those tolerances are exceeded through wear or abuse, the machine must receive some at-

tention if you expect it to continue to operate reliably. This book explains how to measure and check all of the machine's parts to see if they need adjustment or replacement and how to restore the various parts to proper working order. This chapter and the second chapter cover various parts and procedures which are common to all snowmobiles in order to avoid repetition in the chapters on each specific brand. You should read these first two chapters before turning to the chapter which applies to your particular brand and model.

The specifications and procedures cited in this book are the ones most generally accepted by professionals who repair and maintain snowmobiles. The majority of these methods can be accomplished with standard American tools. Special tools are cited where needed, and can generally be obtained from your local dealer. If, at any time, there is confusion with a procedure, consult your local dealer or authorized maintenance manual for your specific model.

GENERAL CARE AND MAINTENANCE

The simplest method of discovering, preventing, and correcting a mechanical failure before it can cause inconvenience or serious damage is periodic, systematic inspection and lubrication. (See unit section lubrication chart.) It should be noted that the specific maintenance and lubrication charts included in this book are based on "average" operating conditions. Under severe usage or continuous heavy-duty or high-speed operation, both inspection and lubrication should be more frequent. (Refer to specific unit chapter for maintenance details.)

OFF-SEASON STORAGE

For the snowmobile, out-of-season storage is a battle to keep rust and corrosion from attacking the machine. The corrosive forces which can attack an incorrectly stored unit are sufficient to cause irreparable damage which will lead to added repair costs. Anyone can see the necessity of sufficiently preparing the snowmobile for storage. This process is as follows:

1. Close the fuel tank shut-off valve and run the engine until it stops. (If the tank is not fitted with a valve, siphon the tank and run the machine until the engine stops.) Fuel must be removed from the tank and carburetor to prevent the formation of gum (varnish).

2. Siphon all possible fuel from the tank.

3. Remove the spark plug wire(s), making sure that the ignition is turned off.

NOTE: *Mark these wires to prevent confusion when they are reconnected.*

4. Remove the spark plugs. Spray approximately one ounce of a rust preventive lubricant or light engine oil into each spark plug hole.

5. Turn the engine over several times to distribute the lubricant in each cylinder.

6. Reinstall the spark plugs and plug wires.

7. Remove the variable-speed drive belt. Wipe the belt contact surface of the driven sheave with light oil to prevent it from rusting.

8. Ease the track tension. (Refer to the specific model section for the procedure.)

9. By placing the vehicle on stand, or supporting it in a similar manner, release its weight from the track.

10. Thoroughly clean the snowmobile, including the engine. Apply a thin coat of light oil to the bottom of the skis and also to such items as the ski pivots, steering spindle bushings, etc.

11. Remove the battery and store it. (Refer to battery testing and maintenance procedures.)

12. Follow the periodic maintenance recommendations and thoroughly lube the machine.

PLACING SNOWMOBILE BACK IN OPERATION

In returning the snowmobile to active service, it is necessary to clean the lubricant from those parts which were stationary during storage. The driven sheave surfaces must be cleaned and the drive belt must be reinstalled.

The final steps before the initial start are the addition of fresh fuel, the opening of the fuel shut-off valve (if the vehicle is so equipped), and the reinstallation of the battery.

TWO-STROKE ENGINE OPERATION

Each cylinder of a snowmobile's two-stroke engine has mainly three moving parts: the piston (which moves up and down), the crankshaft (which revolves) and the connecting rod (which connects the piston to the crankshaft). A two or three-cylinder two-stroke engine has two or three times as many pistons and connecting rods as a single-cylinder engine, but just one crankshaft. A basic understanding of the simple operating cycle (sometimes two-strokes are called "two-cycles") of the two-stroke engine will help you to better comprehend what is right or what is wrong with the engine.

The carburetor on any two-stroke engine feeds its mixture of fuel and air into the crankcase rather then directly into the combustion chamber. Some engine designs mount the carburetor on the side of the cylinder and others mount the carburetor directly on the crankcase. The upward path of the piston creates a vacuum inside the crankcase which draws the fuel and air from the carburetor into the crankcase. Some engines use a reed valve with spring-like flat petals to control the flow of fuel and air into the crankcase—the same vacuum which pulls the

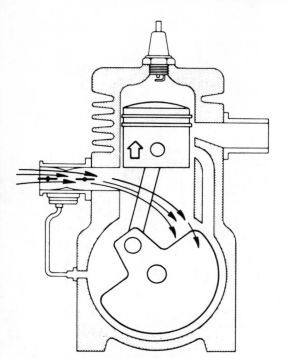

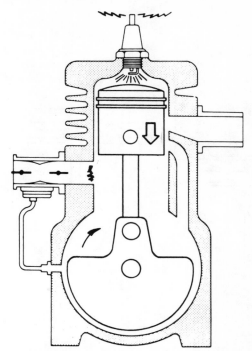

Fuel and air mixture is delivered to crank case below the piston

Spark plug ignites the fuel and air mixture from the previous cycle

fuel and air in opens the reed valve's petals. The petals are normally closed with their built-in self-springing pressure. Other types of two-stroke engines have a hole, or "port," leading from the carburetor to the crankcase with the hole near the bottom of the cylinder bore. The side or "skirt" of the piston opens and closes this intake port as the piston moves up and down in the cylinder. When the bottom edge of the piston skirt reaches the bottom edge of the intake port, the port is just beginning to open; it is fully open about the time the piston reaches the top of its stroke.

A "charge" of fresh fuel and air has been transferred into the combustion chamber at the same time that the intake port is being opened by the piston. This mixture of fuel and air is compressed inside the combustion chamber and, just a fraction of an inch before the piston reaches the top of its stroke (Top Dead Center), the spark plug sparks to begin to burn the charge of fuel and air. The fuel and air begin to burn and expand at a predetermined rate so that their maximum rate of expansion is reached just as the piston swings over top dead center and begins its path downward. The expanding fuel and air which have been ignited by the spark plug then push the piston on down the cylinder to pro-

duce the engine's power. Notice that the fuel and all mixture does *not* explode, but burns. The whole process occurs in just an instant, however, so the sound is like that of an explosion when heard from the tip of an unmuffled exhaust pipe. The burning effect, rather than an explosive effect, is why the spark is timed to fire just *before* the piston reaches top dead center.

The exhaust port, in a two-stroke engine, is also located in the wall of the cylinder bore. This port is located about two-thirds of the way down the cylinder bore so that the piston can move about an inch or so before the top (crown) of the piston begins to uncover the exhaust port. This small amount of movement gives the burning and expanding fuel and air just enough time to expend most of their energy before being forced out of the exhaust port under their own pressure. The design of the exhaust system produces an additional blocking effect on these exhausting gases.

There are at least two additional ports or holes in the walls of the cylinder bore of a two-stroke engine. These ports are called "transfer ports" because they transfer the fresh fuel and air mixture from the crankcase below the piston to the combustion chamber above the piston. The transfer ports are actu-

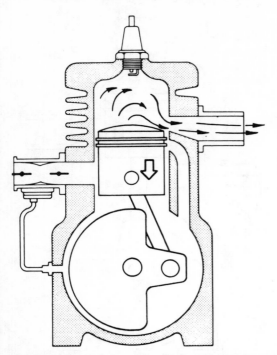

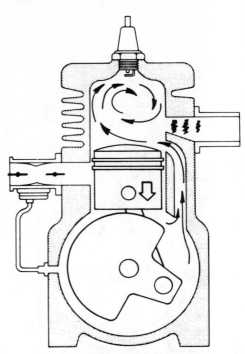

As piston travels down the cylinder bore it opens the exhaust port

Fuel and air is transferred from the crankcase to the combustion chamber

ally located on the sides of the cylinder walls about 90 degrees from the exhaust and intake ports' centerlines. The crown of the piston uncovers the transfer ports just a few fractions of an inch (or fractions of a second) after the exhaust port is uncovered (opened). The shape and angle of the transfer ports directs the fresh fuel and air away from the exhaust port and upward so that very little of this fresh charge is pushed out the exhaust pipe with the previously burned fuel and air charge. The design of the exhaust system, again, helps to keep the fresh fuel and air charge in the cylinder. The downward path

of the piston reduces the volume of the area in the crankcase to compress the fresh fuel and air so that it is forced up the transfer ports and into the combustion chamber above the piston.

The spark plug fires and produces a power "stroke" every time the piston rises and falls (one complete turn of the crankshaft). The upward path of the piston is called a "stroke" and the downward path a "stroke" to explain the use of the term "two-stroke."

The exhaust system on any modern two-stroke engine contains a bulge which looks like a muffler. This bulge allows the exhaust

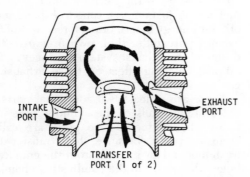

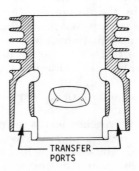

Cutaway shows fuel air path and transfer ports

to expand temporarily and to bounce off the walls of the chamber (often called an "expansion chamber"). That bounce of the exhaust and its sound waves is directed all the way back up the exhaust pipe to the combustion chamber. The pressure from that bounce-back exhaust is what helps to keep the fresh charge of fuel and air from the transfer ports from escaping with the exhausting burned charge of fuel and air. The exact shape and length of that expansion chamber are extremely critical to ensure that the timing of the backpressure exactly coincides with the opening of the transfer ports. Some form of secondary muffler is fitted to the end of the exhaust pipe or wrapped directly over the expansion chamber to muffle the exterior sound level of the exhaust system. Any change in the muffler system of a two-stroke engine, then, will affect the timing and often reduce the amount of power the engine will produce. Removing the muffler, or any part of it, might make the machine noisier, but don't mistake that extra noise for extra power.

Troubleshooting

This general troubleshooting chart is arranged in the order of most likely occurrence. It must be noted, however, that this is a *general chart*. To obtain full details, refer to the specific book section for complete repair procedures.

ENGINE RUNS ERRATICALLY

Condition	Check for	What to Do
1. Won't idle or idle smoothly	a. Carburetor maladjusted	a. Adjust correctly
	b. Fouled or wrong type spark plugs	b. Replace
	c. Lack of fuel	
	d. Air leak in carburetor and/or intake manifold	d. Repair or replace
	e. Engine overheated	
	f. Faulty fuel primer check valve	f. Repair or replace
	g. Loose cylinder head and/or blown head gasket	g. Repair or replace
	h. Crankcase vacuum leak	h. Repair leak
	i. Plugged or wrong type exhaust system	i. Repair or replace
2. Low-speed miss	a. Carburetor maladjusted	a. Adjust correctly
	b. Fouled or wrong type spark plugs	b. Replace
	c. Lack of fuel	
	d. Air leak in carburetor and/or intake manifold	d. Repair or replace
	e. Faulty high-tension lead and/or spark plug	e. Repair or replace
	f. Faulty magneto component(s)	f. Repair or replace
	g. Faulty low-speed stator winding	g. Replace stator
	h. Short circuit in wiring harness	h. Repair or replace
	i. Faulty ignition coil	i. Replace
	j. Faulty trigger coil	j. Replace
	k. Faulty fuel primer check valve	k. Repair or replace
	l. Crankcase vacuum leak	l. Repair leak
	m. Faulty switch box	m. Replace
3. High-speed miss	a. Faulty high-speed stator winding	a. Replace stator
	b. Voltage leak at white starter lockout switch terminal	b. Repair or replace
4. Poor acceleration or loss of power	a. Carburetor maladjusted	a. Adjust correctly
	b. Lack of fuel	
	c. Air leak in carburetor and/or intake manifold	c. Repair or replace
	d. Incorrect ignition timing and/or ignition advance lever not positioned properly	d. Re-time engine or position lever correctly
	e. Drive clutch malfunctioning	e. Repair or replace
	f. Faulty high-speed stator winding	f. Replace stator
	g. Voltage leak at white starter lockout switch terminal	g. Repair or replace
	h. Engine overheating	

Troubleshooting (cont.)

ENGINE RUNS ERRATICALLY

Condition	Check for	What to Do
4. Poor acceleration or loss of power	i. Loose cylinder head and/or blown head gasket j. Crankcase vacuum leak k. Low compression l. Loose, wrong type, or plugged exhaust system	i. Repair or replace j. Repair leak k. Repair l. Repair or replace
5. Surges, backfires, and loses speed	a. Carburetor maladjusted b. Lack of fuel c. Faulty high-tension lead and/or spark plug d. Faulty high-speed stator winding e. Improper ignition timing and/or ignition advance lever not positioned properly f. Drive clutch malfunctioning g. Voltage leak at starter lockout switch terminal h. Air leak in carburetor and/or intake manifold i. Engine overheating j. Crankcase vacuum leak k. Loose, wrong type, or plugged exhaust system	a. Adjust correctly c. Repair or replace d. Replace stator e. Re-time engine or position lever correctly f. Repair or replace g. Repair or replace h. Repair or replace j. Repair leak k. Repair or replace

VEHICLE LIGHTS DO NOT OPERATE PROPERLY

Condition	Check for	What to Do
1. Headlamp(s) and/or taillamps(s)	a. Light switch off or faulty b. Burned out lamps c. Dead battery d. Wrong type bulbs e. Short circuit and/or faulty connection in wiring harness f. Headlight and/or taillight harness disconnected g. Faulty generator coil or stator h. Faulty light regulator	a. Turn on or replace b. Replace c. Charge d. Replace e. Repair or replace f. Connect g. Replace h. Replace
2. Intermittent lights	Short circuit and/or faulty connection in wiring harness	Repair or replace
3. Premature lamp failure	a. Wrong type bulb b. Cracked or broken, caused by vibration and/or improper mounting c. Short circuit and/or faulty connection in wiring harness d. Faulty light regulator e. Faulty generator coil or stator	a. Replace b. Replace and properly install new lamps c. Repair or replace d. Replace e. Replace

ABNORMAL PERFORMANCE AND HANDLING CHARACTERISTICS

Condition	Check for	What to Do
1. Engine runs but vehicle does not move	a. Track and/or skis frozen to ground b. Worn or broken drive belt c. Track binding, due to incorrect adjustment and/or plugged with foreign material d. Loose or broken drive chain and/or sprockets e. Inoperative drive or driven sheave assembly f. Broken driveshaft and/or drive sprockets	a. Free track and/or skis b. Replace c. Adjust or clean d. Repair or replace e. Repair or replace f. Replace

Troubleshooting (cont.)

ABNORMAL PERFORMANCE AND HANDLING CHARACTERISTICS

Condition	Check for	What to Do
2. Poor vehicle acceleration	a. Track binding, due to incorrect adjustment and/or plugged with foreign material	a. Adjust or clean
	b. Worn and/or slipping drive belt	b. Replace
	c. Drive and/or driven sheave not functioning properly	c. Repair or replace
	d. Sprocket ratio not suited to operating conditions	d. Replace
	e. Improperly adjusted brake	e. Adjust
	f. Improperly adjusted throttle	f. Adjust
3. Vehicle does not develop normal speeds	a. Track binding, due to incorrect adjustment and/or plugged with foreign material	a. Adjust or clean
	b. Worn and/or slipping drive belt	b. Replace
	c. Drive and/or driven sheave not functioning properly	c. Repair or replace
	d. Sprocket ratio not suited to operating conditions	d. Replace
	e. Improperly adjusted brake	e. Adjust
	f. Improperly adjusted throttle	f. Adjust
	g. Improperly adjusted drive chain	g. Adjust
	h. Bogie wheel set inverted and/or faulty bogie wheel bearing	h. Repair or replace
	i. Also refer to "Engine runs erratically"	
4. Vehicle does not maintain normal speeds	a. Track binding, due to incorrect adjustment and/or plugged with foreign material	a. Adjust or clean
	b. Drive and/or driven sheave not functioning properly	b. Repair or replace
	c. Also refer to "Engine Runs Erratically"	
5. Unusual handling and/or rough riding	a. Foreign material on bottom of skis	a. Clean
	b. Wear skeg worn or broken	b. Replace
	c. Loose steering system components	c. Repair or replace
	d. Improper ski alignment	d. Align
	e. Bogie wheel sets inverted and/or Missing bogie wheel	e. Repair or replace
	f. Broken rear axle and/or suspension springs	f. Replace

NO START

Condition	Check for	What to Do
1. Lack of fuel or excessive fuel	a. Fuel tank empty	a. Replenish fuel supply
	b. Fuel shut-off valve closed	b. Open fuel shut-off valve
	c. Carburetor maladjusted or inlet needle stuck	c. Adjust to specifications
	d. Improper use of choke and/or fuel primer	d. Check service manual for proper use
	e. Plugged fuel filter(s) or fuel cap vent	e. Clean or replace
	f. Leaking fuel line or connections	f. Repair or replace
	g. Pinched or kinked fuel line	g. Eliminate pinch or kink
	h. Leaking diaphragm—fuel pump or carburetor	h. Replace
	i. Faulty fuel primer system	i. Repair or replace
	j. Water in fuel	j. Drain fuel system and refill
	k. Crankcase vacuum leak	k. Repair leak

Troubleshooting (cont.)

NO START

Condition	Check for	What to Do
2. No spark—weak or intermittent spark	a. Ignition switch "off" b. Emergency stop switch "off" c. Faulty or wrong type spark plugs d. High-tension leads reversed e. Faulty ignition switch and/or wiring f. Faulty high-tension lead wire and/or spark plug g. Incorrect ignition timing h. Faulty magneto component(s) i. Faulty stator j. Faulty or maladjusted trigger coil k. Faulty ignition coil l. Faulty switch box m. Faulty flywheel and/or fan magneto	a. Turn on ignition switch b. Turn on stop switch c. Replace d. Switch leads around e. Repair or replace f. Repair or replace g. Re-time engine h. Repair or replace i. Repair or replace j. Repair or replace k. Replace l. Replace m. Replace flywheel
3. Rewind and/or electric starter inoperative	a. Broken rewind rope and/or spring b. Rewind starter does not engage c. Battery faulty or not fully charged d. Poor battery cable connections e. Faulty ignition switch and/or wiring f. Faulty starter solenoid g. Faulty starter h. Faulty starter lockout switch and/or starter protector i. Faulty forward/reverse switch j. Faulty voltage regulator and/or rectifier k. Faulty stator or generator coil	a. Repair or replace b. Repair or replace c. Replace or charge battery d. Clean or repair connections e. Repair or replace f. Repair or replace g. Repair or replace h. Replace i. Replace j. Replace k. Replace
4. Engine overheated	a. Restricted air flow and/or circulation b. Incorrect ignition timing c. Wrong type spark plug d. Faulty fan and/or fan belt e. Carb too lean f. Fuel pump	a. Eliminate restriction b. Re-time engine c. Replace d. Repair or replace e. Repair or replace f. Repair or replace

GENERAL TUNE-UP

A periodic tune-up will ensure reliability and good performance from the snowmobile. It is important that a thorough sequence of tune-up procedure be followed in order that no important step be forgotten. It should be noted, once again, that this is a general outline. For the specifics of each step, consult the appropriate section of the desired model.

A recommended sequence for a general tune-up is to check:
1. Compression
2. Fuel System
3. Ignition and Electrical System
4. Lighting System
5. Drive System
6. Suspension and Track
7. Test Run

Compression

Taking a compression test consists of removing the spark plugs and noting which came from which cylinder (in multi-cylinder engines) in order to aid in troubleshooting. Install a compression gauge in the spark plug hole. (Use a compression gauge with at least 225 psi.) Rotate the engine through at least four compression strokes of the piston to obtain the highest reading. Record the total compression in each cylinder. The maximum variation allowable between cylinders is 15 psi. A variation greater than 15 psi between

cylinder or a reading of 20 lbs lower than the recommended average, indicates that the engine is in need of service.

Fuel System

Recommended manufacturers' procedures consist of removal and inspection of both air and fuel filter elements and the cleaning or replacement of them. Since a lack of fuel is an often overlooked source of trouble, inspection of the fuel lines for leaks and possible kinks is important. Following the fuel flow, remove the carburetor(s) and adjust the float(s). (Refer to Chapter 2.) Reinstall the carburetor, adjust high and low-speed on the carburetor(s), and check the throttle cable, making sure that there is free operation. Re-

move the fuel pump and reinstall it only after the installation of a new diaphram and the appropriate gaskets.

Ignition and Electrical System

The electrical and ignition systems play a most important part in the operation of the snowmobile. Since this is true, frequent routine checks are important to maintain the machine in top running condition. A thorough check of the electrical system includes the removal and examination of spark plugs, with concentration on electrode gap and tip condition. Also included is a visual inspection of the breaker point contact surface for pits or fused metal deposits and an inspection of the electric-start system (if so equipped) for proper operation. Finally, in order for the battery to function at its full potential, electrolyte level should be checked and the terminals should be checked to make sure that they are clean and tight.

> NOTE: *Also check the battery hold-down for tightness but do not tighten the hold-down to the point of distorting the battery case.*

Make a check of the timing and adjust it as necessary.

SPARK PLUG ANALYSIS

It is important to note, in this general electrical section, a spark plug analysis chart because spark plug failure is the most common cause of a snowmobile malfunctioning. In nearly every case of spark plug failure, the cause must be corrected before new or reconditioned spark plugs are installed. Otherwise, servicing will again be needed in a short time.

The spark plug heat range has a very important effect on two-cycle engine performance. A hotter-than-normal plug may be necessary for continuous low-speed operation to prevent spark plug fouling. For long, sustained, cross-country operation or racing,

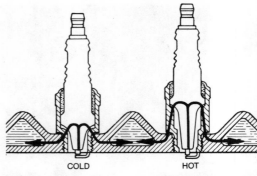

Heat being transferred through a hot and cold spark plug

a colder plug is best because it prevents the engine from overheating.

By varying the construction of the insulator, the spark plug manufacturers are able to vary the heat-dissipating characteristics of a specific plug.

Surface Gap Spark Plugs

Remove the spark plugs and inspect the center electrode. If worn or burned back more than $1/32$ in. (0.8 mm) below the insulator, it will not function properly. Do not replace surface gap plugs for any other reason than this. Be sure that the plugs being replaced are definitely misfiring; the accumulation of deposits can be deceiving.

> CAUTION: *Due to the high voltage requirements with surface gap spark plugs, do not use this type of plug, unless specifically recommended by the manufacturer.*

Surface gap style spark plug

Normal Ignition

Normal ignition occurs when a spark of adequate energy is delivered at the correct instant across the electrode gap. Normal ignition is characterized by a spark plug tip with brown or gray-tan color, few combustion de-

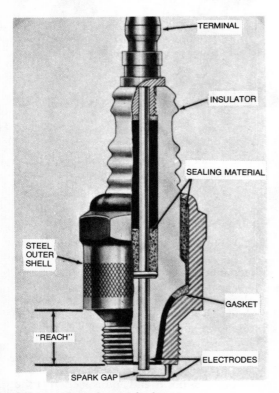

Cutaway view of a spark plug

posits, and with electrodes not burned or eroded.

Regular tip type spark plug

Worn-Out Spark Plug

Eventually, corrosive exhaust gases and high-voltage spark will erode the electrodes. Spark plugs in this condition require more voltage to fire and can cause hard starting and engine misfire. The solution to this is to replace them with new plugs of the proper heat range.

Worn out spark plug

Overheated Spark Plug

This condition is characterized by a spark plug with light gray or chalky-white color, and with excessively burned electrodes. This

Overheated spark plug

can be caused by a carburetor setting that is too lean, air leaks at the intake manifold or carburetor gasket, engine overloading, or clogged exhaust ports. A spark plug with too hot a heat range could be the cause.

Gap-Bridged Spark Plug

This is a spark plug that has been shorted out by combustion deposits fused between the electrodes. This condition is caused by excessive carbon in the cylinder. A rich fuel mixture, improper gasoline/oil mixture, poor quality gasoline or oil, or plugged exhaust ports could be the cause of excess carbon.

Gap Bridged spark plug

Wet-Fouled Spark Plug

Evidence of this condition is a black color and a dark, oily film over the firing end. This is caused by excessive oil in the fuel mixture, a carburetor adjustment that is too rich, too cold a spark plug, or weak ignition output. Excessive idling also could be the trouble.

Wet fouled spark plug

Aluminum Deposit on Spark Plug

A somewhat large deposit of gray metal adhering to the electrodes and plug core characterizes this type of malfunction. The cause

Aluminum throw off on spark plug

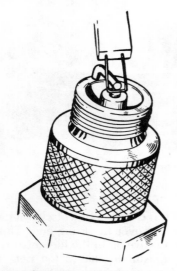

Using a wire type spark plug guage

the piston is at its highest point, known as Top Dead Center (TDC). Retarded timing (ATDC), is the number of degrees of timing after TDC.

Energy Transfer Systems

Energy transfer systems are composed of either breaker points mounted on a stator plate or a capacitive discharge type. The action of the opening and closing of the breaker points regulates the current which is generated by the coil(s). The breaker points are opened and closed by a rotating cam inside the flywheel. The gap between the points is a critical setting. If the setting is too close, the spark will jump across the gap when the points are open. If the point gap is too large, the current is not sufficient to fire the mixture completely.

BREAKER POINT ADJUSTMENT

To adjust the points, find the place where the lift of the flywheel cam opens the points to their widest gap. Check the gap with a feeler-type gauge and, if the points need adjustment, adjust them through the window in the flywheel by loosening the point locknut and by adjusting the points to the correct gap. After adjustment is made, tighten the locknut.

> NOTE: *Always check the gap again, after locking the point set, as tightening may have affected the gap.*

A centrifugal advance mechanism is included in the flywheel. This is used to gain added power and economy at higher rpm. When the engine is running at idle, the spark plug fires at approximately top dead center (TDC). As the engine speed increases, the spring on the advance is overcome and the weight on the advance is thrown outward, rotating the cam lobe. This action causes the ignition system to fire earlier or farther advanced.

Ignition timing on any two-cycle engine with aluminum components must be exact. For this reason, use of a timing gauge which is inserted into the cylinder and shows the exact location of the piston is recommended.

To time the engine, use the following procedure.

1. Remove the recoil starter, starter pulley, and the breaker cover on the flywheel.

2. Hold the centrifugal advance in the advanced position.

3. Being sure that the points are set at specifications, remove the spark plugs and

of this condition is excessive heat in the combustion chamber which melts the piston causing the loose metal to adhere to the plug. This excess heat can be caused by too hot a spark plug, incorrect ignition timing, carbon deposits in the combustion chamber, or a carburetor setting that is too lean.

IGNITION TIMING

The correct ignition timing is of paramount importance to the performance and life of the snowmobile engine. Improper timing can cause misfiring, excess fuel consumption, loss of power, and overheating which may result in severe engine damage, possibly irreparable.

Advanced timing or the number of degrees Before Top Dead Center (BTDC) is the number of degrees the timing is set before

Surface Gap Spark Plug Analysis

NORMAL
Light tan or gray colored deposits indicate good engine and ignition system condition. Electrode wear indicates normal spark rotation.

WORN OUT
Plugs with excessive electrode wear may cause misfire during acceleration or hard starting. Replace with the recommended plug.

COLD FOULED
Wet fuel/oil deposits can be caused by "drowning" with raw fuel mix during cranking, rich carburetion or improper fuel/oil ratios. Weak ignition can also contribute to this condition. Clean or replace.

LOW TEMPERATURE FOULING
Soft, sooty deposits indicate incomplete combustion. Probable causes: rich carburetion; weak ignition; retarded timing or low compression. Continuous low-speed operation or, with oil injection systems, gunning throttle at idle. Clean or replace.

CARBON TRACKING
Electrically conductive deposits on the firing end provide a low-resistance path for the voltage. Carbon tracks are formed and misfire could occur. Plugs should be serviced or replaced.

CHANNELING
Is sometimes incorrectly diagnosed as cracking. Believed to be caused by extreme spark heat. When deposits cover the shallow channels, the rate of insulator erosion is multiplied, the spark is masked and misfire may occur. If so, plugs should be replaced.

CONCENTRATED ARC
Multi-color appearance is a normal condition. Caused by electrical energy consistently following the same firing path. Arc path will change with deposit conductivity and gap erosion.

ALUMINUM THROW-OFF: Danger
Preignition has occurred. Not a plug problem . . . check engine to determine cause and extent of damage. Replace plugs.

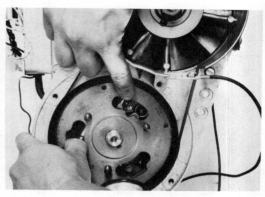

Dial indicator and adaptor installed in spark plug hole

Breaker point adjustments are accessible through flywheel slots

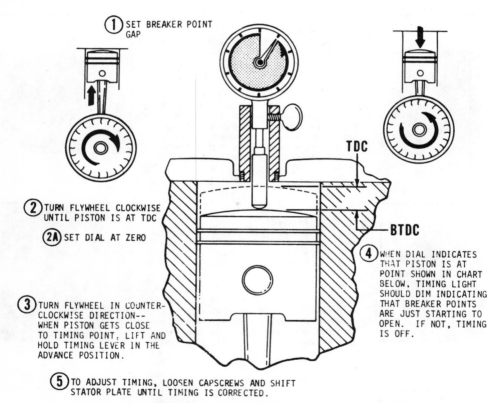

① SET BREAKER POINT GAP

② TURN FLYWHEEL CLOCKWISE UNTIL PISTON IS AT TDC

②A SET DIAL AT ZERO

③ TURN FLYWHEEL IN COUNTER-CLOCKWISE DIRECTION-- WHEN PISTON GETS CLOSE TO TIMING POINT, LIFT AND HOLD TIMING LEVER IN THE ADVANCE POSITION.

TDC

BTDC

④ WHEN DIAL INDICATES THAT PISTON IS AT POINT SHOWN IN CHART BELOW, TIMING LIGHT SHOULD DIM INDICATING THAT BREAKER POINTS ARE JUST STARTING TO OPEN. IF NOT, TIMING IS OFF.

⑤ TO ADJUST TIMING, LOOSEN CAPSCREWS AND SHIFT STATOR PLATE UNTIL TIMING IS CORRECTED.

Finding Top Dead Center (TDC) using a dial indicator

place the timing gauge into the No. 1 cylinder.

4. Using a battery-powered continuity tester, hook one lead of the tester to the wire leading from the No. 1 cyclinder breaker points set and the other lead to a good ground.

5. Rotate the engine by hand and watch the timing gauge. Eventually the needle on the gauge will stop moving in one direction and will begin to move in the other. The exact point where this change takes place is TDC. Place the zero mark on the timing gauge so it aligns with the gauge's needle.

6. From TDC, rotate the engine counterclockwise the specified number of inches to put the timing before TDC. At the specified setting before TDC, the light should

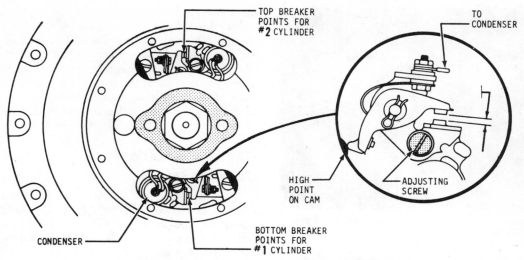

Adjusting points on a breaker point type ignition system

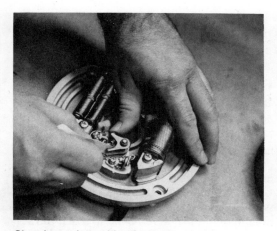

Cleaning points with a business card

begin to flicker. If it does not, make slight adjustments to the point gap.

7. If adjusting the points will not make the test light flicker, reset the points and make adjustments to the stator by rotating it until the light goes out. To check the setting, rotate the engine past the specified setting and turn the engine slowly in the other direction. At the specified setting, the light must begin to flicker.

8. Once the No. 1 cylinder is adjusted correctly, perform the same adjustment on the No. 2 cylinder.

If the light does not flicker, adjust the No. 2 cylinder points only to get the light to flicker. Do not adjust the stator because this will change the timing of the No. 1 cylinder.

Loosen the adjusting screw then set point gap

Capacitor Discharge System

Capacitor discharge systems vary from those mentioned before in that they have no contact points or condensers. The electrical impulse to the spark plug is controlled by a small box usually mounted on the chassis. This box varies the electric current produced by the magnets attached either to the flywheel or to the crankshaft which, when the engine is running, produces this charge.

The only way of checking for a possible malfunction without special test equipment

Some capacitor discharge systems have a timing mark on the flywheel

Loosen adjusting screw on the sending unit

Pry the sending unit into the correctly timed location

is to replace one part at a time. Replace them in the following order; kill switch; control unit; field coils; stator plate; flywheel rotor.

The capacitor discharge systems on most snowmobiles are preset at the factory and cannot be adjusted. Some brands, however, can be adjusted to vary the BTDC ignition timing by loosening a pair of screws and levering the tip of a screwdriver into a slot to move the unit back and forth a fraction of an inch. The specific ignition adjustment sections of each chapter will indicate which type of unit is on your particular machine.

Chassis Electrical
LIGHTING SYSTEM

A general inspection of the lighting system consists of a check of headlight and taillight operation and an adjustment of the headlights if necessary. Visually check the wiring harnesses for wear or chafing points and, with the appropriate equipment, test the wiring to make sure that there are no open or short circuits.

PISTON AND RING REPLACEMENT

Removing the Cylinder Head and Barrel

1. The simple design of the two-stroke engine makes it a relatively easy task to gain access to the piston and rings for replacement or to check them for wear. The cylinder head and the cylinder barrel are instantly accessible on the "free air-cooled" engines; engines with fan-cooling have a metal shroud over the engine that must be removed to reach the actual cylinder head and cylinder barrel. The chapter which applies to your brand of machine will indicate the steps necessary to remove the shrouding pieces from a fan-cooled engine.

2. The engine can remain in the chassis if the crankshaft and connecting rods and their bearings are still within serviceable limits. Failures in these lower end components are extremely rare as long as you remember to add oil to the fuel (or to the oil tank on machines with oil injection style lubrication systems). Generally, the crankshaft and connecting rods and their bearings and seals will last through two or more sets of pistons and piston rings. If the engine is to remain in the chassis, then the various carburetor connections like fuel lines and cables can remain in place and the carburetors can be unbolted from the engine. The air intake silencer box,

on later snowmobiles, will sometimes have to be removed to allow enough free movement so that the carburetors can be pulled back and away from their attaching studs without disconnecting any of the fuel lines or control cables.

3. The complete exhaust system must be removed from most machines. Remove the two or three bolts and, in some cases, the attaching springs which retain the muffler to the snowmobile chassis and to the header pipes which bolt directly to the cylinder barrels. The header pipes can then be unbolted from the cylinders. You may have to tap the side of the header pipe lightly with a rubber or plastic-headed hammer to free the seal at the gasket so that the header pipe can be lifted away.

4. The bolts which retain the cylinder head must be loosened gradually, about one-sixth turn at a time, to relieve the stress on the cylinder head evenly so that the head cannot warp. This should be done on a cold engine. Work in the same numbered sequence shown in the manufacturer's chapter for retightening the cylinder head hold-down nuts when you are loosening those nuts. Turn each that sixth-turn in the sequence shown and repeat the sixth-turn until all of the nuts are finger-tight. The nuts can then be removed from their studs with the washers which are beneath them. Make a careful note of any longer nuts that may be used, on some engines, to hold the shrouding or some other bracket.

5. The cylinder heads can now be removed. Each cylinder has its own individual cylinder head so remove them one at a time. If the cylinder head is stuck tightly to the engine, you may be able to free it by pulling on the starter rope (with the spark plugs still in place, but *not* connected to the ignition) so that the engine's internal parts move through one or two operating cycles. The compression should be enough to free the cylinder heads from their gaskets. If the pistons have no marks indicating "front" for installation, make some.

6. The intake manifold, on some types of two-cylinder engines, connects the two individual cylinder barrels. This manifold must be removed before the barrels can be lifted from the engine. The chapter which describes your particular brand will show how the intake manifold is attached to the cylinder barrels on two-cylinder engines.

7. The cylinder barrels on some engines

Scrape carbon from the exhaust ports

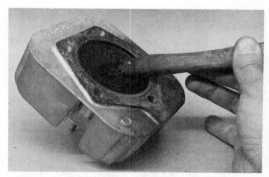

Use a scrap of wood to remove carbon from the combustion chamber

have separate nuts which hold their bases to the crankcase and those nuts must be removed before the barrels are ready for removal. The same nuts which hold the cylinder head hold the cylinder barrel on most brands. If the cylinder barrel is stuck to its base gasket on the crankcase, you may have to tap it lightly with a rubber or plastic-headed hammer to free the seal. Tap only around the heavy flange at the base of each cylinder barrel, however, never on the fragile cylinder fins. Slide the barrel up about two in. so that you can reach beneath it to hold the piston while you slide the barrel the

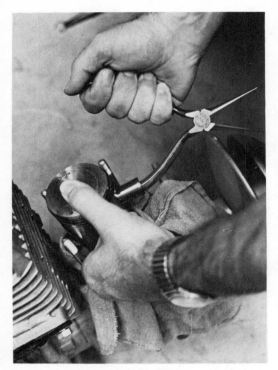

Rubber covered plier handle being used to pull a piston pin out

rest of the way up and off. Stuff a clean, lint-free rag around the opening in the cylinder barrel to protect the piston and to minimize the chances of dropping any small parts down inside the crankcase.

8. Coat the exhaust port and the combustion chamber with some type of carbon-dissolving fluid, but be certain that the label states that the fluid is designed for use on aluminum. Use a wooden hammer handle or a

Using a socket wrench extension to drive a piston pin out

doctor's tongue depressor to scrape away the carbon from the combustion chamber so that there is no chance of nicking the metal's surface. A knife can be used in the exhaust port, but be careful so that you don't scrape the metal along with the carbon. Scrape any remaining residue with an old toothbrush dipped in solvent. Remove the base gasket with a piece of wood and solvent and clean the sealing surface at the base of the cylinder barrel.

9. The fit of the piston pin in the piston will vary from one brand to the next. Some can be pushed out with a suitable size socket and extension or pulled out with the rubber handle end of a pair of pliers. A tiny spring clip retains both ends of each piston pin and it must be removed, with needlenose pliers and, in some cases, a small screwdriver, before the piston pin is ready for removal. If the piston pin is too tight to be pushed or pulled from the piston, then you may have to rent or buy a piston pin puller. Never use a hammer or excessive force to remove the piston pin or you may bend the connecting rod. There is a bearing in the hole in the top of the connecting rod and it, too, should be removed for cleaning and examination for wear.

Installing New Pistons and Rings

The condition of the piston will give some indication of how much wear or damage has occurred. The cause of the piston failure may also be evident, in some instances, from the wear or deterioration which is visible on the piston's surfaces. An ignition system which was set to fire the spark too early can literally melt a piston. It obviously must be replaced and, likely, the cylinder barrel rebored or replaced. Too much oil or, perhaps, too rich a mixture through the carburetor will leave marks on the cylinder walls. If the lines will wash away with solvent to leave no trace of scratches, it is possible that the piston could be reused with only new piston rings. The most common cause of two-stroke engine failure is piston seizure due to an overheated engine. When the engine overheats, the piston expands enough to jam inside the barrel and all oil is squeezed away so that a metal-to-metal contact results. The overheating can be caused by extended full-throttle running, by a carburetor with too lean a fuel/air ratio, or by a lack of adequate lubrication. The simple act of replacing any of these three pistons would only be a temporary solution to the problem; the ignition, carburetion, and oil supply should be checked and adjusted before the machine is placed back in operation.

Measuring Piston, Bore, and Ring Wear

The clearance between your piston and the cylinder bore will, in part, determine whether you need a new piston, a new or rebored cylinder, or both. A flat steel-bladed feeler gauge of the same type used to measure the ignition point gap and piston ring end-gap will give a rough idea of the clearance between the piston and the cylinder bore. This is *not,* however, the method that you should use in fitting the new piston or in determining if the cylinder is worn enough to require reboring or replacement—it is virtually impossible to insert the feeler gauge far enough to get an accurate reading. The general principle of piston-to-bore clearance is a bit easier to understand if you consider the feeler gauge method as a double-check on micrometer measurements.

1. You'll need two types of micrometers to measure the tolerance or clearance between the piston and the cylinder bore; a conventional micrometer and an "inside micrometer," like that in the drawing. The cost of these two tools will likely exceed the cost of having your dealer do the complete engine

overhaul—your dealer will usually be willing to "mike" the piston and the cylinder bore to tell you if a new piston, new cylinder, and/or a new piston and a cylinder rebore will be required. The piston and cylinder maximum and minimum tolerances for your engine are listed in the later chapters. Be sure that you measure the piston and cylinder sizes at four different points to determine if the piston or the cylinder is worn to an oval or a taper. Check each diameter near the top of the piston and cylinder bore and near the center. Check, again at both points, 90 degrees around from the first measurement to determine if either diameter is oval rather than perfectly round. If any of these four measurements on the piston or the four similar measurements in the cylinder bore exceeds the tolerances shown in the chapter which applies to your engine, then a new piston and, likely, a new or rebored cylinder will be required.

2. A cylinder boring bar is not the type of tool found in most home workshops. A dealer or a nearby machine shop which has experience in ths type of work can help here. If you determine that the cylinder must be rebored, then let your dealer select a piston to fit the necessary rebore size. In some instances, the cylinder may be worn enough to require replacement (or it may have been previously rebored to the maximum limits). Some engines have a cylinder liner which cannot be rebored; these machines require a new cylinder if the bore has worn beyond the manufacturer's suggested limits. Be sure to buy a correctly-sized set of piston rings to fit the new piston. Buy a set of piston pin-retaining clips as inexpensive insurance in case the old retainers have lost their proper spring

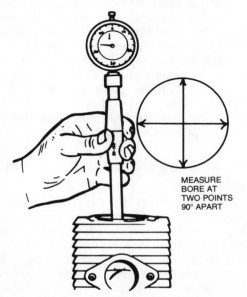
MEASURE BORE AT TWO POINTS 90° APART

Using an inside micrometer to check cylinder bore wear

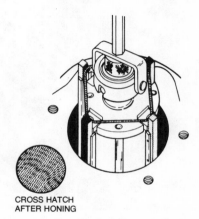
CROSS HATCH AFTER HONING

Hone cylinders to this cross hatch pattern

tension. Most new pistons are furnished with new piston pins and new pin retainers but ask to be certain when you purchase the pistons.

3. Some engine manufacturers suggest that any rebored cylinder be honed to slightly roughen the surfaces of the cylinder bore. The drawing illustrates the honing pattern that is recommended for most engines. The shop which bores the cylinder should have a honing tool. The honed surface helps to break-in the new piston rings so that they'll seal tightly in the least amount of time.

4. It is essential that new piston rings be fitted if new pistons or a rebored cylinder is installed on the engine. In some cases, the wear on the piston and cylinder bore may be slight enough so that only new piston rings need be fitted. In any case, the new piston rings should be fitted to the cylinder with a proper end-gap. The fit of the rings in the piston's ring grooves should be double checked as well. Compress the piston ring just enough to insert it squarely inside the cylinder bore. Use the top (crown) of the piston to push the ring down into the bore an inch or so and to ensure that the ring is abso-

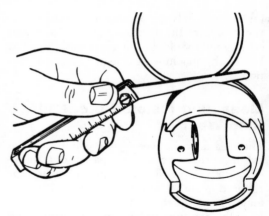

Measuring the piston ring groove clearance

lutely square with the walls of the cylinder bore. A flat feeler gauge can then be inserted in the gap between the ends of the piston ring to measure the end-gap of the piston ring. The specifications on your engine should give the end-gap; if not, consider about 0.008 in. to be the minimum end-gap and 0.014 in. to be the maximum. If the gap is less than 0.008 in., the ends of the ring can be filed slightly. If the end-gap is greater than 0.0016 in. then you likely have the wrong size piston ring for your cylinder bore size. An excessive end-gap measurement can also indicate that a standard-size bore has worn more than you thought and that a rebore (and a new piston and piston rings) are needed.

5. If you purchased a complete set of pistons and piston rings, the rings should be a proper fit. New rings on old pistons, however, can create an unexpected problem if the ring grooves in the piston have worn. Check the clearance between the ring and its groove with a feeler gauge as shown in the drawing. Your dealer should be able to supply the maximum and minimum dimensions for piston ring-to-groove fitting.

Assembling Pistons, Rings, and Cylinders

1. There are three different styles of piston rings in the various brands of snowmobile engines. Some pistons, with two rings, take two of the three different styles. A careful visual inspection of your piston and piston rings should be enough to determine which of the three styles fit each of the ring grooves in your piston. The "plain" type piston ring is generally found in the lower ring groove of

Measure the gap between the ends of the ring

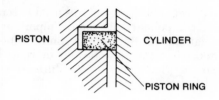

Plain type piston ring in its ring groove

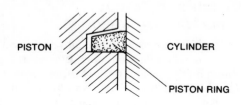

Keystone type piston ring in its ring groove

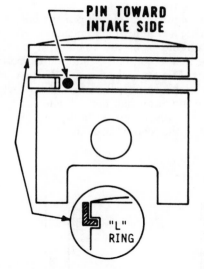

Dykes type piston ring in its ring groove

Two strips of wood being used to support the piston when installing the cylinder

two-ring pistons. The top ring may be either the tapered "keystone" style or the "L"-shaped (also called "Dykes") style. Note that the keystone and Dykes type rings are designed to fit with a "correct" side up. The "keystone" rings usually have a marking to indicate their top side; the top of the Dykes ring should be obvious enough from the drawing and the shape of the ring and its groove in the piston.

2. There is a tiny pin located in each of the piston ring grooves. The ends of the piston rings *must* butt against these pins to prevent the piston ring from moving around the circumference of the piston. The pins are located so that the ends of the rings cannot catch on the ports in the sides of the cylinder barrel. There is often a mark of some type on the top of the piston which indicates the way the piston should be installed. The mark is usually on the exhaust port side of the piston, but double check the specifications on your machine to be sure. The rings can be spread by forcing their ends apart with your two thumbs while you gently slide them over the piston and on into their grooves.

3. It is possible to compress the piston rings tightly against their stop pins by hand while you slide the cylinder barrel over them. It is far easier, though, to use a ring compressor. Push the cylinder down until it contacts the compressor, then push the piston up, out of the compressor, and into the cylinder bore. Two pieces of wood can be used to support the piston near the top of its stroke while the cylinder barrel is fitted. Be sure to install a new cylinder base gasket between the cylinder barrel and crankcase.

4. The cylinder head and gasket (if one is installed on your engine) can now be installed. Turn all the nuts (and the washers beneath them) down fingertight. Use a torque wrench, a six in. extension, and a socket to fit your cylinder head's nut size to tighten each nut down a sixth-turn at a time, working back and forth across the cylinder head. The chapter which applies to your machine will give the proper final torque for your cylinder head nuts. Torque each nut down to specification, working in the pattern shown in the manufacturer's chapter. Check the torque of each nut (with the engine cold) after you have operated the machine for a few hours.

5. The exhaust pipe, muffler, intake manifold, carburetors and engine shroud (for fan-cooled engines) can be installed in the re-

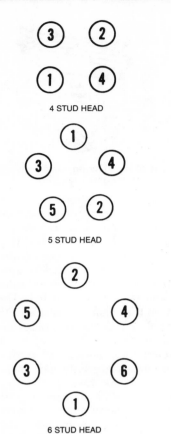

4 STUD HEAD

5 STUD HEAD

6 STUD HEAD

Typical cylinder head tightening sequence

verse order of the procedures used to remove these components. It is most important that the ignition timing and carburetor be adjusted whenever new pistons or rings have been installed. Those procedures are covered in later chapters.

AUTOMATIC TRANSMISSION SYSTEM
Clutch and Torque Converter Operation

The rubber drive belt beneath the hood of your snowmobile connects the centrifugal clutch on the engine to the torque converter. This belt and two-pulley system constitutes the complete automatic transmission system on most snowmobiles. A few machines replace the centrifugal clutch and torque converter units with a hydraulic transmission and a drive belt.

The centrifugal clutch is just what its name implies; a clutch which engages or diengages the engine from the track with centrifugal force as the source of "automatic" action. A series of levers and cams, inside the centrifugal clutch's outer half, are set at the factory to move the outer half inward when the engine speed reaches a prescribed point. The outer half of the centrifugal clutch includes the

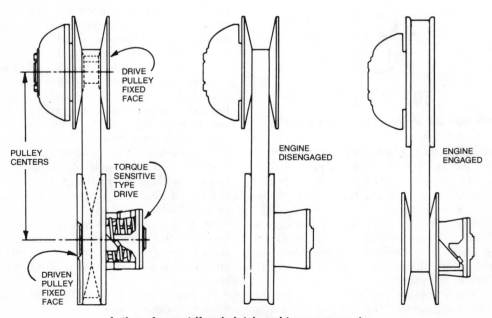

Action of a centrifugal clutch and torque converter

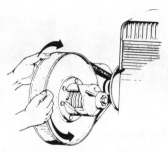

Rotate converter halves in opposite directions

outer half of the pulley on the engine which drives the drive belt; the inner half of the pair of pulley halves rotates with the engine's crakshaft. When the two halves are apart, the engine spins freely inside the drive belt; when the two halves are pressed together they grip the sides of the drive belt to set the machine into motion. The inherent slippage of the drive belt on the centrifugal clutch's pulley gives a slight delay to the engagement to prevent jerky starts.

The second pulley (the larger of the two which are connected by the drive belt) is the torque converter. The inner and outer halves of the torque converter's pulley are spring-loaded to force them together. A set of angled cams near the torque converter's shaft force the two halves of the pulley apart (against the spring pressure) when there is a difference between the machine speed and the speed of the engine. The design makes the torque converter sensitive to the machine's speed and the load which hills and acceleration place on the engine. A low gearing is needed for acceleration and to climb hills. When the two halves of the torque converter's pulley are pressed together, this low ratio is provided. When the machine's speed increases, the two halves of the torque converter's pulley spread apart so that the belt can drop down deeper into the groove between the pulley to provide an "overdrive" drive ratio.

Drive Belt Maintenance

The drive belt, centrifugal clutch and torque converter types of automatic transmission require two types of maintenance; lubrication of the various working parts of the two pulleys and a periodic check of drive belt alignment and tension. The primary cause of most drive belt wear and failure is a misalignment of one or both of the two pulleys, the

centrifugal clutch, and the torque converter. Misalignment of the two pulleys can create improper tension and/or create an angle or an offset between the two pulleys which can chafe and wear the drive belt.

DRIVE BELT REMOVAL

The drive belt must be removed to check the alignment of the two pulleys. The two halves of the larger pulley can be rotated in opposite directions to overcome their spring-loading so that they will spread apart. With the torque converter pulley halves apart, there is enough slack in the drive belt so that it can be easily pried over the edge of the pulley and off. Never use a screwdriver or metal pry-bar. Rotate the two pulley halves in opposite directions with the hand brake lever on to stop the torque converter from rotating. Hold the drive belt itself against one of the pulley halves to hold the pulley half against its spring pressure while you pry the drive belt over the pulley. The loose drive belt can then be lifted from the smaller pulley (the centrifugal clutch) and off.

DRIVE BELT ALIGNMENT

Most manuals refer to the alignment of the two pulleys as drive belt alignment even though it is the pulleys themselves, not the drive belt, which are adjusted. Your dealer uses a metal gauge to provide a visual check for the proper center-to-center distance between the two pulleys and a means of checking how far the pulleys should be offset from one another. Most machines are designed so that drive belt alignment is accomplished by moving the complete engine so that the centrifugal clutch is positioned properly. A few brands, however, have adjustable mounts for the idler shaft inside the torque converter. The offset between the two pulleys is necessary so that the two pulleys can spread and contract (as the machine speed increases or decreases) without moving the belt too far to one side or the other.

Drive System Inspection

General maintenance of the drive system serves as an important part of the overall reliability of the machine. In the inspection of the drive system, the variable-speed drive belt should be checked for wear. (See "Belt Malfunctions.") The drive and driven sheaves should be checked for burrs or any other obstructions which could cause belt

Compare width of old worn belt to a new one

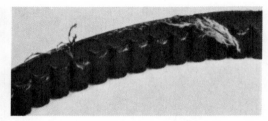

Belt with frayed edge

Turn belt inside out to check its inner surface

wear. Driven sheave wear plates should be examined for wear.

Because lubrication is extremely important in a snowmobile, it is recommended that the level of the chaincase lubricant be checked. The brake should be adjusted along with the drive chain tension.

Drive Belt Analysis

Since drive belts and tracks serve as the major components in the movement of the snowmobile, failure of these will incapacitate the machine with little notice. The ability to foresee these failures, through the use of preventive maintenance can totally eliminate this type of failure. The replacement of a worn or frayed drive belt or track could save much despair in the event of an unexpected breakage. The ability to recognize these defects is the key. Some of the major kinds of malfunctions are listed below.

DRIVE BELT WITH FRAYED EDGE

If the drive belt wears rapidly, exposing frayed edge cord, the belt is misaligned. This could be caused by loose engine mounting bolts which allow the engine to twist and misalign the belt.

BELT WORN NARROW IN ONE SECTION

This sectional wear indicates excessive slippage due to a stuck or frozen pulley. An engine idle speed that is too high could also be a possible cause—especially if more than one narrowed section is evident.

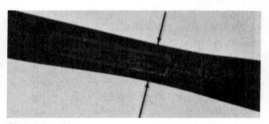

Narrowed belt

DRIVE BELT DISINTEGRATION

This type of damage may be the result of a misaligned belt, an incorrect drive belt, or oil on the sheave surfaces. If the belt is badly misaligned, it will have the tendency to roll over at high speed, causing belt disintegration.

Disintegrated belt

DRIVE BELT WITH SHEARED COGS

This condition would indicate violent engagement of the drive sheave caused by binding or improperly installed drive sheave components.

Sheared drive belt cogs

SUSPENSION AND TRACK SYSTEMS

The system of springs, levers, wheels, and slides which guides the track also serves as the rear suspension for any snowmobile. There are three basic types of snowmobile suspension systems; the bogie wheel style, the slide rail style, and the various types which combine the features of both slide rail and bogie wheel suspensions.

Bogie Wheel Suspension

The bogie wheel style suspension design is derived directly from the type of suspension seen beneath army tanks and civilian bulldozers. A series of wheels guide the track and press it against the surface of the snow. The levers which support the bogie wheels are spring-loaded. Each wheel moves upward as the machine's track moves over a hump or rock with little effect on the total machine; the springs and levers absorb the impact of the bump. This type of suspension is generally believed to provide a smoother ride at slow speeds than any other type. The bogie wheel suspension works quite well on frozen ice because no snow powder is needed for lubrication; the wheels roll in their own bearings to guide the track along.

Slide Rail Suspension

The slide rail suspension systems use a plastic-lined rail to press against the inside of the track to guide the track over the snow. There may be a guide wheel pair or sprocket at either end and, perhaps, at several other locations, but the machine's weight is carried by the slide rail. This type of suspension keeps the track relatively flat as long as the snow is smooth or the machine speed is high. The slide rail suspension is used on virtually all racing machines and is considered the most effective in deep snow. Levers, with spring-loading, press the slide rail against the track much like the bogie wheel suspension's levers operate on the individual bogie wheels. The slide rail suspension provides a smoother ride because the entire slide rail may move up and down or tilt back and forth to ride up and over any bump. A certain amount of powdered snow is necessary to help lubricate and cool the plastic slide which is in constant contact with the inside of the track.

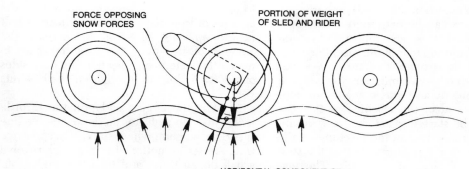

FORCE OPPOSING
SNOW FORCES

PORTION OF WEIGHT
OF SLED AND RIDER

HORIZONTAL COMPONENT OF
FORCE REQUIRED TO MAKE
WHEEL ROLL "UP HILL"

Action of bogie wheel type suspension

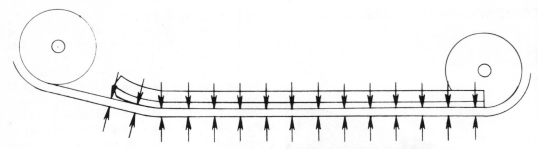

Slide rail suspension contacts most of the tracks surface

Combination Suspension Systems

Many snowmobile manufacturers have attempted to combine the traction advantages of the slide rail suspension with the ride of the bogie wheel suspension. Generally, these types of combination suspensions mount a series of bogie wheels on a single rail rather than on individual levers. The track is then able to undulate to match the changing shape of the snow's surface while maintaining an even front-to-rear pressure on the track.

Track Tension and Alignment

The same springs which press the bogie wheels or slide rails against the track provide enough tension to keep the track in position. The rear idler wheels or gears which guide the track are adjustable, fore and aft, to provide more or less track tension. The same adjusting bolts which move the rear idler are used to maintain the track's self-centering. If the spring tension on the right and left-side of the track is nearly equal, then the track will have little or no tendency to drift to the left or right.

1. The track must be placed in operation, after any adjustments are made in its tensioning bolts, to ascertain if it is self-centering. A spinning track can be extremely dangerous, however, so that it is most important that you keep away from the rear of the machine when the engine is driving the track. An automobile tripod-style bumper jack is the most convenient and stable means of supporting the rear of the machine so that the engine can be started to set the track in motion. Support the rear of the machine on the jack (or on a heavy platform) so that the supports are well clear of the track. The machine's weight will rest on the skis and the support. The track should be at least six in. above the floor.

Track tensioning bolts are located near the rear idler

2. Pull the bottom of the track down so that all of the slack is on the lower run.

3. Consult the chapter which applies to your machine to determine exactly where to measure the amount of free-play in the track. Be sure to measure the free-play on both the left and the right sides of the track.

4. Loosen the locknut on the adjusting bolt near the right rear of the machine and the similar nut near the left rear of the machine. Turn the adjusting bolt in (clockwise) to increase the track tension and reduce the amount of free-play. Turn the adjusting bolt in the opposite direction to increase the amount of free-play. Set the free-play to match the factory specifications on both sides of the track, but do not tighten the locknuts yet.

5. Start the engine and pull the throttle lever just enough to increase the engine speed to the point where the clutch and drive train are set in motion. Let the track revolve a half dozen times and turn the engine off. Do *not* apply the brake; let the track coast to a stop.

6. Look at the extreme rear of the track to

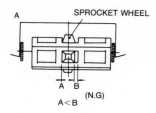 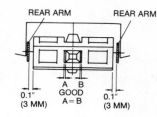 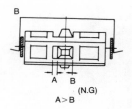

WHEN SHIFTED TO RIGHT.
PROPERLY TIGHTEN THE RIGHT TRACK ADJUST SCREW
AND LOOSEN THE LEFT TRACK ADJUST SCREW.

WHEN SHIFTED TO LEFT.
PROPERLY TIGHTEN THE LEFT TRACK ADJUST SCREW
AND LOOSEN THE RIGHT TRACK ADJUST SCREW.

Adjusting sequence for centering the track

see if there is as much space between the sides of the track and the frame on the left as there is on the right. If the track is not centering itself, you must make some further adjustments on the track-tensioning bolts.

7. If the track is running too far to the right, for example, then the right track tensioning bolt must be tightened a half-turn or more. Loosen the left track tensioning bolt that same half-turn and start the engine once again to set the track in motion. Let the track run for a few revolutions, shut the engine off, and allow the track to coast to a stop. Examine the clearance between the sides of the track and the sides of the frame to see if the track is now centering itself. Repeat the process of loosening one track tensioning bolt and tightening the opposite bolt until the track is self-centering.

8. Recheck the free-play on the right and left sides of the track. If an adjustment is indicated, tighten or loosen *both* the right and left bolt the same amount to retain the self-centering adjustment. You may find that one side of the track has a bit more free-play than the oppsoite side; as long as the free-play is within the tolerance specified by the manufacturer, the adjustment is correct and the locknuts can be retightened. If you find it impossible to achieve both proper free-play on both sides of the track and self-centering, there may be a bent arm or some other fault in the suspension itself.

Track and Suspension Inspection

Efficient performance of both front suspension and track is the key to handling and stability of the snowmobile. More often than not, serious accidents, resulting from mechanical failure, will have as their cause, some type of suspension failure. It is recommended that some type of general inspection be performed before each snowmobile trip. A thorough inspection like this should include a check of the ski wear rods, pivot bushings, and wear plates for loose, worn, or broken parts. Ski alignment, bogie wheels, suspension tubes, and springs should also be checked for worn or broken components.

Because of the severe stress under which the main drive track operates, both the track itself and its components should be checked frequently. The sprockets in particular should be examined for worn, missing, or chipped teeth along with the tension, alignment, and general condition of the track. Equally important is an inspection of both front and rear axles for bent or broken parts, making certain that the axle bearings are in good condition and properly locked on the axle. Finally, an inspection for loose or missing sprocket clips is also important.

Track Analysis

Track composition varies greatly from model to model and there has been much experimentation done to find a substance that has good wear characteristics and yet is still flexible. One of the best materials used now is polyurethane, which exhibits both of these characteristics. Provided that track tension and alignment are properly maintained, the track should be a long-lived component.

CUTS AND PUNCTURES IN THE TRACK

This is the most prevalent condition and is caused by striking sharp objects.

TRACK WITH CRACKS AND WORN CROSS BARS

The occurrence of small cracks and worn cross bars is considered normal after many hours of use. Rapid wear is prevalent if the machine is used on surfaces other than snow.

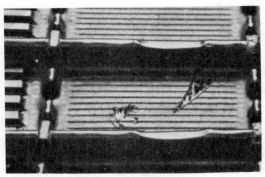

Cuts and punctures in the track

Cracks and worn bars on the track

WORN DRIVE LUGS

Once again, the wearing of drive lugs is common after considerable use. Rapid wear is common if the unit is used on a surface other than snow.

NOTE: *The track may be reversed to obtain maximum life from drive lugs.*

Worn drive lugs

TRACK WITH TORN EDGE

The cause of this condition is the track being greatly out of alignment. It runs to one side and frays the track edges. Eventually, the track will catch in the rear idler pivot arms and cause excessive damage.

Torn track edge

TESTING

The final step in a general tune-up is the test run. Before testing, however, inspect your machine thoroughly for loose or missing fasteners, then test-run the snowmobile and make final adjustments.

REPAIRING DAMAGED THREADS

Several methods of repairing damaged threads are available. Heli-Coil® (shown here), Keenserts® and Microdot® are among the most widely used. All involve basically the same principle—drilling out stripped

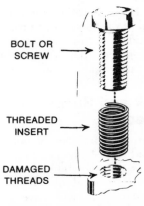

BOLT OR SCREW

THREADED INSERT

DAMAGED THREADS

Damaged bolt holes can be repaired with thread repair inserts

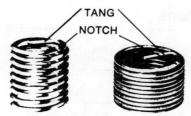

TANG
NOTCH

Standard thread repair insert (left) and spark plug thread insert (right)

threads, tapping the hole and installing a pre-wound insert—making welding, plugging and oversize fasteners unnecessary.

Two types of thread repair inserts are usually supplied—a standard type for most Inch Coarse, Inch Fine, Metric Coarse and Metric Fine thread sizes and a spark plug type to fit most spark plug port sizes. Consult the individual manufacturer's catalog to determine exact applications. Typical thread repair kits will contain a selection of pre-wound threaded inserts, a tap (corresponding to the outside diameter threads of the insert) and an installation tool. Spark plug inserts usually differ because they require a tap equipped with pilot threads and a combined reamer/tap section. Most manufacturers also supply blister-packed thread repair inserts separately in addition to a master kit containing a variety of taps and inserts plus installation tools.

Before effecting a repair to a threaded hole, remove any snapped, broken or damaged bolts or studs. Penetrating oil can be used to free frozen threads; the offending item can be removed with locking pliers or with a screw or stud extractor. After the hole is clear, the thread can be repaired, as follows:

Drill out the damaged threads with specified drill. Drill completely through the hole or to the bottom of a blind hole

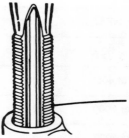

With the tap supplied, tap the hole to receive the thread insert. Keep the tap well oiled and back it out frequently to avoid clogging the threads

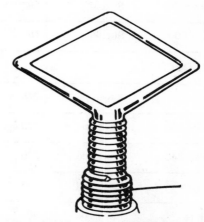

Screw the threaded insert onto the installation tool until the tang engages the slot. Screw the insert into the tapped hole until it is ¼–½ turn below the top surface. After installation break off the tang with a hammer and punch

1980 Specifications

Brand and Model	Engine Make	Weight	Track Width	Suspension	Fuel Capacity	Length	Width
ARCTIC CAT							
Lynx 2000S	Suzuki	322	15	Slide	6.5	95	33
Lynx 2000T	Suzuki	345	15	Slide	6.5	95	33
Jag 2000	Suzuki	363	15	Slide	6.5	102	34
Jag 3000	Suzuki	370	15	Slide	6.5	102	34
Jag 3000 F/C	Suzuki	369	15	Slide	6.5	102	34
Trail Cat 3000	Suzuki	380	15	Slide	7.0	102	38
Trail Cat 4000	Suzuki	387	15	Slide	7.0	102	38
Panther 5000	Suzuki	387	15	Slide	7.0	105	38
Pantera 5000	Suzuki	395	16	Slide	7.0	102	38
El Tigre 5000	Suzuki	389	15	Slide	6.5	104	41
El Tigre 6000	Suzuki	393	15	Slide	6.5	104	41
Kitty Cat 60	Suzuki	NA	10	Slide	0.5	56	23
JOHN DEERE							
Spit Fire	Kawasaki	275	15	Slide	5.5	98	33
Trail Fire 340	Kawasaki	370	15	Slide	7.7	102	37
Trail Fire 440	Kawasaki	375	15	Slide	7.7	102	37
Sport Fire	Kawasaki	385	15	Slide	7.7	102	37
Liqui Fire	Kawasaki	404	15	Slide	7.7	102	37
KAWASAKI							
Drifter F/A	Kawasaki	365	15	Slide	9.0	101	36
Drifter 340	Kawasaki	370	15	Slide	9.0	101	36
Drifter 440	Kawasaki	380	15	Slide	9.0	101	36
Invader 340	Kawasaki	415	15	Slide	8.0	103	41
Invader 440	Kawasaki	430	15	Slide	8.0	103	41

1980 Specifications (cont.)

Brand and Model	Engine Make	Weight	Track Width	Suspension	Fuel Capacity	Length	Width
KAWASAKI							
Intruder	Kawasaki	430	15	Slide	8.0	103	41
Invader L.T.D.	Kawasaki	440	15	Slide	8.0	103	41
POLARIS							
Gemini 244	Polaris	355	15	Slide	7.0	102	32
Gemini 250	Polaris	365	15	Slide	7.0	102	32
Apollo 340	Polaris	375	15	Slide	7.0	102	32
Galaxy 340	Polaris	380	15	Slide	7.0	104	32
Galaxy 440	Polaris	400	15	Slide	7.0	104	32
Centurion	Polaris	420	15	Slide	7.0	104	38
TX 340	Polaris	373	15	Slide	7.0	104	38
TX 440	Polaris	375	15	Slide	7.0	104	38
TX-C 340	Polaris	385	15	Slide	7.0	104	38
TX-L 340	Polaris	NA	15	Slide	7.0	104	38
TX-L Indy	Polaris	NA	15	Slide	7.0	107	41
SKI DOO							
Elan 250	Rotax	281	15	Bogie	3.6	89	31
Citation 3500	Rotax	327	15	Slide	7.5	95	34
Citation 4500	Rotax	353	15	Slide	7.5	101	34
Citation SS	Rotax	352	15	Slide	7.5	95	37
Everest 500	Rotax	449	16½	Slide	7.8	109	39
Everest L/C	Rotax	496	16½	Slide	7.8	109	39
Blizzard 5500	Rotax	420	15	Slide	7.8	104	39
Blizzard 7500	Rotax	442	15	Slide	7.8	104	39

1980 Specifications (cont.)

Brand and Model	Engine Make	Weight	Track Width	Suspension	Fuel Capacity	Length	Width
SKI DOO							
Blizzard 9500	Rotax	442	15	Slide	7.8	104	39
Elite	Rotax	790	2 x 15	Slide	8.1	107	44
YAMAHA							
Enticer 250	Yamaha	308	15	Slide	4.7	94	36
Enticer 300	Yamaha	343	15	Slide	6.0	94	37
Enticer 340	Yamaha	362	15	Slide	6.0	101	38
Enticer Deluxe 340	Yamaha	388	15	Slide	6.0	101	38
Excel V	Yamaha	431	16.5	Slide	7.0	109	41
Exciter	Yamaha	387	15	Slide	8.0	99	39
SRX	Yamaha	398	NA	Slide	7.0	99	40
SS 440	Yamaha	374	NA	Slide	7.0	104	39

NA info not available
L/C engine cooled with liquid
F/C fan cooled engine
F/A free air cooled engine

2

Carburetors

There are only a few different brands of carburetors used on all the various machines in this manual. Some manufacturers have used two or three different brands of carburetors on their various models and some brands of carburetors appear on several different types of machines. The general description, rebuilding, and tuning steps for all snowmobile carburetors, are in this chapter. It's easy enough to identify which carburetor is installed on your machine; the brand and type are cast into the side of the carburetor and the charts in the chapter which pertain to your brand list the carburetor which should be on your machine. Refer to the later chapters for specific carburetor adjustments and tuning data.

GENERAL THEORY OF OPERATION

All carburetors, on any type of engine, rely on two fundamental physics principles in their operation: vacuum and what is called the "venturi effect." The vacuum, created inside the engine's crankcase when the piston rises, serves to pull the air through the carburetor throat. The throat (the carburetor's main and largest opening) is a bit larger on the air intake side and, again, on the engine side than it is in the center of the carburetor. The incoming air speeds up when it passes through that smaller diameter section of the carburetor throat. The necked-down diameter is called the venturi and the acceleration of the air is called the venturi effect.

The venturi effect is greatest and the incoming air's speed the highest at the point where the gasoline is added to the air. A tiny passage or port, which feeds the fuel into the venturi area of the carburetor throat, is angled so that the airstream passes directly over its opening. The speed of the air and the vacuum inside the engine combine to pull the fuel out of the nozzle and to mix it thoroughly with the air. The high velocity of the airflow also serves to help vaporize or atomize the gasoline. The carburetor's internal passages and external adjustments maintain a proper balance of fuel and air for maximum power and fuel economy.

The handlebar throttle cable is linked to a valve which opens and closes the carburetor throat to allow more or less air to flow through the throat. The engine's speed and the resulting vacuum pressure combine with the amount of throttle valve opening to determine the volume of air which enters the engine. That volume of air and the air's speed through the venturi pull just the right amount of fuel into the air/fuel mixture.

There is no direct driver control over how much fuel is supplied to the engine; only the control over how much air, the carburetor does the mixing and blending of fuel and air automatically. It is extremely important, then, to see that the carburetor is functioning correctly.

CARBURETOR TYPES

Even though there are many different brands and models of carburetors used on snowmobile engines, all of them can be divided into three basic types depending on how the throttle valve operates to control the air supply and on how the fuel is delivered to the nozzle to be mixed with that air. Polaris, Arctic Cat, John Deere, Kawasaki and some Yamaha snowmobiles use a Mikuni slide-type carburetor with a float bowl type of fuel supply. The throttle is a round slide which moved up and down in a circular slot when the lever on the handlebar is pulled. The fuel is held in an aluminum cup in the base of the carburetor where it is always available to the nozzle to feed fuel into the carburetor throat. The most common type of carburetor on the other brands of snowmobile engines is the diaphragm type. The Keihin, and Tillotson,

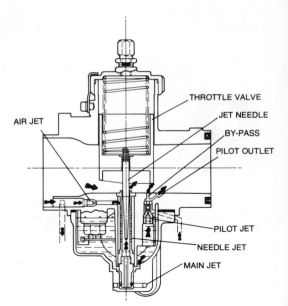

Mikuni Slide type carburetor

carburetors are diaphragm types as are the Mikunis used on some Yamaha snowmobile engines. All of these carburetors have a throttle valve about the size and shape of a half-dollar. This throttle valve is pivoted open, whenever the handlebar lever is pulled, to open the carburetor throat. A rein-

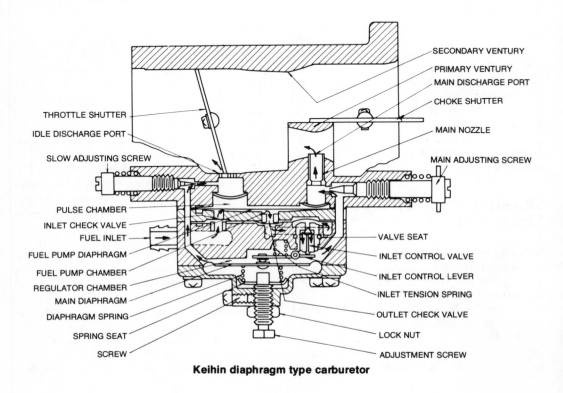

Keihin diaphragm type carburetor

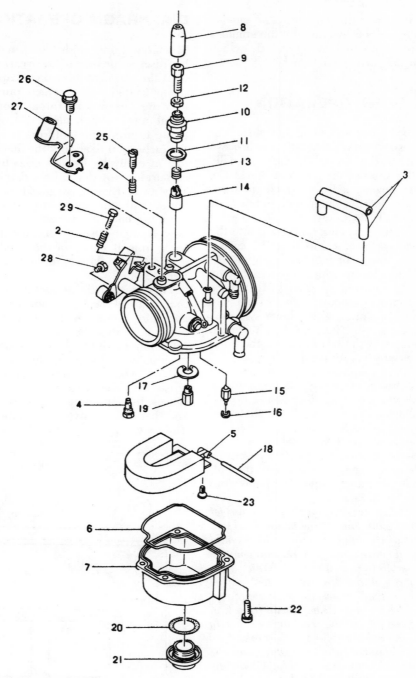

1. Carburetor assembly	11. Washer	21. Drain bolt
2. Clip	12. Nut	22. Screw
3. Hose	13. Spring, starter plunger	23. Screw
4. Idle jet	14. Starter plunger	24. Spring
5. Float	15. Valve seat assembly	25. Adjusting screw
6. O-ring	16. Clip	26. Screw, bolt
7. Float body	17. Clip	27. Stay
8. Cover, starter plunger cap	18. Float pin	28. Bolt
9. Adjuster, cable	19. Main jet	29. Screw
10. Cap, starter plunger	20. O-ring	30. Spring

Mikuni Float-Butterfly type carburetor used by Yamaha

forced rubber-like diaphragm in the base of these carburetors is actuated by the engine's vacuum to pump fuel to the nozzle which feeds into the carburetor throat.

FLOAT BOWL OPERATION

The float bowl derives its name from the fact that it is a small bowl and that there are two small floats in that bowl. The floats literally float on the gasoline in the float bowl. The floats push against a lever which, in turn, pushes a needle valve open or closed to allow fuel to enter the float bowl. The float bowl is much like a tiny gas tank built right into the base of the carburetor and it is the carburetor's only source of fuel. It is important, then, that the levers which are actuated by the floats be adjusted properly so that there is always a proper amount of fuel in the float bowl. The adjustment of the lever is generally referred to as a "float level" adjustment even though it is the lever and not the floats themselves which is adjusted. A separate fuel pump (often a diaphragm-type) is mounted near the crankcase to pump the fuel into the float bowl whenever the float bowl's needle valve is allowed to open by a "low" fuel level in the float bowl. All of the engine's fuel is picked up from the float bowl by a single small pipe (or orifice). A nut with a precisely-sized hole or orifice is threaded into the bottom of that fuel pickup tube. The hollow nut is called a "main jet."

> WARNING: *Never remove the main jet cover bolt while the engine is hot. Fuel will flow out of the float chamber which could ignite and cause damage to the snowmobile and possibly injury to the mechanic.*
> *Place a rag under the carburetor so fuel does not spread. Place the main jet cover bolt in a clean place. Keep away from fire. After assembling the carburetor, firmly tighten the rubber joint screw. Make sure the throttle outer tube is in place and the throttle cable moves smoothly. Clean the carburetor and allow it to dry.*

Replacing the main jet with one having a smaller or a larger orifice determines how "rich" (more fuel) or how "lean" (less fuel) the engine will run at half to full-throttle settings. The needle which moves in and out of the fuel nozzle with the throttle slide and other adjusting nuts regulate the fuel and air mixture at partial throttle operation on the Mikuni slidetype carburetors.

DIAPHRAGM OPERATION

The large round sandwich of metal and rubber discs in the base of these carburetors contains the various rubber-like diaphragms and spring-loaded valves which pump the fuel into the carburetor's throat. Some of these metal and rubber discs constitute a fuel pump to bring the fuel from the fuel tank to the carburetor itself, but the fuel pump could just as easily be located elsewhere and the carburetor would still be a diaphragm type. Tiny air and fuel passages (orifices) virtually honeycomb the carburetor to separate the pumping flow of vacuum (air) from the fuel flow. A single hose which looks like a fuel line leads from the base of the crankcase to the carburetor in addition to the hose which supplies the fuel.

There are usually at least three diaphragms in the base of the carburetor. One of these diaphragms pumps the fuel from the tank, another regulates the fuel pressure, and the third pumps the fuel into the nozzle which eventually delivers it to the carburetor throat. The constantly surging vacuum (created by the piston's upward movements) causes the pumping diaphragms to flutter and that action provides the pumping effect. The faster the engine runs, the faster the dia-

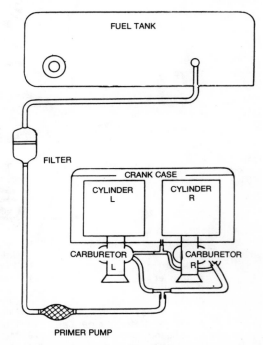

Fuel supply diagram for diaphragm type carburetors

phragms flutter to automatically provide more fuel for higher engine speeds. A needle valve prevents too much fuel from reaching the carburetor throat in much the same manner as the similar valve on a carburetor with a float bowl. The pressure-regulating diaphragm serves much the same purpose as the floats; to actuate the needle valve. There is a small fuel supply chamber inside the diaphragm-type carburetor which stores the engine's immediate supply of fuel much like the float bowl stores fuel in that type of carburetor. The flow of fuel from the fuel supply chamber is regulated by a simple needle valve with an external screwdriver slot or tee handle to provide for adjustments.

KEIHIN CARBURETORS

The Keihin diaphragm-type carburetors are fitted to some of the engines in Yamaha snowmobiles. Its appearance differs from other diaphragm-type carburetors only in that there is an external tube on the left-side of the carburetor for checking the level of the fuel in the fuel chamber.

Removal and Installation

The carburetor should be cleaned with fresh gasoline before it is removed so that there is less chance of any dirt finding its way inside the tiny orifices. The air intake silencer box lid must be removed by prying back the spring clips or by removing the bolt. The screws which retain the air intake silencer will be visible on each side of the carburetor; they can be removed. Disconnect the fuel line and seal its open end (or drain the gas tank) so that no fuel can escape. Remove the vacuum line from the carburetor. The rod which actuates the oil pump will have to be disconnected on Yamahas. The nuts which hold the carburetor to the engine can now be removed and the carburetor pulled away from the intake manifold. The throttle cable (and choke cable, if one is fitted) must be disconnected at their screw-clamps to free the carburetor from the engine. Installation is simply the reverse of this procedure.

Disassembly

1. Scribe a line across the carburetor casting to aid in reassembly alignment. Remove the six screws which hold the pump section to the main body of the carburetor.

Removing the six screws from the base of the carburetor

Remove the spring and spring seat from the base cover

2. Locate the pump diaphragm and check it for possible damage. If it is not damaged, handle it with extreme care.

3. Remove the two gaskets (one between the pump and the mixing body and the gasket inside of the pump body).

4. Release the O-rings which are stationed in the mixing body and the pump body.

5. At this point, if the check valve is known to be defective, it must be removed

Handle the delicate rubber diaphragms carefully

Remove the screws which retain the float arm

and replaced. If, however, it works sufficiently, do not remove it. At no time should the check valve be pulled or rolled as this might damage the valve's synthetic rubber material.

6. Once the valve is removed, check the condition of the valve seat. If it is defective, the pump body has to be replaced as the seat is bonded to the body and cannot be removed.

7. Remove the regulator diaphragm, taking extreme care in handling it. It should never be pulled or rolled. If it is defective, replace it.

Inlet Control Level Adjustment

To make certain that the inlet control lever is adjusted properly, see that the lever itself is flush with the floor of the regulator chamber.

Assembly

When reassembling the carburetor, make sure that all fuel passages through the gaskets, pump diaphragm, pump body, and the mixing chamber are aligned.

1. Position the regulator diaphragm into the mixing body and place the diaphragm spring on the center of the diaphragm. Put the two screws through the pump cover and, using them as a guide, compress the spring

Pump body and rubber check valve

Upper portion of pump body and gasket

Pump diaphragm

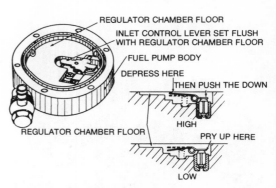

Fuel level lever adjustment

Check fuel level in the plastic tube

Adjusting screw and lock nut for fuel level adjustment

evenly. Once this is done, turn the assembly over onto a clean, level surface, still applying enough pressure to keep the spring compressed.

2. With the assembly in the position described above, install the new O-rings into the fuel passages and put the new check valve in position if a new one was needed. Position the body gasket.

3. Place the pump body on the top of the staked pieces. Make sure that the groove for the O-rings are in the "up" position. Install the new O-rings in the pump and the mixing bodies.

4. While holding the guide screws in position, place the stainless steel diaphragm and the gasket on the pump body.

NOTE: *When performing this procedure, make sure that the dowel pin holes and the fuel passages are in alignment.*

5. Align the mixing body and the stacked assembly, and then secure them with the six screws which hold the pump section to the main body. Tighten these screws evenly and slowly to prevent warpaging or breaking the casting.

Fuel Level Adjustment

The carburetor has a level pipe which is used in fuel level adjustment. To adjust the fuel level, remove the level pipe cap and start the engine. While keeping the idle speed up to 1,800 rpm, loosen the fuel level locknut on the lower part of the carburetor and adjust the fuel level by turning the fuel level adjusting screw.

Accelerator pump cover and gasket

Carefully remove pump diaphragm to check for wear or cracks

Accelerator pump body

Regulator

The fuel regulator in this unit will not work when the engine is stopped. In the case of reassembly after parts have been replaced, the adjusting screw should first be turned in about one turn. The engine should be started and the fuel level should be adjusted at idle speed.

NOTE: *The adjusting screw can be turned from the lower side of the pump body.*

The internal pressure in the regulator chamber can be freely controlled by the adjusting screw. Regulating the adjusting screw changes the amount of fuel pressure in the regulator chamber and, therefore, the amount of pressure delivered to the engine.

Accelerator Pump

Some of the later-model Keihins are fitted with this acceleration pump. The screw assembly is designed for easy replacement of worn or punctured diaphragms and to clean the orifices.

Idle Adjustment (Low-Speed)

The correct idle adjustment varies from engine to engine. It is generally accepted that the correct idle adjustment is obtained when the screw is adjusted to obtain smooth running. Turning the screw clockwise results in a leaner mixture while rotation of the screw counterclockwise results in a richer mixture. Manufacturers have found that the approximate adjustment is 1½ turns counterclockwise from a fully closed position.

High-Speed Mixture Adjustment

The high-speed mixture screw is adjusted with the snowmobile in motion under half-throttle. The best method is: drive the snowmobile, then stop and adjust the carburetor,

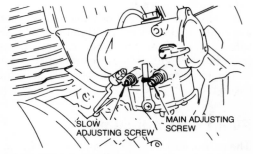

Adjusting screw locations

and make another run. This should be done until peak performance is obtained. The average adjustment is approximately 1⅝ turns counterclockwise from a fully closed position.

Synchronizing Twin Carburetors

The carburetor throttle valves (butterfly valves or throttle shutters) must work in exactly the same manner to synchronize the two carburetors. The slightest variation in the throttle valves' action or opening can upset the carburetion and performance. Some Yamaha snowmobile dealers and a few sports car accessory shops sell an inexpensive vacuum gauge for checking the flow of air through the carburetor throats at most throttle valve settings. These vacuum gauges are sold under various brand names including the Unisyn®. The vacuum gauge is hand-held over the carburetor throat while the engine is running. The vacuum (or airflow) through that carburetor registers on the glass tube beside the vacuum gauge as the fluid in the tube rises or falls. The vacuum gauge is then moved to the second carburetor throat, with the engine running at exactly the same speed, and the reading on the glass tube is compared to the reading from the first cylinder. The vacuum gauge might have to be moved back and forth, from the one carburetor throat to the next, several times while the throttle valves on each carburetor are adjusted to open slightly more or less. The throttle valves will be synchronized when the readings on the vacuum gauge's glass tube are identical for both carburetors. The gauge is shown, here, on the Keihin carburetor, but it can be used on virtually any snowmobile engine with twin carburetors.

1. Attach the carburetor vacuum gauge (Unisyn® or its equivalent) to the left carburetor throat.

2. Set the idling speed screw (the throttle stop screw) to give the desired idle speed.

3. Turn the adjusting knob on the vacuum gauge's sight glass until the float is in the center of the scale (the knob or screw in the center of the gauge adjusts the level of the float).

4. Remove the vacuum gauge from the first carburetor and attach it to the throat of the second carburetor. The engine idle speed should remain as it was with the gauge on the first carburetor.

5. Mark the position of the float on the

Using a vacuum gauge to synchronize carburetors

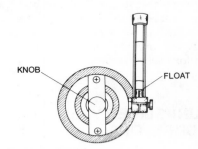

Turn knob to center float

Adjust each cable to synchronize the throttles

vacuum gauge's sight glass with a grease pencil. If the float is higher than it was on the first carburetor, then the second carburetor's throttle valve should be adjusted to close that throttle valve slightly. A single knob in the linkage between Keihin's on Yamahas is used to synchronize the throttle valves. Turn that adjusting screw clockwise to lower the position of the float on the vacuum gauge or counterclockwise to lower the float's position in the sight glass.

6. Speed up the engine by pulling on the handlebar throttle a few times to help clean the spark plugs to give a smoother idle speed.

7. Let the engine return to idle speed (with the vacuum gauge removed from both carburetor's throats). Adjust the idle speed. The two carburetors' slow speed and high-speed adjusting screws can then be set individually to provide the optimum performance for each cylinder.

MIKUNI SLIDE-TYPE CARBURETORS

The Mikuni carburetor, which is used on all Polaris, Kawasaki, Arctic Cat, John Deere and most other late model snowmobiles consists of four main systems which allow smooth operation at varying engine speeds. The first is the initial starter system which will allow smooth starting in cold weather because the fuel and air are always in the correct ratio. The pilot system allows gasoline to be delivered constantly at idle and low-speed operation. Third is the main system, which delivers the air/fuel mixture between low and high-speed driving. The float system maintains a constant flow of gas to the other systems.

Removal and Installation

The air silencer box must be removed (from machines which are equipped with the devices) before the carburetors can be removed from the engine. A pair of bolts, one on each side of the carburetor throat, hold the back panel of the air silencer box to the carburetor. The knurled round collar at the very top of the Mikuni slide-type carburetor must be removed by turning it in a counterclockwise direction. This collar, the round throttle slide, needle, and return spring can then be pulled from the top of the carburetor. Compress the spring to allow enough slack in the throttle cable so that it can be slipped free from its retaining notch in the

throttle slide. The choke cable (if fitted) can be removed by unscrewing the choke assembly slide from the side of the carburetor. The carburetor can now be removed from the engine by loosening and removing the two nuts on each side. The carburetor should be thoroughly cleaned in fresh (oil-free) gasoline if it is to be disassembled. Installation is simply the reverse of this procedure.

Disassembly

It should be mentioned that most carburetor malfunctions are caused by component wear or by the systems being clogged with dust or dirt.

These problems are remedied by replacement. A clogged valve is fixed by cleaning. A float malfunction due to a bent guide pin can be remedied with an adjustment.

To adjust the float, remove the float chamber, invert the mixing body, and remove the float chamber packing. Measure the distance from the float arm to the float chamber. It must be within 17.0–17.5 mm.

NOTE: *When using gasoline for a cleaner, always work in a ventilated area and keep the solution away from fire or flames. (Do not smoke in the area.)*

In the maintenance of the starter carburetor system, it should be noted that the jets should never be cleaned with drills or wire. In handling the starter plunger, exercise great care not to scratch the circumference or the base; this may cause a fuel leak. A routine part of every carburetor disassembly is the replacement of the rubber starter cap to prevent moisture from seeping inside.

When disassembling the pilot system, care should be taken to prevent scratching the casing. Wash out the pilot jet in gasoline and dry it thoroughly. Watch for disfigured air screws and replace them if necessary. While servicing air screws, clean the passages on the side of the body (pilot outlet, by-pass).

In disassembling the main jet, do not pry to separate the parts as large scratches will result. It should be noted that upon assembly the throttle screws should not be torqued too tightly.

In float system maintenance, be careful not to bend the float guide pin. When the needle valve is damaged, the entire system should be replaced with a new needle valve assembly.

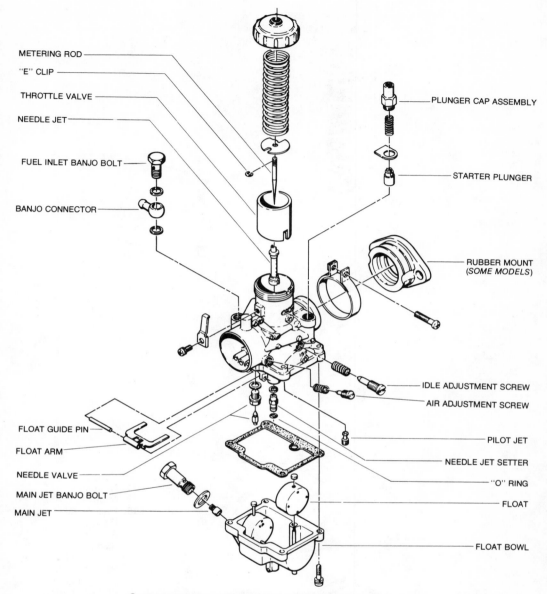

METERING ROD

"E" CLIP

THROTTLE VALVE

NEEDLE JET

FUEL INLET BANJO BOLT

BANJO CONNECTOR

PLUNGER CAP ASSEMBLY

STARTER PLUNGER

RUBBER MOUNT
(*SOME MODELS*)

IDLE ADJUSTMENT SCREW

AIR ADJUSTMENT SCREW

FLOAT GUIDE PIN

FLOAT ARM

NEEDLE VALVE

MAIN JET BANJO BOLT

MAIN JET

PILOT JET

NEEDLE JET SETTER

"O" RING

FLOAT

FLOAT BOWL

Components of a (Polaris type) Mikuni slide carburetor

Checking the Float System

Overflowing during operation is usually caused by some malfunction in the float system, such as a worn needle valve. The most common needle valve conditions are: wear, spring damage, worn seat, worn float pins or worn float pin holes in casting. If any of these conditions exist worn parts must be replaced.

Adjustment of the Choke and Throttle Cables

When adjusting the choke, there must be some play in the cable so that the starter plunger of each carburetor will not rise when the choke is fully closed. There must not be, however, an excess of play which may effect air/fuel mixture.

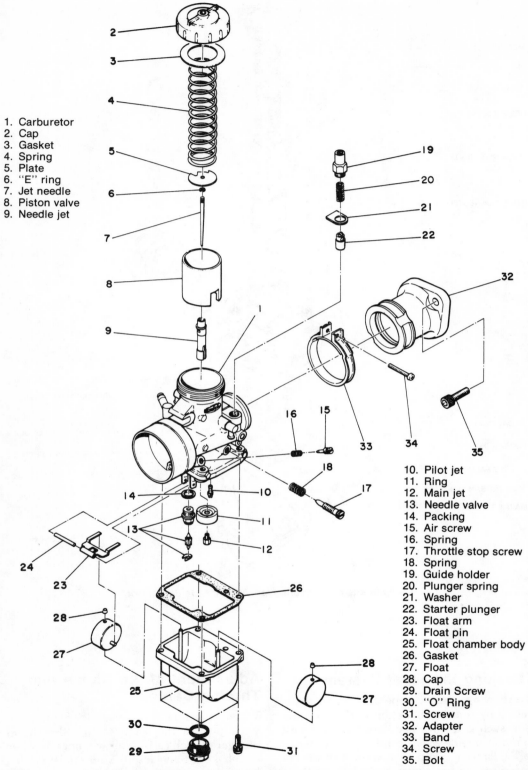

1. Carburetor
2. Cap
3. Gasket
4. Spring
5. Plate
6. "E" ring
7. Jet needle
8. Piston valve
9. Needle jet

10. Pilot jet
11. Ring
12. Main jet
13. Needle valve
14. Packing
15. Air screw
16. Spring
17. Throttle stop screw
18. Spring
19. Guide holder
20. Plunger spring
21. Washer
22. Starter plunger
23. Float arm
24. Float pin
25. Float chamber body
26. Gasket
27. Float
28. Cap
29. Drain Screw
30. "O" Ring
31. Screw
32. Adapter
33. Band
34. Screw
35. Bolt

Components of a (Arctic Cat type) Mikuni slide carburetor

Remove large knurled cover to remove slide and cable

The main jet holder is located on the side of the float bowl (Polaris type)

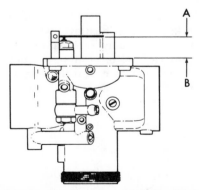

The distance between A and B is the float level

When adjusting the throttle cable, adjust each throttle valve (in multi-cylinder engines) with the throttle cable attached and the throttle completely open.

Adjustment is correct when the corner of the cutaway of the throttle valve matches

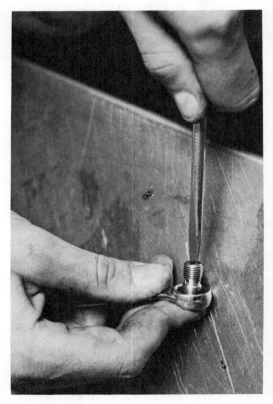

Removing the main jet from holder

Float needle valve

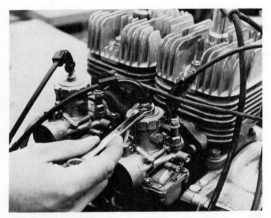

Loosen the locknut to adjust throttle cable

with the upper surface of the main bore. It is very important to be sure to fasten the cable adjuster locknuts securely.

Adjustment of Idling and Synchronization

1. Set the throttle stop screw of each carburetor evenly to maintain an engine idling speed of approximately 1,000 rpm.

2. Run the engine to reach operating temperature.

3. By opening and closing the air screws (each individually about ½ turn at a time) find the position at which the engine is at

Adjusting the air screws (idle) on a Mikuni carburetor (slide type)

maximum rpm. (A tachometer is recommended.)

4. Return each throttle adjustment screw to idle.

5. By rotating the air screw ¹/₁₆ turn each time, find the maximum once again.

6. If there is a change (Step 5) adjust the idle once again.

NOTE: *It must be remembered that at greater altitudes air becomes thinner; at these altitudes it will be necessary to adjust the carburetors to compensate for this thinner air.*

MIKUNI DIAPHRAGM-TYPE CARBURETORS

The Mikuni, diaphragm type carburetor, which is known as a "floatless" type of carburetor, is used on many Yamaha models. This diaphragm carburetor draws the fuel from the tank and meters it into the engine. The Mikuni carburetor has three main mecha-

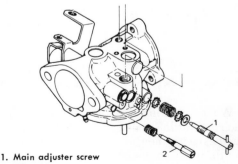

1. Main adjuster screw
2. Pilot screw

Adjusting screws (Mikuni butterfly type)

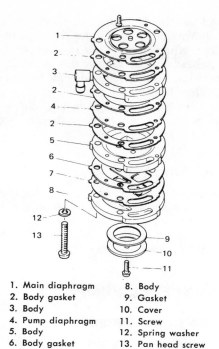

1. Main diaphragm
2. Body gasket
3. Body
4. Pump diaphragm
5. Body
6. Body gasket
7. Check valve
8. Body
9. Gasket
10. Cover
11. Screw
12. Spring washer
13. Pan head screw

Components of the diaphragm type Mikuni carburetor fuel pump

nisms: the mixing body, supplying the fuel air mixture to the engine; the fuel pump, which draws the fuel from the tank to the carburetor; and the regulator, which maintains the fuel pump pressure by reducing or increasing it according to the needs of the engine.

The regulator in a diaphragm-type carburetor is likened to the float in a float-type carburetor. The regulator's internal pressure is the same as the level of gasoline in the float bowl of a float-type carburetor.

Removal and Installation

To remove the Mikuni carburetor, disconnect the fuel line and seal it to prevent gasoline from escaping. Disconnect the pressure pulse line and the oil pump operating rod. Loosen the carburetor mounting nuts and remove the carburetor from the cylinder.

The cleaning of the carburetor, as a unit, or any carburetor parts, should be done with clean solvent. After this is done, all parts must be blown dry before assembly.

Disassembly

1. Remove the single screw from the bottom of the carburetor. Gently lift the bottom

cover and its rubber gasket from the base of the carburetor.

2. Remove the four screws which retain the sandwich of aluminum castings and rubber gaskets to the base of the carburetor. Carefully lift each casting and peel away each rubber gasket or diaphragm to avoid ripping the rubber. Lay the parts on the workbench in their order of removal to help identify each part and its location for later assembly.

3. Remove the phillips head screw which retains the needle valve and arm. The needle valve can then be pulled from its seat.

4. The slow speed and adjusting screw and the high-speed "main" adjusting screw can be removed to inspect their tips for wear. Note that there are two O-rings inside the main adjusting screw's groove, but do not remove them unless they are torn.

Assembly

The various parts can be assembled in the reverse order of their disassembly. Carefully inspect each gasket and each diaphragm for any signs of tears or pinholes. Replace any rubber parts which appear to be worn. Check each of the orifices and the passages inside the castings for any accumulated residue and clean them throughly before assembly. Your dealer can supply a complete "rebuild" kit which contains all the gaskets, diaphragms, and springs which might wear.

Adjustments

There are three places at which the carburetor may be adjusted: the low-speed adjusting screw which controls the air-fuel mixture at idling speed; the idle speed screw (throttle stop screw) which controls the idle speed; and the high-speed adjusting screw which

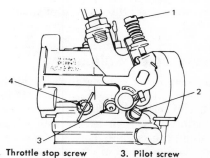

1. Throttle stop screw
2. Slow adjusting screw
3. Pilot screw
4. Main adjusting screw

Adjusting screws

controls the air fuel mixture when the throttle shutter has reached ¼ throttle or above.

The carburetor setting must be performed with the consideration that the snowmobile is used in winter and at low altitudes. If the snowmobile is operated at high altitudes or under special atmospheric conditions, the specifications given may not be suitable. It should be noted that twin carburetors must be adjusted evenly.

All adjustments should be performed after the adjusting screws have been lightly seated. The number of turns to be backed off is listed in the "Carburetor Specifications Chart" in the later chapters.

FUEL LEVEL ADJUSTMENT

No special adjustment of fuel level is needed with the Mikuni carburetor. If the fuel level has to be adjusted, the pump body should be disassembled and the diaphragm control level in the regulator chamber should be corrected.

Idle Speed Adjustment

The idle speed should be set at 1,000–1,100 rpm. The low-speed adjusting screw should be adjusted so that the engine idles smoothly. This low-speed adjustment will affect the engine performance at low and medium speed ranges.

The low-speed is adjusted by turning the adjusting screw in or out slowly in order to attain the maximum engine rpm. Then back the screw out ⅛ turn more to enrich the mixture.

The final adjustment is to readjust the idle speed screw in or out to attain an idle speed of 1,000 rpm. Ride the snowmobile to test the engine performance, accleration, and idle speed. If the engine is not responsive, the fuel-air mixture may be too lean. If the engine runs roughly, the mixture may be too rich. In either case, the carburetor should be readjusted.

Main Adjuster Adjustment

The main adjusting screw adjusts the air-fuel mixture when the engine is running at high speeds. This screw should be adjusted so that the mixture is as rich as possible without overloading the engine. This is necessary to prevent the engine from overheating.

1. Back out the main adjusting screws to specifications.

2. Make further adjustments by running the snowmobile and finding the adjustment position where the engine runs smoothly at the richest setting. To find this position, the adjustment screws should not be turned more than ⅛ turn at a time.

3. After testing at high speeds, check the spark plug coloration for indication of proper carburetor mixture.

Synchronizing

The adjustments on the Mikuni diaphragm carburetors are similar to those on the Keihins in this chapter. The same general synchronizing procedures can, then, be used with Mikuni carburetors.

MIKUNI FUEL PUMPS

Testing Fuel Pump

1. Disconnect impulse line from fuel pump.

2. Use a short piece of fuel line to connect a pressure gauge to the impulse side of fuel pump.

3. Pressurize to 5 or 6 psy and observe guage. Pressure should not drop.

Inspecting Fuel Pump

To inspect fuel pump, separate the castings shown. Check valves should not be bent or have foreign matter holding them off their seat. There should be no liquid in the impulse cavity. All parts must be clean and not discolored.

If any components are damaged, the entire fuel pump must be replaced.

IMPORTANT: *Do not use carburetor cleaner or strong solvents on fuel pump components.*

FUEL PUMP, FUEL TANK, SCREEN AND IN-LINE FUEL FILTER

The fuel tank features a fuel gauge in the cap and a spill ledge. The spill ledge prevents spilled fuel from spilling onto the seat. The fuel tank cap is sealed and the tank is vented by the vent line at the top of the tank.

The fuel pick-up line in the tank is connected to a screen. The fuel shut-off valve

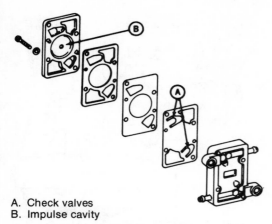

A. Check valves
B. Impulse cavity

Components of remote rectangular fuel pump

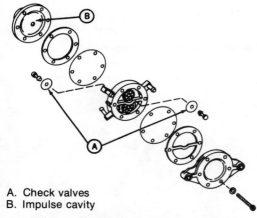

A. Check valves
B. Impulse cavity

Components of remote round type fuel pump

and in-line fuel filter are located in the fuel line between the fuel tank and fuel pump.

The nylon screen in the in-line filter has a self-cleaning action. Pulsation of the screen shakes loose contamination such as dirt, rust and small fibers. Loose contamination collects at the base of the cone.

NOTE: *If snowmobile (some John Deere Models) has been transported on a trailer and the fuel shut-off valve was not closed, the engine may be "flooded".*

Service
SCREEN

To remove pick-up screen, disconnect fuel lines from fitting, and remove fitting from fuel tank. Remove pickup screen from end of line.

Clean screen with gasoline and compressed air. Replace screen if it is damaged.

Replace gasket on fuel line fitting, if necessary.

FUEL TANK

Clean fuel tank if dirt deposits have been detected in tank. Remove tank by disconnecting fuel lines and vent lines. Remove the seat and tank hold-down clips. Slide tank rearward to remove.

If tank has major damage, it should be replaced. Minor damage or leaks can be patched, if practical.

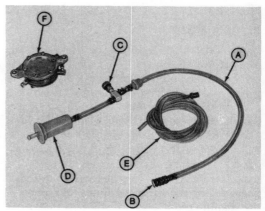

A. Fuel tank
B. Fuel cap and gauge

Typical fuel tank

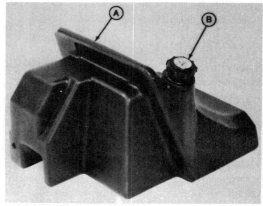

A. Fuel pick-up line   D. Fuel filter
B. Screen   E. Vent line
C. Shut-off valve   F. Fuel pump

Typical fuel lines and pump

IN-LINE FUEL FILTER

Change the filter annually or when packed contamination starts to build up at the base of the cone.

TILLOTSON CARBURETORS

The Tillotson carburetors fitted to some Ski-Doo snowmobiles, are all diaphragm-type carburetors. There are four basic types of Tillotson carburetors; the HD, HR, HL and the newer HRM, but the basic principles of operation are similar. The major differences between the various types are pimarily in the size of the throat, the location of the fuel and air passages inside the carburetor, and the number of turns necessary to adjust the idle and high-speed screws. The precise adjustment figures are listed in the chapter which pertains to each brand of snowmobile.

REMOVAL AND INSTALLATION

The air silencer box should be unbolted from the intake side of the carburetor to allow better access for tuning and disassembly. The fuel line must be disconnected and its end plugged to prevent any fuel from escaping and the vacuum line to the crankcase disconnected from the base of the carburetor. The clamp screws which connect the throttle and choke cables to the carburetor must be loosened so that the cables can be removed from the carburetor. Finally, the nuts which hold each carburetor to the engine must be removed.

HL Series

DISASSEMBLY

It is important, when disassembling the carburetor, to thoroughly clean it before it is disassembled and to perform the disassembly procedure on a clean and level workbench.

1. Remove the lower bowl cover by removing the screw and the plastic cover.
2. Pull out the strainer gasket and screen.
3. Remove the fuel pump body by releasing the attaching screws.
4. Carefully remove the fuel pump diaphragm and the gasket. Do not fold or bend the diaphragm.
5. Pull the main diaphragm out of the casting, along with the cover plate and gasket.
6. Pull out the pin which holds the inlet control lever. Use caution since the spring may fly out. Gather the lever, pin, and tension spring.
7. Remove the inlet needle from the casting. The inlet needle seat can be removed from the carburetor body by using a 5/16 in. socket. Remove the seat gasket. When in-

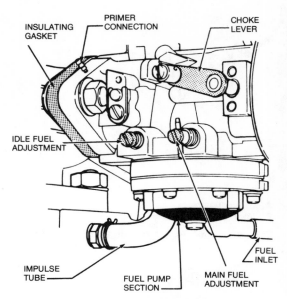

Tillotson diaphragm type carburetor

The adjusting screws on a newer HRM Tillotson

stalling the seat, torque the nut to 25–35 in. lbs of torque.

8. Remove both the idle and the main adjusting screws.
9. Some of the carburetors are equipped with O-ring type adjusting screws. These should be lubricated with SAE 30 oil when reinstalling them. The packing-type adjusting screws do not need lubrication.
10. If the main nozzle must be removed, tap it out of the casting with a small punch. It will fall into the venturi. The new nozzle should be pressed into position with its holes

in line with the main adjustment needle. The brass cage should also be pressed so that it is flush with the metering chamber casting.

11. If the fuel supply channel or the discharge ports are clogged, it may be necessary to remove the welch plug. Use the following procedure to perform the action.

a. Using a ⅛ in. drill, drill a hole in the center of the plug. Drill only enough to just break the inner surface of the plug. To drill deeper will seriously damage the casting and will require its replacement;

b. Pry out the welch plug, being careful not to damage the casting. Clean out the ports and cross channels. Do not use drills or wire to clean the ports as this will change the inner dimensions of the ports;

c. To install the new plug, place it into the casting with the convex side facing upward. Tap it into position with a tool which has a ⁵/₁₆ in. diameter end.

ASSEMBLY

Basically, the HL series carburetor can be assembled by following the disassembly procedure in reverse order. Make certain that all the parts are clean and in good condition before assembly.

All the passages should be free of blockages but, as was mentioned previously, do not clean the orifices with any type of wire or drill.

When installing the inlet control lever with its spring, remember to check to make sure that the spring is located in its place in the casting and that its other end is positioned on the notch of the inlet control lever.

NOTE: *Do not in any way stretch the spring.*

When placing the main diaphragm, its gasket, and covering into position, make certain that all of these are fitted over the three pins which are located at the rim of the metering body. There are three other pins which are in the main diaphragm cover casting which must be positioned under the fuel pump gasket, diaphragm, and the fuel pump body. Tighten the fuel pump body screws.

ADJUSTMENT

After reassembling the carburetor, make the following preliminary adjustments after seating the needle screws. The main adjusting screw should be turned counterclockwise 1¼ turns. Then open the idle adjusting screw ¾ turn.

CAUTION: *Whenever the needle screws*

are adjusted they are to be seated lightly into their seats. If they are forced, both the seat and the needle will be damaged irreparably.

Once these adjustments have been made, start the engine and make any further adjustment after the engine has reached operating temperature. Adjust both of the needle screws so that smooth idle and high-speed running are obtained.

HD Series

Before the carburetor is disassembled, the external surface must be cleaned thoroughly.

CAUTION: *Do not use alcohol, lacquer acetone thinner, benzol, or any solvent which contains these ingredients. These solutions will damage the rubber parts of the carburetor.*

DISASSEMBLY

1. Remove the idle speed screw from its orifice along with the washer and the tension spring. Check the screw for worn or crossed threads.

2. Remove the fuel inlet and the fuel filter along with the filter cover, the cover gasket, and the filter screen. The gasket for the filter screen should be replaced at every servicing. Clean the screen thoroughly before installation.

3. Remove the fuel pump cover casting by removing the six body screws. The fuel pump diaphragm and gasket may be removed. Both the diaphragm and the gasket should be inspected for holes or tears. The order of reassembly is important; the fuel pump is connected to the fuel pump body first, then the inlet diaphragm is positioned next to the gasket.

Peel each diaphragm away from base

By aligning the pegs and holes you correctly align the diaphragms and castings

4. Remove the housing from the pump body and pull out the pump diaphragm and the gasket. Make an inspection of the diaphragm as was done in Step 3. Make a careful inspection of the casting for cracks or nicks. When assembling these units, the pump gasket is attached to the metering diaphragm cover first, then the diaphragm is joined to the gasket.

5. To remove the fulcrum pin, release the retaining screw. This will release the fulcrum pin, the control lever, and the tension spring. Be careful that the inlet lever does not fly from the casting when the pin is released.

Remove the single screw to release the fulcrum lever

Life fulcrum lever and pin from base

CAUTION: *When handling the tension spring, use caution not to alter the compression of the spring. If there is reason to think that the spring has been stretched, it should be replaced.*

6. Remove the inlet seat assembly with a thin-walled ⅜ in. socket. Also remove its gasket.

NOTE: *The assembly is made up of a brass cage and a rubber insert for the needle seat. The insert fits into the cage in only one direction. On the surface of the insert there is a rim around the edge on one side; the ridge must be placed away from the point of the inlet needle when assembled.*

NOTE: *The needle and seat assemblies are sold in matched sets only. Do not force the brass cage into position as the threads will be stripped or the cage distorted.*

ASSEMBLY

To assemble the carburetor, reverse the above procedure.

ADJUSTMENT

All adjustments are made on the needle adjusting screws from the position where the needle just contacts the seat.

CAUTION: *Do not seat the needle screws tightly since severe damage will be done to both the seat and the needle screw.*

The low and the high-speed needle screws are adjusted from this slightly closed position one full turn counterclockwise. It should be noted that these are preliminary adjustments and that further adjustments are necessary once the engine is running at operating temperature. Adjustments vary because of alti-

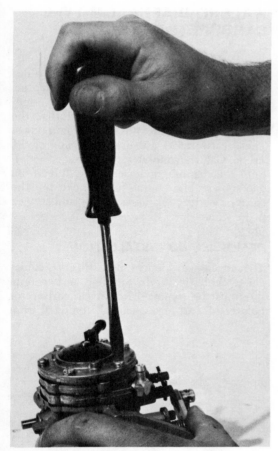

Tighten all six screws equally

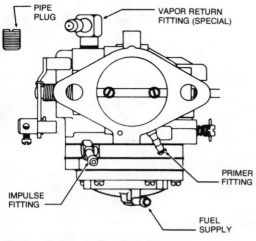

Fuel and vacuum line fittings

PIPE PLUG

VAPOR RETURN FITTING (SPECIAL)

PRIMER FITTING

IMPULSE FITTING

FUEL SUPPLY

tude, climate, and terrain on which the vehicle is used.

The idle speed should be adjusted so that a smooth idle is obtained.

CAUTION: *Because of the centrifugal clutch, the idle should not be excessively high as this will cause the clutch to engage.*

HR Series

DISASSEMBLY

1. Remove the low-speed adjustment screw along with its washer and tension spring. Make an inspection of the threads for cross-threading and other defects.

2. Remove the center screw of the carburetor; this will release the fuel inlet and the filter cover. Once the cover is removed, lift the cover, the cover gasket, and the filter screen from the body. Before assembly, clean and dry the filter screen and replace the screen gasket. Remember to flush the plastic cover with clean gasoline to remove all dirt deposits.

3. Release the six body screws and remove the fuel pump cover from the casting. Remove the pump diaphragm and gasket and make an inspection of the diaphragm and gasket for warpage or cracks.

When reassembling the components listed above, the order is important. The pump gasket should first be assembled to the diaphragm cover, then the fuel pump diaphragm is attached to the gasket and the flap valve, which is located next to the fuel pump diaphragm, because the flap valves must seat against the fuel pump cover.

4. Remove the diaphragm cover casting along with the metering diaphragm and its gasket.

When reassembling the gasket is attached to the body casting and then the metering diaphragm is positioned next to the gasket.

5. Remove the fulcrum pin screw, fulcrum pin, inlet control lever, and tension spring. (See Step 5 of the HD Series.)

6. Remove the inlet needle and seat using a $5/16$ in., thin-walled socket. (Follow Step 6 of the HD Series.) The inlet needle is torqued to 25–30 in. lbs.

7. Remove and inspect the low and high-speed mixture needles for worn or distorted tips. If the seats are damaged, a new body casting is needed since the seat may not be removed from the casting.

8. If it is feared that the idle by-pass ports or the main nozzle are clogged, the welch plugs must be removed. These plugs normally do not have to be removed. (See Step 11 of the HL disassembly section.)

9. Remove the choke and throttle shaft

only if there is evidence of wear or damage. If the body bearings of the shafts are worn, the body casting must be replaced. If the choke shaft has to be removed, make certain that the ball and the friction spring do not fly out of the casting.

ASSEMBLY

Before reassembly, make sure that all the parts are clean and in the best working order, then reverse the disassembly procedure to assemble them.

SYNCHRONIZING

The opening action of the throttle valves, on engines fitted with two Tillotson carburetors, must be synchronized so that each carburetor will supply an equal amount of fuel and air. The procedures outlined for the Keihin carburetor synchronizing (using a vacuum gauge) can be used to adjust the throttle valves on Tillotson carburetors.

WALBRO DIAPHRAGM-TYPE CARBURETORS

The Walbro WDA, WD and WR series carburetors perform much like the other diaphragm-type carburetors in this chapter. These Walbro types can be instantly identified by their square bases rather than the round bases of all the other diaphragm types. These carburetors are used on many of the Arctic Cat snowmobiles. The exact model, from the diaphragm series, may differ from one snowmobile engine to the next, but the basic procedure for dissassembly and service is the same.

REMOVAL AND INSTALLATION

The air intake silencer box, throttle cable, choke cable (if fitted), fuel line and vacuum line must be removed from each carburetor before the carburetor can be removed from

Loosen cross cable clamps to synchronize carburetors

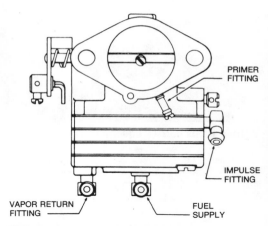

Walbro diaphragm type carburetor

2.	Ring-retaining swivel
3.	Ring-adj. packing-needles
4A.	Cover assy-conversion w/elbow fittings
4.	Cover assembly-fuel pump-straight fittings
5.	Throttle shaft & lever assembly
6.	Choke lever assembly
7.	Choke shaft
8.	Swivel assembly-throttle & choke
9.	Choke valve (WR & WD)
10.	Inlet needle valve
11.	Check valve
12.	Choke friction ball
13.	Circuit plate gasket
14.	Flange-WR gasket
15.	Circuit plate gasket
16.	Fuel inlet gasket
17.	Fuel pump check valve gasket

18.	Fuel pump gasket
19.	Flange gasket WD/WDA
20.	Circuit diaphragm
21.	Diaphragm-metering
22.	Diaphragm-fuel pump
22A.	Diaphragm-fuel pump (WDA-1 only)
23.	Diaphragm-check valve
24.	Screw-idle adj.
25.	Screw-meter lever pin
25A.	Screw-throttle bracket
26.	Screw-circuit plate
27.	Screw-valve
28.	Screw assembly-cover
29.	Spring-valve (Not used in WDA—1)
30.	Spring-idle screw
30A.	Spring throttle return
31.	Spring-pressure
32.	Spring-choke friction

33.	Spring-fuel pump leaf (not used in WDA—1)
34.	Spring-metering lever
35.	Spring-idle & power needles
36.	Needle assembly-power-(top) standard
37.	Needle assembly-power-(side) some OEM models
38.	Needle assembly-idle
39.	Retainer-O-ring (top only)
40.	Washer-adj. packing (side)
41.	Screen filter
42.	Pin-metering lever
43.	Plate-filter
44.	Plate-fuel pump
45.	Plate-circuit
46.	Plate assembly-metering diaphragm
47.	Lever-metering
48.	Bracket-throttle

the engine. Usually, just two nuts hold each carburetor to the engine.

DISASSEMBLY

After the carburetor has been removed from the engine and has been cleaned in a good carburetor cleaner to remove the external dirt deposits, place the unit on a clean and level workbench for further disassembly.

1. Remove the four screws which hold the bottom cover in place. Then remove the filter screen and the screen gasket.

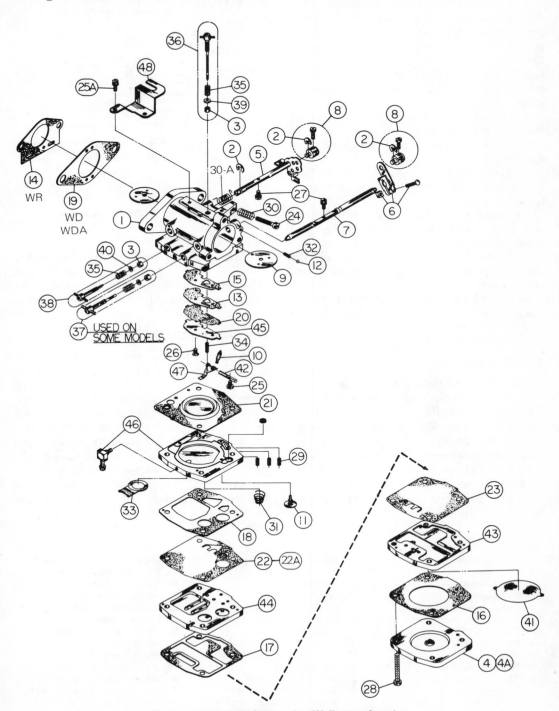

Components of WD/WR series Walbro carburetor

2. Pull the check valve diaphragm and its gasket from the casting along with the fuel pump diaphragm and its sealing gasket.

3. Release and remove the three check valve springs and the one main fuel leaf spring.

4. Remove the metering diaphragm.

5. Release the screw of the metering lever pin. Remove the pin slowly as it is under spring tension. Remove both the spring and the screw.

6. With the spring tension released, remove the metering lever and the inlet needle valve.

7. Release the three circuit plate screws and then remove the circuit plate.

8. Make an inspection of the check valve diaphragm and its gasket.

9. Remove the high-speed needle and spring and also the low-speed needle with its spring.

10. Make a close examination of the choke and throttle shafts for wear. If they are not worn, they need not be removed.

The reassembly procedure is basically the disassembly procedure, but followed in reverse order.

NOTE: *The most important aspect of reassembly is to keep all parts clean. Dirt in carburetor parts is the main cause of carburetor failure.*

ADJUSTMENT

CAUTION: *All the carburetor adjustments are made with the needle screw lightly contacting the needle seat. Do not jam the needle valve against the needle seat as irreparable damage will result and a new carburetor casting will be needed.*

1. The high-speed needle valve is set by opening the needle valve 1¼ turn.

2. The low-speed needle valve is adjusted by opening the valve 1¼ turn.

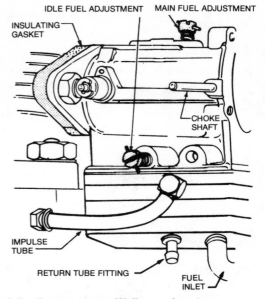

Adjusting screws on Walbro carburetors

These are only preliminary adjustments. Once the engine is running, make the final adjustments to the carburetor so that the engine runs smoothly at all engine speeds.

SYNCHRONIZING

Each carburetor, on engines with two Walbro carburetors, must be adjusted to provide optimum low-speed (idle) and high-speed performance. The action of the throttle valves on the two carburetors must, however, be adjusted so that both throttle valves are perfectly synchronized to supply equal amounts of fuel and air to each cylinder. The procedures in the section describing Keihin carburetor synchronizing can be used, with the vacuum gauge described, to synchronize two Walbro carburetors.

1. Body assembly—fuel pump	15. Ball—enrichment friction	29. Spring—idle air bleed needle
2. Body assembly—carburetor	16. Gasket—jet plug	30. Spring—enrichment friction
3. Ring—retaining	17. Gasket—flange	31. Spring—idle feed tube pressure
4. Bowl assembly—fuel	18. Gasket—pump	32. Spring—fuel pump leaf
5. Cover assembly—fuel pump	19. Gasket—surge chamber	33. Spring—throttle return
6. Shaft & lever assembly—throttle	20. Gasket—fuel pump assembly—	34. Spring—float support
7. Valve—throttle	carburetor body	35. Needle—power adjustment (opt.)
8. Swivel assembly	21. Gasket—fuel bowl	36. Needle—idle
9. Float assembly	23. Diaphragm—surge chamber	37. Needle—idle air bleed
10. Pin—float valve lever	24. Diaphragm—pump	38. Jet—limiting high speed (.076)
11. Pin—float assembly	25. Screw—throttle valve	38. Jet—limiting high speed (.070)
12. Valve—check	26. Screw—fuel bowl assembly	38. Jet—limiting high speed (.068)
13. Valve assembly—enrichment	27. Screw—Fuel pump assembly	38. Jet—limiting high speed (.072)
14. Plug—limiting jet	28. Spring—idle needle	39. Jet assembly (.076)

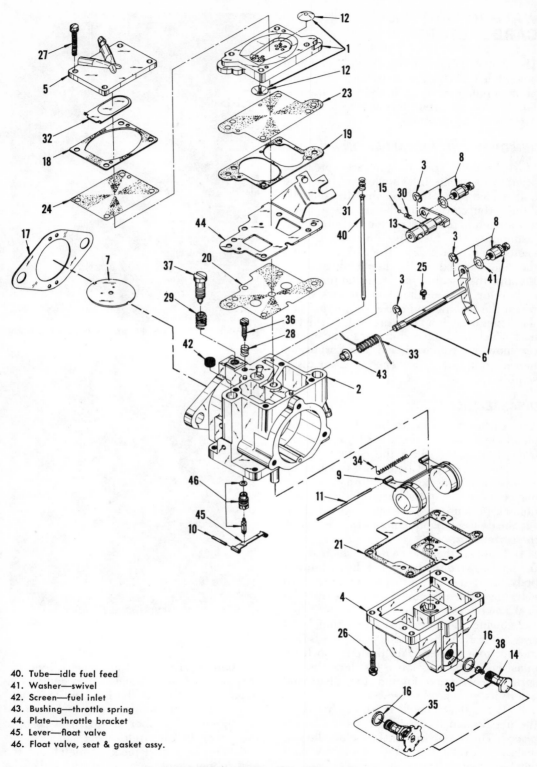

40. Tube—idle fuel feed
41. Washer—swivel
42. Screen—fuel inlet
43. Bushing—throttle spring
44. Plate—throttle bracket
45. Lever—float valve
46. Float valve, seat & gasket assy.

Exploded view of Walbro WF series carburetors

WALBRO WF-TYPE CARBURETORS

The Walbro WF carburetor combines a float bowl style fuel chamber in its base with a diaphragm pumping action in the top of the carburetor. These carburetors are fitted to many Arctic Cat snowmobiles.

REMOVAL AND INSTALLATION

Most of the WF style Walbro carburetors are fitted with an air intake silencer box. The bolts which retain this box must be removed if the carburetor is to be disassembled, but it can remain in place for simple carburetor adjustments. The fuel line must be disconnected from the base of the carburetor and the line plugged or the fuel tank drained. Remove the vacuum line from the top of the carburetor. Loosen the clamp screws which retain the throttle and choke cables and pull the cables away from the carburetor. The two nuts which hold the carburetor to the engine can now be removed and the carburetor moved to a clean workbench area for disassembly.

Remove the float bowl from the carburetor body

DISASSEMBLY

Any carburetor should be cleaned completely in solvent to remove all traces of grit from its exterior. Blow the carburetor dry with an air hose, but be careful to keep the air away from the carburetor throat, the fuel line connection and the vacuum line connection; air pressure in these openings can damage the delicate diaphragms and valves inside the carburetor.

1. Remove the four screws which retain the float bowl to the bottom of the carburetor body. Loosen each screw just a quarter-turn to relieve the pressure evenly so that the float bowl doesn't distort.

2. Swing the brass floats and their float arm up so that the needle valve can be removed from its seat. Pull the pin which retains the floats, but notice just how the coil spring is wrapped around the pivot and where its ends are located.

3. If the float needle is worn, then both the needle and its brass seat should be replaced. The hex on the end of the needle seat makes removal a simple task of unscrewing it with an open-end wrench.

4. The thin strip of metal with the rounded end is bent to adjust the float level. Measure from the base of the carburetor to

the bottom of the float as shown. Bend the strip of metal which touches the needle valve to adjust the level of the floats up or down.

5. Remove the four screws which hold the aluminum and rubber sandwich of parts to the top of the carburetor.

6. The D-shaped piece of metal and the first rubber diaphragm in the very top of the carburetor are the fuel pump parts. Each part has a peg and an aligning hole to help in fitting them back together properly.

Float valve, valve seat and adjusting arm

Measure float level from base of carburetor

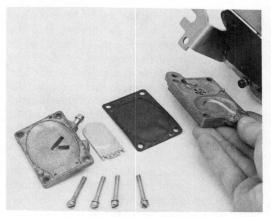

Fuel pump petal and diaphragm parts

Each gasket, diaphragm and casting has aligning pins or holes

ASSEMBLY

Your dealer can supply a complete rebuilding kit for the Walbro WF carburetor which includes all of the diaphragms, gaskets, the float valve, and float valve seat. The various aligning pegs will help to keep the proper gasket side up and they help to determine just where each piece fits. A mixture of 25 parts gasoline to one part oil can be used to hold the fuel pump's metal petal in place while the diaphragm and aluminum cover are installed. There should be a bit of spring tension on the float bowl when it is replaced· if not, check the fitting of the brass fuel pickup tube. The fuel pickup tube rests against a spring in the *top* of the carburetor that spring forces the tube against the bottom of the float bowl; tightening the float bowl's screws compresses that spring.

ADJUSTMENT

1. Adjust the throttle cable for smooth and complete throttle valve action. Loosen the

7. Gently peel back the gaskets and diaphragms so that they won't tear. The parts can be arranged on the workbench in their order of disassembly to help to identify just where each piece will fit together later.

screw which clamps the cable to the pivot arm on the side of the carburetor. Pull the cable so that there is $1/16$ in. of slack before the throttle begins to open and retighten the clamp screw. Remove the air intake silencer box so that you can reach inside the carburetor to feel and see the action of the throttle. Pull the throttle lever on the handlebar fully open and check to see that the throttle valve inside the carburetor is fully open.

2. Check the operation of the throttle safety spring switch. That $1/16$ in. of throttle cable slack should be just enough to actuate the safety switch (the switch shuts off the carburetor in the event that the throttle cable should freeze in the open throttle position).

3. Turn the throttle stop screw in or out to obtain a smooth and even idle speed just slow enough to prevent the centrifugal clutch from engaging (check the tuning specifications on your machine for the correct idle speed).

4. The low-speed needle is the slotted screw on the top of the carburetor which is closest to the air intake silencer (the screw nearest the engine, on the top of the carburetor, is the idle air needle). Rotate the low-speed needle screw clockwise until it is just finger-tight then back it out approximately 1¼ turn.

5. Tighten (clockwise) the idle air needle to a finger-tight setting and back it out 1¼ turn.

6. Rotate the idle air needle *and* the low-speed needle clockwise to increase engine speed and counterclockwise to decrease engine rpm. Turn one of the two screws a quarter-turn and check the machine's acceleration then repeat the test run with the other screw turned a quarter-turn. Repeat the acceleration tests until both screws are set in the position to provide the best low-speed acceleration and idle. Neither screw should be turned much more than a half-turn from that previous 1¼ turn presetting.

7. The brass hex nut on the air intake side

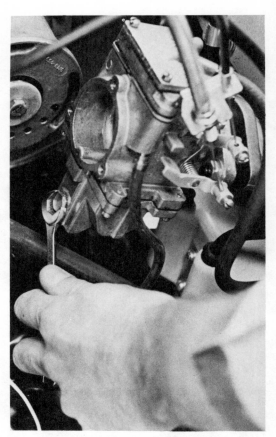

The high speed jet is inside the hex cap

of the float bowl contains the main jet which governs the fuel supply for maximum throttle operation. If the spark plug indicates a too lean condition from high-speed test runs (a clean and white electrode color), then the main jet may have to be replaced with one having a slightly larger orifice. If the engine runs too rich (a black color on the spark plug after a high-speed run), then the main jet may have to be replaced with one which has a smaller orifice. If in doubt, however, it is better to have a slightly rich mixture to minimize the chance of engine seizure during prolonged high-speed operation.

3

Arctic Cat

INTRODUCTION

Arctic Cat snowmobiles are produced by Arctic Enterprises, Incorporated in Thief River Falls, Minnesota. Arctic Cat began production in 1967 although development work on several limited production machines extended back to the late fifties. The owners of Arctic Cat snowmobiles are often far more loyal to the brand than most other snowmobile owners. Arctic produces its own chassis and, since 1973, it has also produced its own drive system. From 1976 through 1980 all Arctic Cat Snowmobiles have been equipped with spirit (Suzuki) engines. The '76 and newer Arctic Cat Snowmobiles have all used Mikuni carburetors and fuel pumps because of their trouble free operating characteristics.

SERIAL NUMBER IDENTIFICATION

Vehicle

There are two identification plates; one on a serial number plate riveted to the frame and the other is stamped into the chassis. The chassis model and serial number plate is riveted to the side of the chassis near the

right foot rest. The body serial number should be stamped in the chassis sheet metal, near the chassis and serial number plate.

Engine

The engine serial number and model number are stamped into a metal plate which is affixed to the engine housing near the recoil starter. All three numbers should be recorded to complete the warranty and to help recover the vehicle in case it is stolen. They can also be helpful when repairing the snowmobile and for ordering the correct repair parts.

ROUTINE MAINTENANCE

General care and maintenance is possibly the most important aspect of owning a snowmobile. Frequent examination of the vehicle's components will keep the unit in the best possible condition. Before using the vehicle, there should be a predriving inspection, a type of check list, where components are checked for workability and possible wear. It is in this manner that possible serious failure can be avoided. Don't be caught out in the cold; make this inspection before each usage.

Listed below is a periodic inspection list which should be used to check the vehicle.

Maintenance Interval Schedule

	Daily	Weekly	Monthly
Fuel	X		
Throttle control freedom	X		
Brake control freedom	X		
Steering movement	X		
Tools	X		
Lights and safety switch	X		
Rear tension arms		X	
Spark plug		X	
Drive belt		X	
Suspension adjustment		X	
Ski Alignment		X	
Ski skag condition		X	
Eccentric bearing			X
Clutch torque converter			X
Chaincase oil level			X
Track tension and alignment			X
Fuel filter			X
Drive chain tension			X
Battery			X

Lubrication

The factory recommends that the eccentric bearing be lubricated at forty-hour running-

time intervals. The lubrication should be done with low-temperature grease.

CAUTION: *Use extreme caution not to damage the seal when inserting the grease. Stop pumping the grease when slight resistance is felt. Do not blow the seal out.*

Using a hand-type grease gun, lubricate (with the same low-temperature grease) the grease fittings on the rear suspension arms.

The driven sheave should be lubricated once each month, as illustrated in the chart. First, remove the drive belt (see "Drive Belt Section") and expand the pulley by moving the movable face. Put a thin coat of the low-temperature grease onto the shaft and move the sheave half in and out to distribute the lubricant. Do not overgrease the shaft, as the centrifugal force will throw the grease onto the belt, which will cause it to slip.

Arctic Cat recommends that the chaincase lubricant level be checked at monthly intervals. The level should be to the lower hole. The factory specifies the use of Arctic Cat Chainlube which is inserted through the upper filler hole until the level reaches the lower hole.

Brake Adjustment

It is recommended that the brake maintain at least ¾ in. of free travel at the hand grip at all

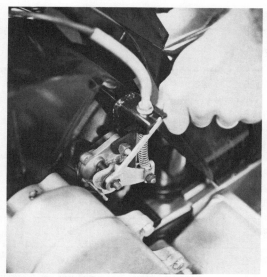
Turning the brake adjusting nut

Locknut on steering tie rod

times. If the brakes need adjustment, it is done by tightening the locknut which is located at the center of the brake lever arm. This will take up the play in the brake line.

Track Tensioning and Alignment

The track tensioning and alignment procedures outlined in Chapter 1 should be used to adjust the track. The track tension is measured at the bottom run of the track with the rear of the machine off the ground so that all of the slack can be pulled to the bottom run of the track. There should be 1¼ to 1½ in. of clearance on the 1976 and 1977 models. The clearance should be the same on both sides of the track.

Ski Alignment

The skis have been aligned at the factory and do not require further attention except in the case of an accident where there is fear of misalignment.

The alignment may be checked by placing the handlebar in the straight driving position with the machine on a level surface. Measure the distance between the skis at the tips and also the distance at the rear spring mounts. The skis should be parallel to each other. Adjustment can be made by loosening the adjusting nut on the steering tie-rod end and moving the rod end inward or outward to gain the paralleled setting. Remember to

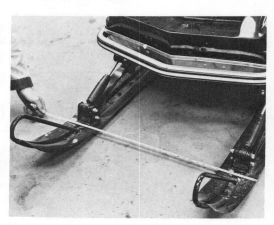
Measuring ski alignment

tighten the locknut after making the final adjustment.

NOTE: *In order to adjust the right side tie-rod end it may be necessary to remove the muffler.*

TUNE-UP

Ignition System

Each of the various brands of engines used in Arctic Cat snowmobiles over the years has its own brand of ignition system. A capacitor discharge ignition (CDI) system appeared on some of the 1973 Kawasaki engines and on most of the later models. All of the other engines used in Arctic Cat snowmobiles have a breaker point type of ignition system. The

Tune Up Specifications

Year	Engine Series	Type Cooling	Spark Plug	Plug Gap	Ign. Timing at 6000 RPM	Eng. Size C.C.
1976–80	2000(T)	F.A.	BR8ES	.020	18°	275
	2000(S)	F.A.	BR9ES	.020	22°	250
	3000	F.A.	BR8ES	.020	18°	339
1976–79	4000	F.C.	BR8ES	.020	18°	431
	4000	F.A.	BR8ES	.020	18°	431
	5000	F.C.	BR9ES	.020	18°	500
	5000	F.A.	BR9ES	.020	20°	500
1979	6000	Liquid	BR9ES	.020	22°	436
1980	6000	Liquid	BR9ES	.020	27°	500
	4000	F.C.	BR9ES	.020	18°	431
	5000	F.C.	BR9ES	.020	18°	500
	3000	F.C.	BR9ES	.020	18°	339

F.A. = Free Air
F.C. = Fan Cooled
*oil injection

general adjustment and removal and installation steps described in Chapter 1 should be used for repair or tune-up of the CDI type of ignition systems. The engine sections in this chapter describe the variations of each engine with specific tune-up specifications for each engine used by Arctic Cat.

The ignition timing specifications on the engines used by Arctic Cat are given in degrees BTDC rather than in inches BTDC as described in Chapter 1. The timing sequence is the same with either type of ignition timing dimensional data. The degrees BTDC timing refers to the number of degrees (of the 360 degree total) of crankshaft rotation while the inches BTDC figures refer to the piston's distance down the cylinder before it moves up to top dead center. There is usually a mark on the flywheel at the specified number of degrees before top dead center. Most snowmobile shops and automotive tool supply stores sell a degree wheel which can be bolted to the end of the crankshaft to verify

the location of the factory ignition timing mark on the flywheel. Locate top dead center, with a dial indicator in the spark plug hole as described in Chapter 1, and rotate the crankshaft backward to the specified degrees of BTDC figure to verify the location of the factory ignition timing mark.

FUEL SYSTEM

Carburetor

Consult the specific section of Chapter 2 which is applicable to the carburetor brand and type used on the engine in your Arctic Cat snowmobile for complete overhaul information.

Fuel Pump

All engines used in Arctic Cat snowmobiles are equipped with a remote mounted diaphragm type fuel pump (Mikuni). The information given in Chapter 2 will be sufficient to repair or replace a faulty fuel pump. When the fuel pump fails it should be removed, after draining the fuel tank. Then it can be repaired or replaced with a new or rebuilt fuel pump available from an Arctic Cat dealer.

Fuel Tank

The fuel tank on most of the Arctic Cat models is located at the front of the machine and is constructed of polyethylene. The tank capacity varies from model to model. For the correct capacity of your model, check the specifications chart.

To remove the tank from the chassis it is necessary to remove the seating cushion and disconnect the gas line hose from the tank. (The tank should of course be drained before this.) Remove the tank from the chassis.

IGNITION SYSTEM

Spirit Engine C.D.I. Test Procedure

Oftentimes, the fuel system will not be functioning properly and, as a result, you may believe there is a problem in the ignition system. Before the ignition system is considered to be malfunctioning, check the fuel system to make sure the engine is getting fuel.

1. Check fuel tank for fuel; remove cap and visually check.

2. Check in-line fuel filter. If filter is dirty, clean or replace.

3. Check fuel delivery to the engine. This can be determined by using a squirt can filled

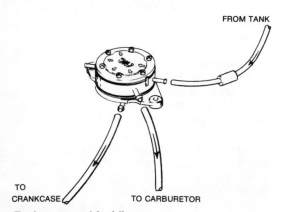

Fuel pump and fuel lines

with a gas/oil mixture. If engine will not start, squirt two or three bursts of fuel into the carburetor bore. Make sure all switches are in the "ON" position. Start engine. If engine runs and then stops, the carburetor is not delivering fuel. If the engine does not at all respond, proceed to step 4.

4. Remove spark plugs and visually check condition. Replace any fouled plug. Attach spark plugs to spark plug wires and lay on the cylinder heads so they are grounded. Make sure all switches are in the "ON" position.

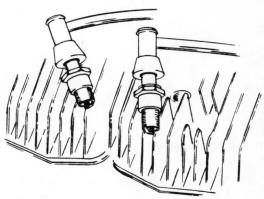

Checking spark

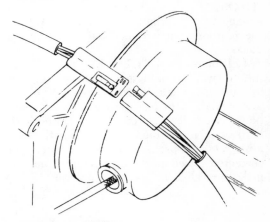

Checking wire harness

5. Grasp recoil and crank engine over quickly. Check spark plugs for spark. If no spark is seen, disconnect the main wiring harness from the engine. Pull recoil rope several times. If there is no spark, the wiring harness is defective. To check wiring harness, proceed to wiring harness test procedure. If there is still no spark, the problem is in the engine ignition system. To check ignition system, proceed to High Voltage Output Test.

WIRING HARNESS TEST

1. Make sure throttle cables are synchronized so throttle safety switch is properly tensioned.

2. Connect one ohmmeter lead to the black lead in the main harness at the engine connector. Attach the other lead of the meter to the double brown wire connection in the same connector.

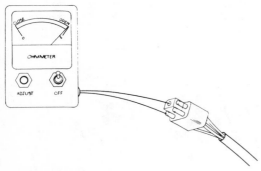

Using an ohmmeter

3. With both the ignition switch and safety switch in the "ON" position, the meter must register "OPEN." If tester reads "CLOSED," disconnect the ignition switch connector. If the meter now reads "OPEN" the ignition switch is bad and must be replaced.

4. If meter reads "CLOSED" with the ignition switch unplugged, then go to the safety stop switch and disconnect it. If the meter reads "OPEN," the safety switch must be replaced. If the circuit is still closed with both switches disconnected, replace the harness. After the problem has been located and corrected, place machine on a test stand and make sure all safety switches are working.

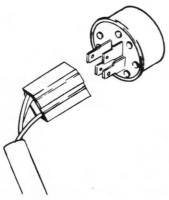

Ignition switch and harness

Safety switch wire harness

IGNITION SYSTEM TEST

To test the ignition system on the new Spirit engines, a service technician must have a CDI tester and a trigger pulse simulator. A new tester is available which incorporates both testers into one. The testers are not available from Arctic but can be ordered directly from the manufacturer: Electro-Specialties, Inc., 11225 W. Bluemound Road, Wauwatosa, WI 53226.

If the engine fails because of lack of spark, check the output of the external coils first.

HIGH VOLTAGE OUTPUT TEST

1. Remove the resistor spark plug and spark plug cap. For test purposes install a B9EV spark plug and an automotive type spark plug wire end.

2. Install the B9EV plug in the MAG side cylinder. Attach plug wire with metal connector. Make sure the PTO side plug wire is attached to a spark plug and properly grounded

NOTE: *Damage to the coils will result if the engine is cranked over when the spark plugs are not properly grounded.*

3. Connect the red lead of the tester to the MM-1 secondary adapter. Connect the adapter to the MAG side high tension lead. Connect the yellow tester lead to ground. Set the tester on 80 and crank engine over quickly. If the red light of the tester illuminates the high voltage output is satisfactory. Repeat the test three times for conclusive results. If the light did not illuminate, proceed to CDI Unit Output Test.

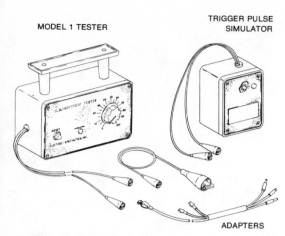

MODEL 1 TESTER

TRIGGER PULSE SIMULATOR

ADAPTERS

C.D.I. test equipment

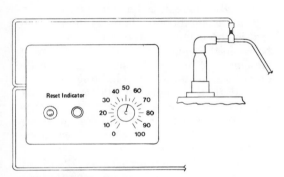

Reset Indicator

40 50 60
30 70
20 80
10 90
0 100

C.D.I. output test

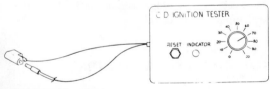

C D IGNITION TESTER

RESET INDICATOR

C.D.I. ignition test

NOTE: *During electrical checks of the engine, the CDI tester leads may be reversed with no effect to the life of the tester. Occasionally reversing the leads will result in better test readings.*

CDI UNIT OUTPUT TEST

1. Disconnect the two wires connecting the CDI unit to the external coil.
2. Connect the red tester lead to the black wire coming from the CDI unit.
3. Connect the yellow tester lead to the remaining white and blue wire coming from the CDI unit. Set the tester on 65 and pull the engine over quickly. If the tester light illuminates, this will indicate that the external coil is bad. If the light does not illuminate, proceed to the Charge Coil Test.

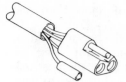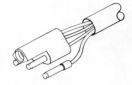

Magneto to C.D.I. harness

CHARGE COIL TEST

1. Disconnect the triple plug from the magneto to CDI unit. Also, disconnect single green wire outside the triple plug.
2. Connect the red lead of tester to the red wire in the triple plug. Connect the yellow lead of tester to the black wire, also located in triple plug.
3. Set tester on 50. Grasp recoil and crank the engine over quickly. If the light illuminates, repeat the test twice for conclusive results. If the light does not illuminate, replace the charge coil.
4. Repeat steps 2 and 3, but connect the red tester lead to the white wire in the triple plug. Light must again illuminate. If the charge coil tests good, proceed to Trigger Coil Test.

TRIGGER COIL TEST

1. Using the wire harness adapter, connect the yellow tester lead to the single green wire coming from the engine.
2. Connect the red tester lead to a good ground on the engine.
3. Set tester selector at 75 on the low scale.
4. Grasp recoil and crank engine over quickly. Light must illuminate if trigger coil is good. Repeat test 3 times to be sure of the results.

NOTE: *If the light illuminates in both the trigger and charge coil test, this would then indicate that the CDI unit which previously tested out satisfactory, is actually bad and must be replaced. If the light on the tester fails to illuminate, replace the trigger coil.*

LIGHT SYSTEM TEST PROCEDURE

Problems in the lighting system can be pinpointed in a relatively short time, if a systematic troubleshooting procedure is followed.

Too many times when a light bulb fails or becomes loose in the socket, the magneto system is blamed. If this happens, and the mechanic spends needless time disassembling the magneto only to find it in good condition, you have lost shop time and money.

When troubleshooting the lighting system, keep these points in mind. Your first approach should be to check the simplest reasons for not having lights. In order to have lights, you first must have current and a good patch for it to follow. Second, you need a workable switch, third, a good ground to complete the circuit, and fourth, a good bulb to provide the light.

The light system troubleshooting chart at the end of this manual will provide you with information that should be used in troubleshooting a lighting problem. It will list the problem, the probable cause, and the remedy. By referring to this chart, your troubleshooting time should be reduced.

LIGHTING COIL TEST

1. Disconnect the main wiring harness from the engine.

2. Connect the red lead of the tester to either of the yellow wires located in the four-prong plug coming from the engine. Connect the yellow tester lead to the remaining yellow wire in the plug.

3. Set the tester at 80 on the LOW scale, grasp recoil and crank engine over quickly. Light must illuminate if lighting coils are in good condition.

LIGHTING COIL RESISTANCE TEST

1. Disconnect the main wiring harness from the engine connector.

2. Connect ohmmeter to the two yellow wires in engine connector.

3. Meter should register 0.145 ohm if coil is good. The coil resistance on this model is 0.18.

4. To check voltage regulator, proceed to Check Voltage Regulator.

CHECK VOLTAGE REGULATOR

1. Raise the rear of the snowmobile off the shop floor, using a safety stand. Make sure track is free to rotate.

2. Connect the main wiring harness connector to the engine connector plug.

3. Remove the voltage regulator from the chassis. Leave it connected to the wire harness, but isolate it from the chassis.

4. Set multitester selector at 100 AC volts. Connect one lead of the AC voltmeter to the yellow wire on the voltage regulator and the other tester lead to GROUND on the steering column.

5. Turn the ignition switch to the run position.

6. Start the engine and allow it to idle rapidly. The voltmeter must register approximately 12–15 AC volts. Grasp the throttle and accelerate slightly. As the engine rpm increases, the voltmeter must register 15 to 25 AC volts.

CAUTION: *Make sure the AC voltmeter has the capacity to test in excess of 30 AC volts. High engine rpm can cause high voltage and, as a result, may damage on-line components (AC voltmeter, etc.).*

7. If the voltmeter registers 12 to 15 AC volts at engine idle, and 15–25 AC volts when engine is accelerated slightly, adequate power is getting to the system. Proceed to step 8. By contrast, if the voltmeter does not register as mentioned, there is either a problem in the magneto alternator wiring circuit between the engine connector and the regulator ground on the chassis or, between the engine connector and the lighting coil.

8. With the engine at idle, and the AC voltmeter as in step 4, connect the voltage regulator to the chassis. Voltmeter must register 12–15 AC volts at idle and when the engine is accelerated.

9. If the voltmeter registers 12–15 AC volts, the voltage regulator is operating correctly. If voltmeter does not register 12–15 AC volts, the voltage regulator is defective and must be replaced.

SERVICING ENGINE ELECTRICAL SYSTEM

Ignition Coil

1. Remove the two screws securing the ignition coil in place on the fan housing.

2. Disconnect the ignition coil wiring harness from the engine wiring harness.

3. Remove the spark plug caps from the coil leads by rotating the caps counterclockwise.

4. Install the caps on the ignition leads by rotating the caps clockwise, then slide cap seals onto caps.

5. Secure coil in place with two cap screws and washers.

6. Connect the coil harness to the engine harness.

CDI Unit

1. Remove the two cap screws securing the CDI unit in place on the fan housing.

2. Disconnect the CDI wiring harness from the main engine harness.

3. Place the new CDI unit in position and secure with two cap screws and washers.

4. Connect the CDI harness to the engine wiring harness.

Magneto Components

1. Remove the four cap screws securing the recoil on the fan housing.

2. Remove the three cap screws holding the pulley starter and fan drive pulley against the flywheel.

3. Remove the nut, lock washer, and spacer washer securing the flywheel on the crankshaft.

NOTE: *If an impact wrench is not available, secure the pulley starter on the flywheel with the recoil bolts; then use the special flywheel spanner to prevent the crankshaft from turning when removing the nut.*

4. Using the special flywheel puller and attachment, remove the flywheel from the crankshaft. Place flywheel on a clean surface with the magnets facing upward.

5. To remove the lighting/charge coil, remove the two screws and washers securing the coil ring to the stator baseplate.

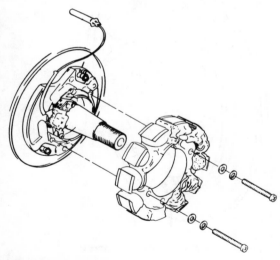

Lighting charge coil

6. Disconnect the wiring harness and guide harness w/grommet through the fan housing.

NOTE: *Be sure to loosen the harness clamp.*

7. To install the coil ring, proceed to step 14.

8. To remove the trigger (timing senser) coil, remove the two screws and washers securing trigger coil to the baseplate.

9. Guide the green wire through the grommet; then remove trigger coil. For assembly, proceed to step 13.

10. To remove the baseplate, remove two screws and washers securing baseplate to the fan housing, Fig. 7-14. For assembly, proceed to step 12.

11. To assemble the magneto components, care must be taken to ensure correct engine timing. On the baseplate are four timing reference marks. When viewing the marks from left to right, the marks correspond to 15, 18, 20, and 22 degrees before top dead center (BTDC). To time the engine for assembly purposes, align second mark from the left with the center of the upper baseplate mounting hole (18 degrees BTDC).

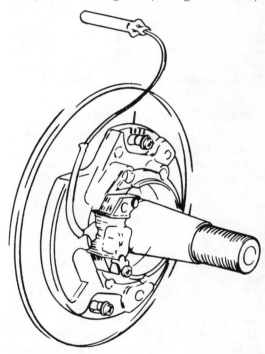

Magneto components

12. Secure the baseplate with two cap screws and washers.

13. Fasten the trigger coil to the baseplate, using two screws and washers.

NOTE: *Apply Loc-Tite® to the screws before assembly.*

14. Fasten the lighting/charge coil ring to the baseplate of the stator, using two screws and washers.

NOTE: *Apply Loc-Tite® to the screws before assembly.*

15. Align the woodruff key in the crankshaft with the slot in the flywheel; then guide the flywheel on to the crankshaft.

NOTE: *Be sure the flywheel magnets are free of any foreign material.*

16. Install the spacer washer, lock washer, and nut on the end of the crankshaft; then tighten the flywheel nut to 65–80 ft-lb (8.99–11.06 kg-m).

NOTE: *The pulley starter may be fastened to the flywheel and used in conjunction with the special flywheel spanner to prevent the crankshaft from turning when tightening the flywheel nut.*

17. Place the fan drive pulley and pulley starter against the flywheel and secure, using three cap screws and washers. Tighten the cap screws to 5–7 ft-lb.

18. Place the recoil in position and secure with the four mounting screws. BEFORE tightening the mounting screws, pull the rope slightly to engage the recoil pawls. This will self-center the recoil on the housing. Tighten screws to 5–7 ft-lb (0.69–0.97 kg-m).

Ignition Timing Adjustment

1. Use the dial indicator to find top dead center (TDC) of the PTO side cylinder.

2. Rotate the PTO end of the crankshaft opposite normal shaft rotation 18° (0.080").

3. When the correct reading is reached, make a reference mark on the drive clutch housing and a corresponding mark on the PTO cylinder. These marks will be used to check timing.

4. Remove the dial indicator and install the spark plug.

5. Start the engine. Check the timing with a timing light. The timing marks must align when the engine is at 6000 rpm.

6. If the timing is off, remove the recoil starter, the starter pulley, and the fan drive pulley.

7. Remove the flywheel nut and lock washer; then remove the flywheel with the aid of a flywheel puller.

8. Remove the two screws securing the lighting coil ring to the baseplate.

9. Loosen the two screws securing baseplate to the magneto case. Rotate the baseplate clockwise to retard the timing or counterclockwise to advance the timing.

10. Tighten the baseplate screws; then install the lighting coil.

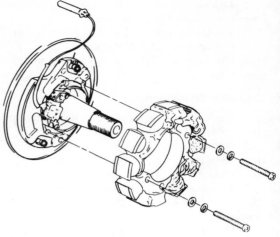

Coil-magneto attaching parts

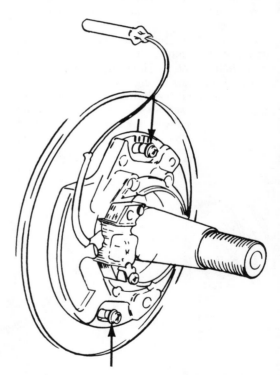

Magneto base plate adjusting screws

11. Install the flywheel, lock washer, and nut; then tighten flywheel nut to 65–80 ft-lb or 8.99–11.06 kg-m.

12. Install the fan drive pulley, axial belt and starter pulley; then install the recoil starter assembly.

13. Recheck ignition timing and readjust if necessary.

ENGINES

Arctic Cat has used a variety of engines in their snowmobiles over the years. But since 1976 they have used the Arctic Cat Spirit engine Suzuki. They have a reputation for performing well and at the same time being quite trouble-free.

Arctic Cat "Spirit" Engines

The following section covers the Arctic Cat "Spirit" engines. The El-Tigre 5000 and 6000 are covered in detail and are typical of Arctic Cat engines. All other model specifications and clearances are listed. By following the step by step procedures shown for the El-Tigre engines and the proper listed specifications and clearances you will be able to repair any Arctic "Spirit" engine.

Engine Specifications

Year	Engine Model	No. of Cylinders	Displacement (C.C.)	Bore (M.M.)	Stroke (M.M.)	Comp. Ratio
1976–80	2000	2	275	54	60	6.5-1
	3000	2	339	60	60	6.8-1
1976–79	4000	2	431	65	65	6.5-1
1976–80	5000	2	500	70	65	6.9-1
1977–80	Kitty Cat	1	60	41	45	N.A.
1976–79	4000 F/C	2	431	65	65	6.6-1
	5000 F/C	2	500	70	65	6.6-1
1976–80	2000 S	1	250	70	65	6.8-1
1978–79	6000 4C	2	435.8	68	60	6.9-1
1980	6000 4C	2	500	70	65	6.9-1
1979–80	3000 F/C	2*	339	60	60	6.8-1
1980	4000 F/C	2*	431	65	65	6.5-1
	5000 F/C	2*	500	70	65	6.6-1

L/C Liquid Cooled
F/C Fan Cooled
All others Free Air Cooled
*oil injection

Engine Specifications—1976–79 El-Tigre

Engine	5000	6000
Model number	AD50F3	AF44L1
Type	2 cycle	2 cycle

Engine Specifications—1976–79 El-Tigre (cont.)

Engine		5000	6000
No. of cylinders		2	2
Lubrication		Gas/oil mix	Gas/oil mix
Manual start		Std.	Std.
Bore	mm in.	70 2.756	68 2.677
Stroke	mm in.	65 2.559	60 2.362
Displacement	cc cu. in.	500.3 30.5	435.8 26.6
Compression Ratio		6.47 : 1	6.89 : 1
Piston ring end gap wear limit	mm in.	0.15–0.83 0.006–0.033	Up to 0.8 Up to 0.033
*Piston skirt cylinder clearance	mm in.	0.04–0.05 0.0015–0.002	0.04–0.05 0.0015–0.002
Piston pin diameter	mm in.	18 0.7085–0.7087	18 0.7085–0.7087
Piston pin bore diameter	mm in.	18 0.7085–0.7089	18 0.7085–0.7089
Connecting rod small end diameter	mm in.	23.00–23.03 0.9059–0.9067	23.00–23.03 0.9055–0.9067
Connecting rod radial play	mm in.	0.017–0.034 0.00067–0.0013	0.017–0.034 0.00067–0.0013
Crankshaft end play	mm in.	0.05–0.10 0.002–0.004	0.05–0.10 0.002–0.004
Crankshaft runout	mm in.	0.05 0.002	0.05 0.002

*The specification given is for new component assembly. The piston skirt/clearance wear limit for both models is 0.15 mm or 0.006 of an inch.

Engine Specifications—1980 El-Tigre

Engine	5000	6000
Model number	AD50F5	AH50L1
No. of cylinders	2	2
Engine lubrication	Gas/oil mixture	Gas/oil mixture
Starter system	Manual recoil	Manual recoil
Bore x stroke	70 x 65 mm (2.756 x 2.559 in.)	70 x 65 mm (2.756 x 2.559 in.)
Displacement	500 cc (30.5 cu in.)	500 cc (30.5 cu in.)
Compression ratio	6.5 : 1	6.9 : 1
Piston-ring end gap	0.15–0.83 mm (0.006–0.033 in.)	0.15–0.80 mm (0.006–0.031 in.)
Piston skirt/cylinder clearance range	0.04–0.15 mm (0.0015–0.0060 in.)	0.095–0.15 mm (0.0037–0.0060 in.)
Piston pin diameter	17.995–18.000 mm (0.7085–0.7087 in.)	17.995–18.000 mm (0.7085–0.7087 in.)
Piston-pin bore diameter	17.998–18.006 mm (0.7086–0.7089 in.)	17.998–18.006 mm (0.7086–0.7089 in.)
Connecting-rod small end diameter	23.00–23.03 mm (0.9056–0.9067 in.)	23.00–23.01 mm (0.9056–0.9059 in.)
Crankshaft end play	0.05–0.10 mm (0.002–0.004 in.)	0.035–0.175 mm (0.0014–0.0069 in.)
Crankshaft runout (max.) (total indicator reading)	0.05 mm (0.002 in.)	0.05 mm (0.002 in.)
Cylinder (max.) out-of-round	0.05 mm (0.002 in.)	0.05 mm (0.002 in.)

Engine Specifications—All Models Except El Tigre 5000 and 6000 Models

NEW CYLINDER DIAMETERS

Engine	Diameter (mm)	Diameter (in.)
AB25F1/F2	70.00–70.015	2.7559–2.7565
AA28F2/F3	54.015–54.030	2.126–2.127
AA34F3	60.000–60.015	2.362–2.363
AC44A3	65.000–65.015	2.559–2.560
AB50A3	70.000–70.015	2.7559–2.7565
AC50F2	70.000–70.015	2.7559–2.7565
AE50A2	70.000–70.015	2.7559–2.7565

ACCEPTABLE PIN BORE DIAMETERS

Engine	Diameter (mm)	Diameter (in.)
AB25F1/F2	18	0.7085–0.7089
AA28F2/F3	16	0.6298–0.6301
AA34F3	16	0.6298–0.6301
AC44A3	18	0.7085–0.7089
AB50A3	18	0.7085–0.7089
AC50F2	18	0.7085–0.7089
AC50A2	18	0.7085–0.7089

ACCEPTABLE PISTON PIN DIAMETERS

Engine	Diameter (mm)	Diameter (in.)
AB25F1/F2	18	0.7085–0.7087
AA28F2/F3	16	0.6297–0.6299
AA34F3	16	0.6297–0.6299
AC44A3	18	0.7085–0.7087
AB50A3	18	0.7085–0.7087
AC50F2	18	0.7085–0.7087
AE50A2	18	0.7085–0.7087

ACCEPTABLE RING END GAP CLEARANCES

New Components

Engine	Clearance (mm)	Clearance (in.)
AB25F1/F2	0.20–0.40	0.008–0.016
AA28F2/F3	0.15–0.36	0.006–0.014
AA34F3	0.15–0.36	0.006–0.014
AC44A3	0.15–0.36	0.006–0.014
AB50A3	0.20–0.40	0.008–0.016
AC50F2	0.20–0.40	0.006–0.014
AE50A2	0.15–0.36	0.006–0.014

Wear Limit

Engine	Clearance (mm)	Clearance (in.)
AB25F1/F2	0.20–0.83	0.008–0.033
AA28F2/F3	0.15–0.80	0.006–0.031
AA34F3	0.15–0.80	0.006–0.031
AC44A3	0.15–0.80	0.006–0.031
AB50A3	0.20–0.83	0.008–0.033
AC50F2	0.20–0.83	0.008–0.033
AE50A2	0.20–0.83	0.008–0.033

ACCEPTABLE PISTON SKIRT/CYLINDER CLEARANCE / WEAR LIMIT CLEARANCE

Engine	(mm)	(in.)	(mm)	(in.)
AB25F1/F2	0.05–0.06	0.0020–0.0025	Up to 0.15	Up to 0.006
AA28F2/F3	0.04–0.06	0.0015–0.0025	Up to 0.15	Up to 0.006
AA34F3	0.04–0.06	0.0015–0.0020	Up to 0.15	Up to 0.006
AC44A3	0.05–0.06	0.0020–0.0025	Up to 0.15	Up to 0.006
AB50A3	0.05–0.06	0.0020–0.0020	Up to 0.15	Up to 0.006
AC50F2	0.05–0.06	0.0020–0.0025	Up to 0.15	Up to 0.006
AE50A2	0.05–0.06	0.0020–0.0025	Up to 0.15	Up to 0.006

ENGINE REMOVAL AND INSTALLATION

5000 Free Air

1. Open hood.
2. Remove the two pins securing clutch guard and remove the clutch guard.
3. Remove the drive belt.

4. Remove the springs securing the expansion chamber and remove the chamber.
5. Remove the spark plug caps.
6. Loosen hose clamps securing the air silencer connectors to the carburetors.
7. Loosen the carburetor flange clamps and slide the carburetors free of the adapters.

8. Disconnect the impulse line from the crankcase fitting.

9. Disconnect the main ignition harness and the ignition coil harness.

10. Remove the four screws securing the recoil starter.

11. Remove the four cap screws securing the motor plate to the tunnel and angle support.

12. Lift engine out of the chassis.

13. Remove the motor plate.

14. Remove the drive clutch.

To install the engine:

15. Install the motor plate. Tighten the screws to 55 ft. lb.

16. Set motor on the motor mounts and secure it with cupped washers, mounts and screws. Tighten screws to 23 ft. lb.

17. Install the recoil starter and screws. Pull recoil rope until pawls engage and then tighten the screws to 5–7 ft. lb.

18. Connect the impulse line to the crankcase fitting.

19. Connect the main wiring harness and ignition coil harness.

20. Install the caps on the spark plugs.

21. Install the carburetors and air silencer connectors. Tighten both the carburetor flange clamps and connector clamps making sure the connector sides are not kinked.

22. Install the pulse charger and secure it with springs and lock nut. Seal the joint of the pulse charger with RTV sealant.

23. Install the drive clutch.

24. Install the clutch guard and secure it with two retaining pins.

25. Check engine timing.

26. Check the clutch alignment and then install the drive belt.

27. Check the operation of the machine.

6000 Liquid Cooled

1. Open the hood.

2. Remove the two pins securing the clutch guard and remove the clutch guard.

3. Remove the drive belt.

4. Remove the springs securing the expansion chamber and remove the chamber.

5. Loosen the hose clamp securing hose to water intake manifold. Use a plastic container to catch coolant and carefully remove hose from intake manifold.

6. Loosen the clamp securing the hose to the thermostat cap and slide the hose off cap.

7. Disconnect the temperature gauge sender from the cylinder head.

8. Remove the spark plug caps.

9. Loosen the hose clamps securing the air silencer connectors to the carburetors.

10. Loosen the carburetor flange clamps and slide the carburetor free of the adapters.

11. Disconnect the impulse line from the crankcase fitting.

12. Loosen the clamp securing the heat exchanger supply hose to the water pump. Slide the hose free of the pump.

13. Disconnect the main ignition harness and the ignition coil harness.

14. Remove the four screws securing recoil starter.

15. Remove the four screws securing the motor plate to the tunnel and angle support.

16. Lift engine out of the chassis.

17. Remove the motor plate from the engine.

18. Remove the drive clutch.

To install the engine:

19. Install the motor plate. Tighten the screws to 55 ft. lb.

20. Install the motor onto the motor mounts. Secure it with cupped washers, mounts and screws. Tighten screws to 23 ft. lb.

21. Move the recoil starter into position. Install the mounting screws. Pull recoil rope until pawls engage and tighten them to 5–7 ft. lb.

22. Connect the impulse line to the crankcase fitting.

23. Connect the main ignition harness and the ignition coil harness.

24. Apply thread sealer to the cylinder head sending unit and install the sender. Use caution when tightening sender unit to prevent damage.

25. Connect the upper radiator hose to the thermostat cap.

26. Connect the hose from the heat exchanger to the water pump fitting.

27. Install the carburetors. Install the air silencer connectors. Tighten the intake flange clamps and the connector clamps.

28. Install the spark plug caps on the plugs.

29. Secure the exhaust manifold to the engine with lockwashers and nuts. Tighten the nuts to 11–14 ft. lb.

30. Install the expansion chamber and secure it with springs.

31. Install the drive clutch.

32. Install the clutch guard and secure it with two retaining pins.

33. Fill the cooling system.

34. Check the clutch alignment. Install the drive belt.

35. Check the engine timing.

36. Test drive snowmobile.

ENGINE DISASSEMBLY

Free Air Engine

1. The engine should be in a clean area.

2. Remove the recoil starter.

3. Remove the flywheel nut, lockwasher and spacer.

4. Remove the three screws holding pulley starter to flywheel.

5. Using an Arctic flywheel special puller, remove the flywheel from the crankshaft. If flywheel does not break loose, give the bolt a sharp rap with a hammer. The shock should free the flywheel. If it doesn't, repeat until the flywheel is free. Set flywheel on a bench with magnets facing upward.

6. Note position of timing marks on stator plate and crankcase. Remove the two screws securing the stator plate to the magneto case.

7. Loosen the stator harness clamp screw.

8. Using an impact screwdriver, remove the eight screws securing the magneto case to the crankcase.

9. Using a soft mallet, tap the magneto case to remove it from the crankcase. Leave ignition intact with the magneto case.

10. Remove the nuts, lockwashers and flat washers securing cylinder heads. Remove the heads and head gaskets.

11. Remove the nuts, lockwashers and flat washers holding the cylinders.

12. Carefully lift the cylinder straight up until it is free of the piston. Remove the remaining cylinder.

13. Remove the piston pin circlip from the outward side of each piston.

14. Using the Arctic special piston pin puller, remove the piston pins and pistons.

NOTE: *Keep the piston, rings, pins and bearings with their respective cylinders.*

15. Use rubber bands over the connecting rods to prevent crankcase damage should the crankshaft be accidentally rotated.

16. Using an impact screwdriver, remove the four screws securing the PTO side seal housing. Carefully remove the housing and the gasket.

17. Remove the screws securing the crankcase halves.

Hold the flywheel with a special wrench to remove the nut

Remove the nuts holding the cylinders

Use a special Arctic puller to remove the flywheel

Carefully, remove the cylinder by lifting straight up

Remove the piston pin circlips

Remove the 4 screws holding the PTO side seal

18. Using a rubber mallet, tap the crankcase halves apart.

NOTE: *DO NOT use a chisel or screwdriver to pry cases apart. Severe damage to the crankcase sealing area will result.*

19. Lift the crankshaft from the crankcase lower half. Don't lose the C-ring in the lower crankcase half.

20. If no further disassembly is needed, see Inspection and Cleaning. Crankshaft bearing service requires special tools and equipment and should not be attempted.

Liquid Cooled Engine

1. Place the engine on a clean workbench.

2. When removing the recoil starter, note its original location.

3. Remove the screws securing the outside magneto cover and carefully lift the cover free of engine.

4. Using the special Arctic wrench to hold the flywheel, remove the three screws securing starter pulley.

5. Carefully pry the belt pulley off magneto and set the belt and pulley aside.

6. Place starter pulley into position. Use the special wrench to hold flywheel and remove flywheel nut, lockwasher and spacer.

NOTE: *When using starter pulley, make sure mounting bolts do not come in contact with the internal magneto coils.*

7. Using the special Arctic flywheel puller, remove the flywheel from the crankshaft. If flywheel does not break loose, give the bolt a sharp rap with a hammer. The shock should free the flywheel. If it doesn't repeat until the flywheel is free. Set flywheel on a bench with the magnets facing upward.

8. Loosen the screw securing the magneto harness clamp.

9. Note the position of the timing marks on the stator plate and crankcase. Scribe matchmarks to aid in correct positioning during engine assembly.

10. Remove the two screws securing stator plate to crankcase. Slide plate free of crankshaft and lay the plate in the magneto housing.

11. Using an impact screwdriver, remove the screws securing magneto housing to crankcase.

12. Disconnect the coolant bypass hose from the cylinder head.

13. Using a rubber mallet, tap the magneto case to remove it from the crankcase.

14. Remove the screws securing the thermostat cap to the cylinder head. Remove the cap.

15. Remove the thermostat.

Remove the outside magneto cover

Loosen the magneto harness clip

Remove the magneto housing from the crankcase with an impact driver

Remove the magneto case

Remove the thermostat and housing

NOTE: *The thermostat used is set to open at 122° F. To test the thermostat, thread a piece of string under the valve. Suspend the thermostat in a pan of water. Begin heating water. As the seal opens the thermostat should fall at about 122° F (50° C). If the valve does not open, replace the thermostat.*

16. Remove the screws, lockwashers and flat washers securing the cylinder head.

17. Using a rubber mallet, tap the cylinder head until it is free of cylinders. Remove the head gaskets.

18. Remove the four screws securing the water intake manifold.

19. Remove the cylinder base nuts, lockwashers and flat washers. Using a rubber mallet, tap the cylinders to free them from the crankcase.

20. Carefully slide the cylinders straight up over the piston assembly. Mark all components so they can be installed with their respective cylinders.

NOTE: *Use extreme care when handling the cylinder to prevent the reed stop from being damaged.*

21. Remove the outward piston pin circlips.

Unbolt the cylinder head

Tap the cylinder free using a rubber mallet

Carefully slide the cylinders straight up

Lift the crankshaft out of the lower crankcase half

Reed block components

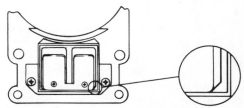

Position the reed with the beveled corner at the lower right hand corner of the block

22. Using the special Arctic piston pin puller, remove the piston pins.

23. Place rubber bands over the connecting rods to prevent rods from damaging crankcase.

24. Lay the engine on its side. Remove the sixteen bolts and washers holding the crankcase halves together.

25. Using a rubber mallet, tap the crankcase halves apart.

NOTE: *DO NOT use a chisel or screwdriver to pry cases apart. Severe damage to the crankcase sealing area will result.*

26. Lift the crankshaft from the crankcase lower half. Be sure you don't lose the C-ring in the lower crankcase half.

27. If no further disassembly is required, see Cleaning and Inspecting. Crankshaft bearing service requires special tools and equipment and should not be attempted.

REED VALVE SERVICING

1. Remove the screws securing the reed block to the cylinder and carefully remove the block.

2. Remove the two screws securing the reed assembly components. Remove the reed block, reed and reed stopper.

3. Inspect the reed block for signs of wear or cracking in the rubber seating area. Replace any damaged reeds.

4. Check the reeds for cracks or signs of warping. Replace if damaged. Apply a light coat of oil to the reeds to prevent corrosion.

5. To assemble the reed block, position the reed with the beveled corner to the lower right hand corner of the block.

6. Move the reed stopper into position on reed. Apply Loc-Tite® to the screws and tighten securely.

7. Place a new reed block gasket on the cylinder base; then install block. Apply Loc-Tite® to the screws and tighten securely.

CAUTION: *When handling the liquid cooled cylinders, do not bump reed stopper. A damaged stopper may eventually cause reed failure, resulting in severe engine damage. HANDLE CYLINDER/ REED CAREFULLY.*

8. Measure from the top of the reed stop to the rubber seating surface of the reed block. Measurement must be 0.362 in. If the reed stop is not within tolerance, do not attempt to bend the reed stopper. Remove stopper and replace with a new part.

CLEANING AND INSPECTION

Whenever a part is worn excessively, cracked, defective or damaged in any way, replacement is necessary.

Cylinder Head

1. Remove any carbon which has collected in the combustion chamber.

NOTE: *Use a plastic or wooden scraper to prevent scratching and scoring of the combustion chamber.*

2. Thoroughly clean the cylinder head in cleaning solvent.

3. Inspect spark plug threaded area for any damage.

4. On the 6000 series engine, place the cylinder head on a glass plate with 400 grit sandpaper to ensure a true sealing surface.

The cylinder head can be surfaced on a glass plate with 400 grit paper

Cylinder

1. Remove carbon from the exhaust port. NOTE: *Use a plastic or wooden scraper removal tool.*

2. Wash the cylinder in cleaning solvent.

3. Inspect cylinder for pitting, scoring, scuffing or corrosion. Replace if damaged.

4. To remove minor imperfections or marks in the cylinder, use a flex hone with 500 grit stones to clean cylinder bore. Use honing oil for lubrication. Move hone so a "crosshatch" pattern will result.

5. Inspect all threaded areas for damage or stripped threads.

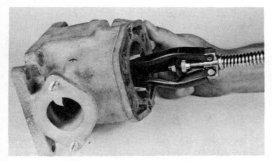

Hone the cylinders with 500 grit stones

Piston

1. Remove carbon buildup from dome of piston using a wooden or plastic tool.

2. Examine the sides of the piston for evidence of excessive "blowby". Excessive "blowby" will indicate worn piston rings or and out-of-round cylinder.

3. Check the sides and skirts for evidence of scuffing. To remove minor marks, use 400 grit sandpaper and lightly sand the affected areas.

4. Check the pistons for signs of cracks in the piston pin and skirt areas. Replace any cracked pistons.

5. Use a piece of an old piston ring to remove any carbon buildup from the piston ring grooves.
NOTE: *Because the Spirit engine uses keystone-type rings, conventional ring groove cleaners must not be used.*

Crankcase Halves

1. Thoroughly wash the crankcase halves, using cleaning solvent.

2. Inspect the crankcase halves for scoring, pitting, scuffing or any imperfections in the casting.

3. Inspect all threaded areas for damaged or stripped threads.

4. Check the bearing areas for signs of cracking or bearing movement; then check retaining dowel pins in bearing areas for wear.

5. Examine the crankcase sealing area. If any nicks or scratches are found in the sealing area, they can be removed with a file. Use the draw file method or use a surface plate. When using the draw file method, push and pull the file the complete length of the crankcase using very light pressure. Continue until high spots are removed. Do not file across the crankcase. If a surface plate is used, rotate the crankcase in a figure eight motion until a uniform finish is noted.

Check the bearing areas for signs of cracks or wear

Crankshaft

1. Thoroughly wash crankshaft and bearings in cleaning solvent.

2. Inspect edges of bearings for external wear, scoring and scuffing. Rotate the bearings by hand to ensure they return freely without binding or roughness.

3. Check the connecting rod using the

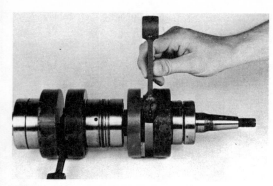

Check the connecting rod bearing play

same method. If binding or roughness is noted, the connecting rod, bearing and crank pin will have to be replaced.

MEASURING CRITICAL COMPONENTS
Checking Cylinder Wear

1. Insert an inside micrometer into the cylinder bore and take six measurements of the bore. Measure front to back and side to side at points below intake port, above exhaust port and ⅜″ below top of cylinder. If measurements vary by more than 0.002 in. the cylinder is either tapered or out-of-round and must be replaced.

2. Check piston skirt clearance. If clearance is more than allowable, the excessive clearance may be reduced with the installation of a new piston. If clearance is still excessive, replace the cylinder.

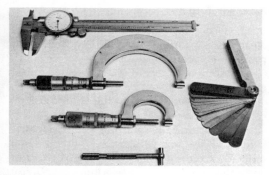

Critical measuring tools

Checking Piston Skirt Clearance

1. Insert an inside micrometer approximately 1 inch from the bottom of the cylinder. Take measurement from front to back.

2. Measure the piston skirt ⅜ in. above the bottom of the piston skirt.

3. Subtract the measurement in step 2 from measurement in step 1. The difference is the piston skirt clearance and must fall within specifications.

NOTE: *If the clearance exceeds the wear limit, the piston must be replaced to bring clearance into the acceptable range. However, if clearance is still excessive, the cylinder will have to be replaced.*

Checking Piston Ring End Gap

1. Insert the piston ring approximately ⅜ in. into the top of the cylinder bore. Position the ring horizontally in cylinder by pressing the dome of the piston against the ring.

2. Slide a feeler gauge between the ends of the ring.

3. End gap must be within specifications. Since the amount of wear at the ends and center of the piston ring arc affects the end gap, replace the ring set if the ring end gap is excessive.

Checking Piston Pin and Piston Pin Bore

1. Measure the piston pin approximately ⅜ in. from each end. Piston pin diameter must be as specified.

NOTE: *If piston pin is not within specifications, replace the piston pin and bearing as a set.*

Measuring the piston pin

Measuring the piston pin bore with a stop gauge or telescope gauge

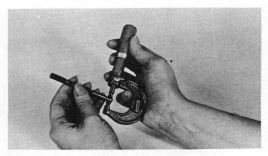

Measuring the gauge with a micrometer

Checking connecting rod play

2. Insert an inside snap gauge ⅜ in. from the outside of the piston pin bore. Carefully remove the snap gauge.

3. Measure the snap gauge with a micrometer. Piston pin bore must be as specified.

Checking Connecting Rod Small End Diameter

1. Insert a snap gauge about ⅜ in into the bore of the connecting rod small end diameter. Lock the gauge and carefully remove it.

2. Measure the snap gauge with a micrometer. The diameter must be as specified. If the diameter is not within specifications, the connecting rod must be replaced.

Checking Crankshaft Runout

1. Firmly mount the crankshaft on V-blocks with a mounting base.

2. Support the crankshaft with the outer crankshaft bearings on the V-block.

3. Mount a dial indicator against the crankshaft at the area of the oil seals. Be sure that the crankshaft is clean. Do not take readings on the tapered areas because an inaccurate reading will be obtained.

4. Slowly rotate the crankshaft and observe the "total" crankshaft runout. This is the difference between the highest and lowest readings. Maximum runout must not exceed 0.002 in. If runout exceeds specifications, the crankshaft must be straightened or replaced.

Checking Connecting Rod Big End Radial Play

1. Use same equipment as preceding.

2. Place the connecting rod at top dead center (TDC).

3. With the crankshaft held at TDC, lift the connecting rod straight up and observe the reading.

4. Push the connecting rod straight down and observe the reading.

5. Big end play must be as specified. If radial play exceeds the maximum limits, the connecting rod, lower rod bearing and crankshaft pin must be replaced.

Checking Crankshaft End Play

The Spirit engine used in the 1978 El Tigre uses a C-ring to locate the crankshaft in the crankcase. The central location of the C-ring eliminates the need for shimmering the end bearings. The bearing dowel pin holes have sufficient clearance to allow easy crankshaft replacement with the need for shims virtually eliminated. Crankshaft end play can be checked and will in nearly every case, be within the specifications. When replacing a crankshaft, install the standard shims and bearings; then assemble the engine.

ENGINE ASSEMBLY

Free Air Engine

1. Place the lower crankcase half on a clean surface. Make sure all bearing dowel pins are correctly positioned.

2. Apply a thin coat of RTV sealer to the crankcase sealing surfaces.

3. Install the C-ring in the center groove of the crankcase halves.

4. Lubricate the inner lip of the Magneto side crankcase seal with grease. Slide the seal onto Magneto end of crankshaft. Make sure spring side of seal faces bearing.

5. Install crankshaft in bottom half of crankcase. Be sure alignment hole in each bearing is positioned over the dowel pin in the crankcase. If the bearings are not properly seated, the case halves will not bolt together tightly. Be sure the half ring is installed in the center of crankcase.

6. To assure a good seal between the two halves, lay number 50 cotton thread

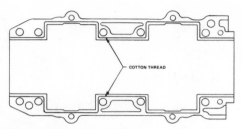

Apply cotton thread to these areas of a Free Air engine

next to the inner edge of crankcase along the full length of the case.

7. Install the top half of the crankcase and start each bolt finger tight only.

8. Tighten the crankcase bolts in small increments to the torques listed. Use the following torque sequence.

CRANKCASE BOLT TORQUE

Bolt Size	ft. lb.
6 mm	6-7
8 mm	13-16
10 mm	23-29

9. Place a thin coat of RTV on both sides of the PTO bearing housing gasket; then place gasket on crankcase. Make sure the oiling hole of gasket is aligned with the hole in crankcase.

10. Apply grease to the double lip of the PTO side seal. Install the seal in the bearing housing. Slide housing into position on the crankcase. Install the four screws and tighten with an impact driver.

11. Oil the lower crankcase bearings and the lower connecting rod bearings.

12. Apply RTV to the base gasket surface. Place gasket in position, and, apply RTV to base gaskets.

13. Install the connecting rod small end bearings. Oil the bearings.

14. Place the pistons over the connecting rods so the arrows on the dome of the piston point to the exhaust port. If there is no mark on the piston dome, correctly position the piston so the top piston ring keeper pin is on the intake side of the cylinder.

NOTE: *If the piston rings were removed, install the piston rings making sure the small letter is positioned on the top side of the ring. If the rings are installed improperly, cylinder installation may be difficult.*

15. Insert the piston pins. Secure them with the piston pin locks. Make sure the open end of the locks are positioned upward.

16. Lubricate the pistons, rings and cylinder walls.

17. If the carburetor flanges were removed, apply RTV sealant to the cylinder intake flanges. Install the carburetor flanges and tighten to 11–14 ft. lb.

18. Place a piston holder or a piece of hi-fax under the piston to hold piston steady. Using the Arctic special ring compressor, carefully slide the cylinders onto the pistons. If the cylinder seems to resist or bind, do not force cylinder. Remove it and try again. If difficulty still occurs, check the piston rings for correct installation. Install remaining piston.

19. Install the exhaust manifold. This will properly index the cylinders on the crankcase. Install the flat washers, lock washers and nuts. Tighten to 22–29 ft. lb. using a crisscross pattern.

20. Apply a thin coat of RTV to the cylinder head gasket sealing surface.

21. Place head gaskets in position. Install the cylinder heads on cylinders.

22. Install the flat washers, lockwashers and nuts. Tighten the nuts to 13–16 ft. lb. Use the torque sequence shown.

23. Place the magneto case in position and secure with the eight screws. Apply Loc-Tite®

Free Air engine crankcase torque sequence

Apply RTV sealant to the cylinder head gasket sealing area of Free Air engines

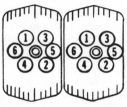

Free Air engine cylinder head torque sequence

Install the flywheel spacer, lockwasher and nut

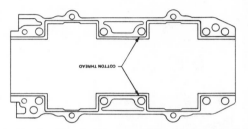

Apply cotton thread to these areas of liquid cooled engines

Position of bearing alignment holes on liquid cooled engine

to the screws and tighten it with an impact screwdriver.

24. Move the stator plate into position. Align the marks noted during disassembly. Install the screws and tighten.

NOTE: *If no timing marks were made during disassembly, refer to the general information section.*

25. Tighten the stator plate harness clamp.

26. Be sure the flywheel magnets are clean. Install the flywheel over the woodruff key. Install the spacer, lockwasher and nut.

27. Install recoil pulley and cap screws. Using the spanner wrench, tighten cap screws to 0.7 kg-m or 5 ft. lb.

28. Tighten the flywheel nut to 65 ft. lb.

29. Install the engine.

Liquid Cooled Engine

1. Place the lower crankcase half on a clean surface. Make sure all bearing dowel pins are correctly positioned in crankcase.

2. Apply a thin coat of RTV sealer to the crankcase sealing surface.

3. To assure a good seal between the two halves, lay number 50 cotton thread next to the inner edge of crankcase along the full length of the case.

NOTE: *Be sure to use cotton thread when sealing crankcase halves. Polyester thread will damage the crankcase halves.*

4. Install the C-ring in the center groove of the crankcase halves.

5. Note the position of the bearing alignment holes and the bearing dowel pins. Be certain that the alignment hole in each bear-

ing is correctly positioned over the dowel pin. If the bearings are not seated properly, the case halves will not bolt together tightly and engine damage will result.

6. Lubricate the crankshaft end seals with a liberal amount of grease between the double lip of the seals. Slide the seals onto the crankshaft. Make sure spring side of the seals faces the bearings.

7. Install the crankshaft in the lower crankcase half. Align each bearing by rotating it until the bearing drops over dowel pin.

8. Install the top of the crankcase. Lay engine on its side and install the bolts finger tight.

9. Tighten the crankcase bolts to the torque listed. Use the following torque sequence shown.

CRANKCASE BOLT TORQUE

Bolt Size	ft. lb.
6 mm	6–7
8 mm	13–16
10 mm	22–29

10. Lubricate the lower connecting rod bearing with engine oil.

11. Apply RTV sealer to both sides of the base gasket in the areas near the transfer ports and reed block. Install the gaskets.

12. Insert the connecting rod small end bearings and lubricate with engine oil.

13. Place the pistons over the connecting

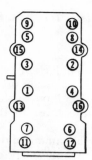

Crankcase torque sequence—Liquid cooled engines

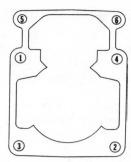

Cylinder base nut torque sequence—Liquid cooled engines

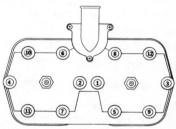

Cylinder head torque sequence—Liquid cooled engines

rods and secure with piston pins. Secure pin with the pin locks, making sure that the open end of the lock is positioned upward.

NOTE: *The arrow on the piston dome must point to the exhaust port. On pistons without an arrow, the top ring retaining pin must be positioned on the intake side.*

14. If the piston rings were removed, install the rings so the letter on the piston ring faces the dome of the piston.

15. Lubricate the rings, pistons and cylinder walls.

16. Place a piston holder under the piston. Using a ring compressor, slide the cylinders over the pistons.

17. Apply RTV sealer to the water manifold flanges.

18. To correctly index the cylinders, install the gaskets and the water intake manifold. Tighten to 5–7 ft. lb.

19. Carefully tighten the cylinder base nuts in small increments using the pattern shown.

CRANKCASE BOLT TORQUE

Bolt Size	ft. lb.
6 mm	6–7
8 mm	13–16

20. Place the head gaskets on the cylinders. The head gaskets must be installed so the large water passage holes are positioned to the intake side of the engine. If the gaskets are installed improperly, serious engine damage may result. Use a very thin coat of RTV sealer on the gaskets.

21. Place the cylinder head in position. Install the screws, lockwashers, flat washers and nuts.

22. Tighten head bolts to 22–29 ft. lb. using the torque sequence shown.

23. Install the thermostat. Make sure the coil spring portion is positioned downward.

Secure bypass hose to the fitting on the cylinder head.

24. Install the thermostat gasket. Install the cap so that the outlet points to the PTO side. Apply RTV sealer to the gasket.

25. Install the magneto case. Apply Loc-Tite® to the eight screws and tighten with an impact screwdriver.

26. Move the stator plate into position. Align the marks made during disassembly. Tighten the two screws.

NOTE: *If no marks were made during disassembly, refer to the timing information in general information section.*

27. Tighten the wiring harness clamp.

28. Make sure woodruff key is in place. Check to ensure the flywheel magnets are clean and install the flywheel. Install the spacer, lockwasher and nut.

29. Install the belt, belt pulley and starter cup. Use the special wrench to hold flywheel, and tighten flywheel nut to 65 ft. lb. Tighten starter cup bolts to 5–7 ft. lb.

30. Check belt deflection. Deflection should be no more than ¼ inch at midspan. Belt tension can be adjusted with the bolt located on the rear side of the water pump housing.

31. Install the belt cover and tighten all screws.

32. Connect hose to water intake manifold and tighten the clamp.

33. Install the engine.

CHECKING ENGINE SEALING

In a two-stroke engine it is extremely important that there are no air leaks in the engine. An air leak may result in poor engine performance, overheating or severe engine damage.

Following engine service, it is wise to have the engine pressure checked.

Oil Injection

Oil injection is fast becoming a very popular addition to many new model snowmobiles. Some late model Arctic Cat engines are equipped with oil injection. One of its advantages is more efficient use of oil. Another is not having to mix the oil and gas.

Oil Injection Pump

REMOVAL AND INSTALLATION

1. Disconnect the oil supply hose from the pump and plug it to prevent oil drainage.
2. Remove the two bolts, lockwashers, and washers securing oil injection pump and retainer to the crankcase.
3. Remove the two bolts securing oil delivery hoses to the oil injection pump. Note the check valve gaskets.
4. Disconnect the oil injection linkage.
5. Remove the oil injection pump and retainer. Note the two gaskets.

NOTE: *If a problem occurs with the oil-injection pump, the complete pump assembly must be replaced since the pump is a nonserviceable component.*

To install the pump:

6. Apply silicone sealer to both sides of the retainer gasket. Place the gasket and retainer on the crankcase.
7. In order, slide a gasket, check valve, and gasket onto each union bolt. Install union bolts onto oil injection pump and tighten securely.
8. Apply silicone sealer to the oil injection pump gasket. Place the gasket and pump into position making sure the oil injection pump gear is correctly aligned with the oil injection pump drive gear.
9. Install the pump with two bolts, lockwashers, and washers. Tighten bolts to 5 ft. lb.
10. Connect the oil injection linkage to the pump.
11. Connect oil supply hose to the pump inlet fitting.
12. Check oil injection system synchronization.
13. Bleed oil injection system.

SYNCHRONIZING THE OIL INJECTION SYSTEM

Checking

To check the oil injection system synchronization, use the following procedure.

1. With the ignition switch key OFF, move the throttle lever to the wide open throttle position.
2. Check the alignment of the mark on the pump housing and the mark on the control arm. If marks align, the oil-injection system is synchronized with the carburetor and no adjustment is necessary. If the marks do not align, adjust synchronization.

Pencil points to alignment marks on oil injection pump linkage

Adjusting

1. Move the throttle lever to the wide open throttle position.
2. Loosen the jam nut holding the adjustment rod.
3. Rotate the adjustment rod in the proper direction until alignment is achieved.
4. Lock the jam nut to secure adjustment.

BLEEDING OIL-INJECTION SYSTEM

CAUTION: *Whenever bleeding the oil-injection system, use a 50:1 gas/oil mixture in the gas tank to ensure adequate engine*

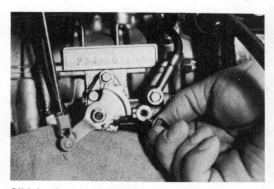

Oil injection pump bleed screw

lubrication. Failure to use the 50:1 mixture during oil injection system bleeding will result in severe engine damage.

1. Fill oil reservoir with Arctic Spirit Injection Oil.

2. Place a rag below the oil injection pump bleed screw, remove the bleed screw from the pump, and allow the oil to flow through the oil supply hose until the hose is filled with oil and free of air. Install the bleed screw.

3. Using a shielded safety stand, raise the rear of the snowmobile off the floor. Start the engine and allow it to idle.

4. Pull the adjustment rod upward to the wide-open position.

WARNING: *Keep hands and clothing away from all moving or rotating parts.*

5. Idle the engine until oil flows out of the oil delivery hoses free of air bubbles.

6. When oil flows to the top of both oil delivery hoses, shut the engine off.

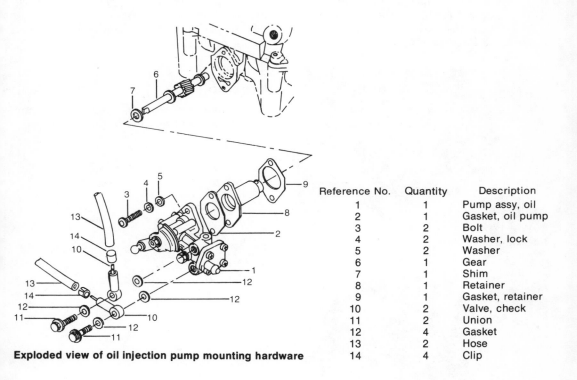

Reference No.	Quantity	Description
1	1	Pump assy, oil
2	1	Gasket, oil pump
3	2	Bolt
4	2	Washer, lock
5	2	Washer
6	1	Gear
7	1	Shim
8	1	Retainer
9	1	Gasket, retainer
10	2	Valve, check
11	2	Union
12	4	Gasket
13	2	Hose
14	4	Clip

Exploded view of oil injection pump mounting hardware

RECOIL STARTER

Removal

1. Remove the four bolts and lock washers securing recoil assembly to the fan case.

CAUTION: *Before removing last bolt, grasp the recoil to prevent a sudden retraction of the recoil.*

2. Tie the slipknot in the recoil rope below the console and allow the rope to slowly retract against the recoil case.

3. Remove the knot at the starter handle; then thread rope through the recoil bushing in the console.

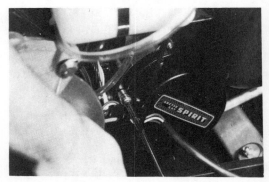

Removing starter

Disassembly

1. Clamp the recoil in a vise.
2. Rotate the recoil reel counterclockwise until the notch of the reel is near the recoil rope guide in the case. Guide the rope into the notch and slowly allow the reel to retract until all recoil spring tension is released.
3. While exerting downward pressure on the drive plate, remove the nut, lock washer, and washer.
4. Slowly release the drive plate and lift the plate free of the reel.
5. Remove the spring and the return spring. Account for the washer.
6. Remove the three pawl springs; then remove the three pawls.

Removing drive plate

Removing recoil spring

7. Carefully lift the recoil reel free of case making sure the recoil spring does not accidentally disengage from the recoil case.
8. Remove the recoil spring from the recoil case by lifting the spring end up and out. Hold remainder of recoil spring with thumbs and alternately release each thumb to allow the recoil spring to gradually release from the recoil case.
9. Unwind the rope from the recoil reel, untie the knot, and remove the rope.

Inspecting

NOTE: *Whenever a part is worn excessively, cracked, defective, or damaged in any way, replacement is necessary.*

1. Inspect all springs, washers, and pawls for wear or damage.
2. Inspect the recoil reel and case for cracks or damage.
3. Inspect the center hub for wear, cracks, or damage.
4. Inspect the recoil rope for breaks or fraying.
5. Inspect the recoil spring for cracks, crystalization, or abnormal bends.
6. Inspect the starter handle for damage, cracks, or deterioration.

Assembly

1. Hook the end of the recoil spring around the mounting lug in the recoil case.

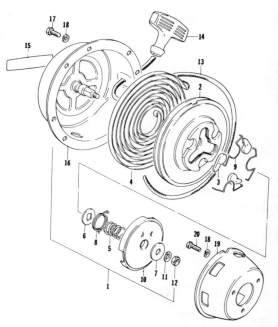

1. Starter assembly	11. Lockwasher
2. Reel	12. Nut
3. Pawl	13. Starter rope
4. Spring	14. Handle
5. Spring	15. Decal
6. Washer	16. Case
7. Washer	17. Bolt
8. Return spring	18. Lockwasher
9. Pawl spring	19. Pulley
10. Drive plate	20. Bolt

Recoil assembly drawing

Install recoil spring

Rewinding recoil rope

2. Insert the recoil-spring winding into the recoil case in a counterclockwise direction until the complete recoil spring is installed.

NOTE: *Recoil spring must seat evenly in the recoil case.*

3. Insert the rope through the hole in the recoil reel and tie a knot in the end; then wrap rope counterclockwise around reel leaving about 20 in. of rope free of reel.

NOTE: *Light oil may be used to lubricate both the spring and reel hub to prevent corrosion.*

4. Align the hook in the end of the recoil spring with the notch in the recoil reel.

5. Carefully slide the recoil reel over hub and engage the spring with the reel.

6. When the recoil reel is seated correctly in the recoil case, place the washer on the hub.

7. Install the return spring and spring; then place the three pawls in position.

8. Slide end of recoil rope through rope guide of the case; then tie a slipknot in the recoil rope.

9. Install the three pawl springs.

10. Using a hooked wire to guide the return spring, install the drive plate.

NOTE: *Return spring pointed end must seat in the recoil reel. Loop must be facing upward.*

11. Rotate the drive plate until return spring is in position and secure drive plate in place with washer, lock washer, and nut. Tighten nut to 2.2 kg-m (16 ft-lb).

12. With about 20 in. of rope exposed, hook the rope in notch of the recoil reel.

13. Rotate the recoil reel three or four turns counterclockwise; then release the recoil rope from the notch and allow the rope to retract.

14. Pull recoil rope out two or three times to check for correct tension.

NOTE: *Increasing the rotations in step 13 will increase spring tension; decreasing the rotations will decrease spring tension.*

Installation

1. Place recoil assembly into position against the fan case.

2. Secure recoil with four bolts and lock washers. Tighten bolts to 5 ft-lb.

NOTE: *Before tightening the bolts, slowly pull recoil rope until the pawls engage;*

Installing pawl springs

Installing recoil starter

then tighten bolts. This will center the recoil on the fan case.

3. Thread recoil rope through recoil bushing in the console and install the handle. Secure with a knot.

4. Release the slipknot in the rope.

DRIVE SYSTEM

All Arctic Cat Snowmobiles in 1976 and after were equipped with Arctic Cat drive clutches and torque converters. The following instructions will enable you to maintain and repair your Arctic Cat drive system.

The maximum allowable bearing wear or clearance between the hex shaft and bearing is critical for correct drive clutch operation. The flats on the drive clutch are directly associated with the large bearing area. This bearing area, added to the high bearing load capacity and low co-efficient of friction, results in improved life expectancy of the clutch.

For assembly purposes, radial clearance between the hex shaft and bearing is necessary, and a slightly greater clearance does not adversely affect clutch operation. However, the maximum allowable bearing wear tolerance is limited by the clearance between the ramp and inside surface of the roller arm.

If the bearing is considered to be worn, roller arm and ramp clearance can be visually inspected by looking into the clutch, or the clutch can be removed from the crankshaft and measured.

The visual inspection method and measurement method are explained below.

VISUAL INSPECTION METHOD

1. Look into the clutch and rotate it clockwise and counterclockwise; a flashlight may be necessary to see inside the clutch. Look at the inside surface of the roller arm; there must not be any contact between the roller arm and ramp.

2. If there is no contact between the roller arm and ramp, the maximum allowable drive clutch bearing wear is within tolerance. The drive clutch is acceptable.

3. If there is contact between the roller arm and ramp, the maximum allowable drive clutch bearing wear is not within tolerance. Drive clutch moveable sheave and cover must be replaced.

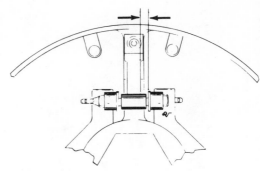

Checking drive clutch bearing wear

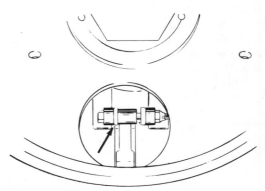

Roller arm must not contact ramp

MEASUREMENT METHOD

1. Remove the drive clutch from the crankshaft.

2. Remove cover housing and spring.

3. Install cover housing with three socket head cap screws, using a ¼-inch wrench.

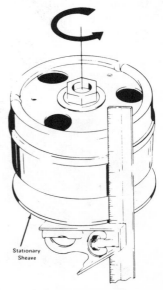

Stationary
Sheave

Checking bearing wear with clutch assembled

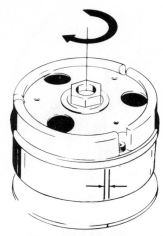

Checking bearing wear with clutch assembled

4. Keeping the stationary sheave fixed, rotate the moveable sheave counterclockwise until all clearance is taken up. Scribe a line on the moveable sheave, using a tri-square and scribe.

5. Keeping the stationary sheave fixed, rotate the moveable sheave clockwise until all clearance is taken up. Scribe another line on the moveable sheave, using a tri-square and scribe.

6. Measure the distance between the two scribe marks, using a caliper or scale.

7. If distance between the two scribed lines is less than $^5/_{32}$-inch (0.156″), the maximum allowable drive clutch bearing wear is within tolerance. Drive clutch is acceptable.

8. If distance between the two scribed lines is more than $^5/_{32}$-inch (0.156″), the maximum allowable drive clutch bearing wear is not within tolerance. Drive clutch moveable sheave and cover housing must be replaced.

REMOVAL

1. Unlatch the clutch shield and tilt it upright.

2. Remove the drive belt.

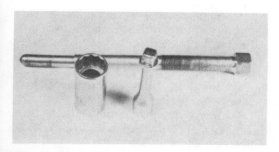

Clutch puller bolt

3. Remove the bolt and lock washer securing the drive clutch on the crankshaft.

4. Insert the special Arctic clutch puller bolt. Use either an impact wrench or a breaker bar and a chain wrench to tighten the puller bolt. If the clutch will not release, sharply strike the head of the puller bolt. If clutch does not come loose, tighten the puller bolt and again strike the bolt. Repeat until clutch becomes loose on shaft.

DISASSEMBLY

1. Remove the three socket head cap screws holding outer housing to the moveable sheave.

2. Remove the clutch spring; then remove the cupped washer.

3. Loosen the three jam nuts and the three set screws holding spider assembly on the hex shaft.

4. Push spider toward stationary face just far enough so the split ring is free.

5. Remove the split ring halves from the groove in the hex shaft.

6. Mark the spider in relation to the hex shaft.

7. Slide moveable sheave off hex shaft.

8. If the spider, rollers or weights are to be serviced, use the following procedure:

   A. Remove the lock nut and cap screw holding weights, rollers and bushing to the roller arm.

   B. Slide roller with bushing from between roller arm.

   C. Perform steps a and b on remaining roller arms.

NOTE: *A complete roller kit with bushings is to be installed, even if only one roller with bushings is worn or damaged. If new rollers with bushings are to be installed, new ramps are also to be installed.*

9. Remove the socket head cap screws retaining the ramps to the moveable sheave. Slide ramp out of "ramp setting" in moveable sheave.

NOTE: *A complete set of ramps is to be installed, even if only one ramp is worn or damaged. If the ramps are to be replaced, new rollers with bushings are also to be installed.*

CLEANING

1. Wash grease, dirt and foreign matter off all parts, using cleaning solvent. Dry the parts with compressed air.

2. If drive belt accumulations are on the stationary sheave, or on moveable sheave duralon bushing, remove the accumulations using cleaning solvent only.

CAUTION: *DO NOT use steel wool or a wire brush to clean parts having a duralon bushing; damage will result if bushing is contacted.*

INSPECTION

1. Inspect stationary sheave, moveable sheave and cover housing for cracks and imperfections in casting.

NOTE: *Whenever a part is worn excessively, cracked, defective or damaged in any way, replacement is necessary.*

2. Inspect the spider for cracks and imperfections in the casting. Arms, weights and rollers must be free of damage or wear.

3. Inspect the ramp settings on the inside of the moveable sheave for wear and cracks.

4. Inspect the spring for proper compression qualities. (See: Spring Compression Test). If spring compression is not as specified or damage is evident, replacement is necessary.

5. Inspect the ramps for any uneven wear pattern.

6. Inspect all threaded areas for any stripped threads.

7. Inspect the hex shaft; no burrs or rough edges are to be evident. Use a fine file to remove any burrs or rough edges. Thoroughly clean and dry the hex shaft if any filing was done.

SPRING COMPRESSION TEST

This spring is to be a specific length and have definite pressure characteristics to ensure proper drive clutch engagement. Spring pressure reading must be as specified when checked with a spring pressure tester. If the pressure is within tolerance and an engagement problem still exists, another part in the drive clutch is affecting engagement rpm. To find the correct pressure valves, refer to the spring chart on page 56.

1. Place spring between compression pad and scale contact surface.

2. Push compression arm down 1.25 inches; then read the number of pounds registered on the indicator. Indicator reading is to be as specified. If reading is less than specified spring pressure, install a new spring.

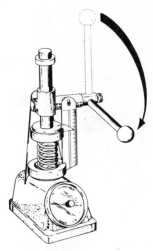

Spring compression tester

ASSEMBLY

1. Install the ramps in the moveable sheave. Tighten the three screws to 25–30 in. lb.

NOTE: *Ramps must be replaced as a set even if only one is worn. Also, if new ramps are being installed, a new roller set with bushings must also be installed.*

2. Slide the moveable sheave onto the stationary sheave. Make sure alignment marks on both sheaves are aligned.

3. If the spider, rollers or weights were serviced, assemble the spider assembly using the following procedure:

A. Slide a bushing into a roller; then insert both parts between the roller arm. Make sure bushing "cut-outs" slide over the two small ears on the inside surface of the roller arm.

B. Slide a weight onto the cap screw; then push cap screw through roller arm, roller and bushing.

NOTE: *Head of cap screw must be positioned on side of roller arm having the two small ears.*

C. Slide another weight onto opposite end of cap screw; then install a lock nut. Tighten lock nut to 35–45 in. lb.

D. Perform steps a, b and c on remaining rollers, bushings and weights.

E. Install the three set screws with lock nuts in the spider.

4. Slide the spider assembly onto the hext shaft. Make sure marks made during disassembly are aligned. Side with stamped part number must face up.

5. Install the split ring halves in the groove on the hex shaft.

6. Pull the spider up against the split ring halves. Tighten the set screws to 35–40 in. lb; then bottom the set screw jam nuts.

7. Slide the cupped washer and spring onto the hext shaft.

8. Place the cover housing on the spring and align the marks with those on the stationary and moveable sheaves.

9. Carefully push down the cover housing and lift up the moveable sheave until the parts contact; then install the three socket head cap screws. Be sure to use care when installing cover so that duralon bushing is not damaged. Tighten the cap screws to 15–17 ft-lb.

INSTALLATION

1. Move the drive clutch into position.
2. Install the drive clutch bolt and lock washer. Tighten the bolt to 7.6–8.3 kg-m or 55–60 ft-lb.

3. Check alignment between the drive clutch and driven pulley.

4. Install the drive belt.

Driven Pulley

Specifications

Driven Pulley Specifications		
Cam Angle		30°
Spring Preload—		2nd hole
Counterclockwise		120°
Spring Color		Black
Spring Part Number		0148-070
Spring Length w/No Load	-cm	11.7
	-in.	4.60
Spring Diameter	-cm	7.3
	-in.	2.88
Spring Wire Diameter	-cm	0.4
	-in.	0.156

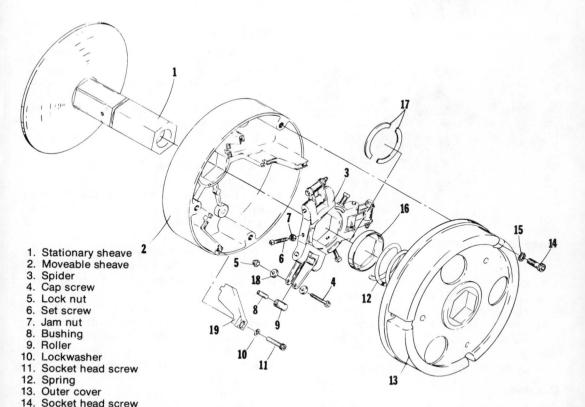

1. Stationary sheave
2. Moveable sheave
3. Spider
4. Cap screw
5. Lock nut
6. Set screw
7. Jam nut
8. Bushing
9. Roller
10. Lockwasher
11. Socket head screw
12. Spring
13. Outer cover
14. Socket head screw
15. Lockwasher
16. Cupped washer
17. Split ring
18. Weight
19. Ramp

Drive clutch assembly

DISASSEMBLY

1. Rotate the clutch sheaves in opposite directions just enough so that the shoe ramps are not contacting the torque bracket.

2. Force the torque bracket downward slightly; then remove snap ring from the groove in the stationary sheave hub.

3. Carefully allow the torque bracket to slide off the stationary sheave hub; then slide spring off hub.

Removing snap-ring

Moveable sheave removed

4. If cam bracket sliding shoes need servicing, remove them with pliers.

5. Slide moveable face off stationary hub.
NOTE: *Woodruff key does not have to be removed to pull moveable sheaves.*

6. Remove woodruff key from stationary hub.

7. Slide bearing off stationary hub.

CLEANING

1. Wash grease and foreign matter off all parts, using cleaning solvent.

2. If drive belt accumulations are on stationary sheave, hub or moveable sheave, remove the accumulations using cleaning solvent only.

CAUTION: *DO NOT use steel wool or wire brush to clean driven pulley parts. A wire brush or steel wool will cause the sheaves to be gouged, thus, the drive belt may not slide properly between sheaves. Decreased performance and possible accelerated belt wear will result.*

INSPECTION

Whenever a part is worn excessively, cracked, defective or damaged in any way, replacement is necessary.

1. Inspect sliding shoes for damage or wear.

2. Inspect the stationary and moveable sheaves for any broken or loose bolts or rivets.

3. Check torque bracket for cracks, wear and other noticeable damage.

4. Inspect sheaves for rough surfaces, grooves or scratches. Use fine emery cloth to repair minor damage.

5. Inspect spring for distortion, crystallization or breaks.

ASSEMBLY

1. Seat cam bracket sliding shoes in position in casting.

2. Slide bearing onto the stationary sheave hub.
NOTE: *Make sure notched end is facing woodruff key slot.*

3. Install woodruff key in stationary sheave hub.

4. Slide moveable sheave onto stationary sheave hub.

5. Place the spring over the staionary sheave hub and hook the turned down end into the hole in the casting on the moveable face.

6. Place the torque bracket over the spring and hook the turned up end into the second hole (standard spring tension) of the troque bracket.

7. Line up the keyway in the torque bracket with the key in the shaft. Also align the spring pin with the notch in the bearings.

8. Carefully push the torque bracket onto the shaft just far enough to contact the woodruff key.

9. Rotate the moveable sheave counterclockwise until there is a slight resistance (spring pressure); then rotate the moveable face an additional 120°.

10. Make sure the spring pin is still aligned with the notch in the bearings; then push the torque bracket down on the shaft until it bottoms on the bearing.

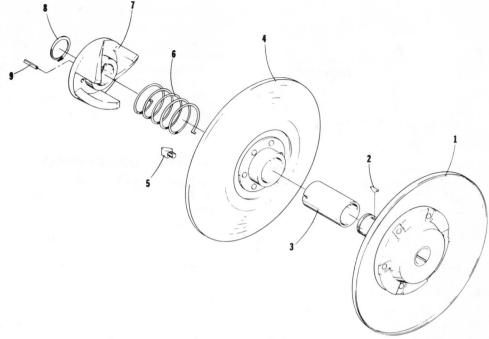

1. Sheave, *Stationary*
2. Key
3. Bearing
4. Sheave, *Movable*
5. Slide, Shoe-Ramp
6. Spring
7. Bracket, Torque (incl. 9)
8. Ring, Retaining
9. Pin, Spring

Driven clutch assembly

11. Install the snap ring in the groove of the stationary sheave hub.

12. Slowly release the torque bracket against the snap ring.

Drive Clutch/Driven Pulley Alignment

The center-to-center distance and the drive clutch alignment are set at the factory and

Installing torque bracket

checked during pre-delivery. Normally, no adjustment is required unless the driven pulley or drive clutch is removed or disassembled. However, if premature drive belt failure is experienced or if the drive belt turns over, the alignment must be checked.

Two dimensions that must be checked are PARALLELISM and OFFSET. The first dimension to check and adjust, if required, is parallelism.

1. Unlatch belt guard and remove the drive belt.

2. Install the clutch alignment bar (part no. 0149-099) between the sheaves of the driven pulley. Allow sheaves to release and hold alignment bar in position.

3. Allow the bar to rest on the hex shaft.

4. Measure dimension X and Y at front and rear edge of drive clutch. Take all measurements with bar on hex shaft. Compare dimension X and Y with Rule A and B.

   Rule A—Dimension Y must be more than dimension X.

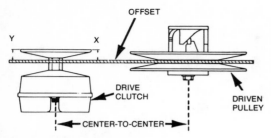

Checking clutch alignment

Rule B—Dimension Y must never exceed dimension X by more than $1/16$-inch (0.0625).

5. If dimension Y is less than dimension X, parallelism between engine crankshaft and driven pulley shaft is not correct. Adjust so that the parallelism is within tolerance and proceed to Offset Check.

OFFSET CHECK

Install clutch alignment bar between clutch sheaves as in steps 2 and 3.

NOTE: *Alignment bar must exceed beyond the front edge of the drive clutch.*

1. Measure dimension X and Y at the front and rear edge of the drive clutch. Both dimensions must be between 0.954 of-an-inch and 1.024 inches.

OFFSET CORRECTION

1. Remove cap screw and washers holding driven pulley on driven shaft.

2. Add or remove washers until correct offset is obtained; then install cap screw and washers.

3. Install the drive belt and secure the clutch guard in place.

PARALLELISM ADJUSTMENT

1. Loosen the bolts and lock nuts securing motor plate to front end.

2. Loosen the lock nuts on the rear motor mount studs.

3. Insert a shim between the bottom of the left rear motor mount (PTO side) and the motor mount bracket on the front end assembly.

4. Tighten all lock nuts; then check parallelism and offset.

NOTE: *Continue to add or remove shims until parallelism is obtained.*

Chain and Sprockets
INSPECTION

1. Thoroughly wash chain and sprockets using cleaning solvent.

2. Thoroughly dry chain and sprockets using comressed air.

3. Inspect sprockets for damaged or missing teeth.

4. Inspect chain for loose rivet pins or cracked link plates.

5. Replace any damaged, worn or defective parts.

Drive Train Disassembly

1. Remove the pulse charger.

2. Remove clutch shield retaining pins; then remove shield.

3. Remove the drive belt.

4. Remove cap screw and flat washer securing driven pulley on driven shaft.

5. Slide driven pulley off driven shaft; then account for driven shaft key.

NOTE: *Account for any shims that were removed during disassembly.*

6. Tip the snowmobile onto the PTO side. This will keep chain lube from spilling into the belly pan.

7. Remove the four bolts and lock washers holding chain case cover to chain case; then remove cover and gasket.

8. Remove cotter key and washer securing tensioner spring to link pin; then slide end of spring free of link pin.

9. Remove the cap screws and washers holding both top and bottom sprockets in position.

NOTE: *If sprocket will not slide off shaft, thread cap screw back into the shaft; then use a puller to remove the sprocket. The cap screw is used for bottoming puller bolt.*

10. Slide both sprockets and chain off the shafts.

NOTE: *Account for any spacer washers removed during disassembly.*

11. Remove the three lock nuts holding

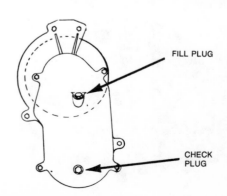

Drive chain lube plugs

Drive chain and chain tensioner

both the upper and lower MAG side bearing flanges in position. Remove flanges, O-rings and bearings.

12. Loosen the set screw on the PTO side driven shaft bearing; then drive the lock collar opposite the direction of rotation until it turns freely.

NOTE: *A small file should be used to remove any burrs left on the shaft by the lock collar set screw.*

13. Force the driven shaft toward the PTO side.

NOTE: *Rotate the shaft while driving to prevent brake disc from binding on shaft.*

14. Slide brake disc free of driven shaft; then remove the woodruff key from the shaft.

15. Remove the skid frame from the tunnel.

16. Remove the three lock nuts from the PTO side bearing holder carriage bolts.

NOTE: *Bearings have radial outers which allow them to swivel, providing clearance for removal.*

17. Tilt driven shaft and remove it from MAG side.

18. Remove the three PTO side lock nuts securing lower drive shaft bearing.

19. Slide track drive shaft toward Mag side until PTO end of shaft is out of front end mounting hole. Tilt end of shaft away from tunnel; then slide track out of tunnel.

NOTE: *If track is to be removed, the idler axle assembly will have to be removed.*

INSPECTION

NOTE: *Whenever a part is worn excessively, cracked, defective or damaged in any way, replacement is necessary.*

1. Thoroughly wash all metallic drive train components in cleaning solvent.

2. Wash all plastic or rubber parts with soap and water.

3. Check drive shaft and driven shaft for damaged splines or stripped threads.

4. Check bearings for any roughness or damage.

5. Examine O-rings and chain case cover gaskets for any breaks or damage.

6. Examine the track for cuts, gouges or broken cleats.

7. Examine the keyways in both the driven shaft and the brake hub.

8. Examine the brake disc for excessive wear or cracks.

9. Examine the brake pads for wear.

10. Examine chain tensioner components.

BRAKE SYSTEM

Do not operate the snowmobile when parking brake is engaged or when any component in the brake system is damaged, worn or adjusted improperly because personal injury could result during an (emergency) stop.

Check

1. Compress the brake lever fully

2. Observe the distance between the lever and brake handle "stop". Correct travel is ¼ to ½ inch.

3. If travel is not as specified, adjust brake

Adjust

1. Open hood and loosen brake adjusting cap screw.

2. To increase brake lever movement, rotate the brake adjusting arm one position in a clockwise direction.

3. To decrease brake lever movement or "set-up" the brake, rotate the brake adjusting arm one position in a clockwise direction. This will decrease the amount of brake lever travel.

4. Repeat the above adjustments until the specified amount of brake lever "free travel" is obtained.

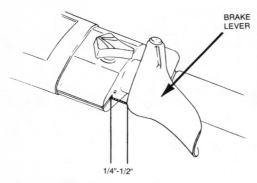

Adjust free travel

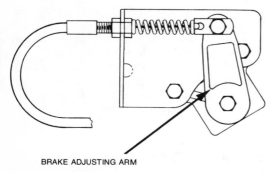

Adjust brake arm

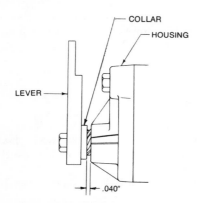

Checking lever clearance

5. Tighten adjusting cap screw.

6. Check the clearance between the housing and brake arm collar. If clearance is less than (.040 in.) with brake applied replace both brake pucks. If both brake pucks are not replaced, loss of brakes could result and cause property damage and or personal injury.

SLIDE RAIL SUSPENSION

Removal, installation and adjustment procedure for Arctic Cat type slide rail suspension follows.

Skid Frame

REMOVAL AND INSTALLATION

5000, 6000, El Tigre

1. Remove the rear suspension springs from the adjustment cams using the suspension spring tool. To facilitate rear suspension spring removal, be sure the adjusting cam is in the number "2" position.

2. Remove the cap screws securing skid frame to tunnel.

3. Tip the snowmobile on its side using a piece of cardboard to protect against scratching.

4. Remove skid frame.

To install:

1. Tip snowmobile onto side using a piece of cardboard to protect against scratching.

2. Pull track away from body tunnel and install skid frame. Slide axles through front and rear arms of skid frame.

3. Move front of skid frame into position with front mounting hole in the tunnel. Slide lock washer onto cap screw; then secure front arm to tunnel. Thread screw in only halfway. DO NOT TIGHTEN

NOTE: *To aid in centering front arm with holes in tunnel, position skid frame and track at a 45° angle to bottom of tunnel.*

4. Push skid frame and track into the tunnel. Tip snowmobile onto opposite side.

5. Secure front arm to tunnel following instructions in step 3.

6. Place sleeves and springs on rear inner axle housing.

7. Move rear arm of skid frame into position with rear mounting holes in tunnel. Slide lock washer onto cap screw; then secure rear arm to tunnel. Thread in only halfway. DO NOT TIGHTEN.

NOTE: *Rear arm of skid frame may not align with mounting holes in tunnel. To obtain proper alignment of rear arm, drive arm in proper direction until alignment is obtained.*

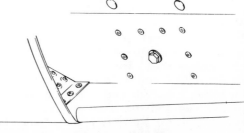

Start bolt through tunnel into axle (frt)

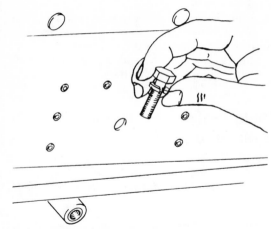

Start bolt through tunnel into (rear) axle

8. Tip snowmobile onto opposite side using cardboard to protect against scratching.

9. Fasten rear arm to tunnel following directions in step 6.

10. Tighten front and rear mounting cap screws to 23 ft-lb.

11. Using the rear spring suspension tool, place suspension springs on the adjustment cams.

NOTE: *Springs are easier to install when adjustment cam is in the number "2" position. Make sure both sides are adjusted equally.*

12. Check track tension and alignment.

Lynx, Pantera

1. With the snowmobile on the shop floor, remove the two cap screws securing the upper axle.

NOTE: *Removing the upper axle is not necessary but will aid in ease of installation.*

2. On the Lynx models, remove the lock nuts securing the rear suspension eyebolts to the chassis.

3. On the Pantera, tip the snowmobile on its side. Use cardboard to protect against scratching. Using the special spring tool, remove the rear springs from the adjustment blocks.

4. Remove the four cap screws and lock washers securing skid frame to tunnel.

5. Remove the skid frame from the tunnel. Account for the axles.

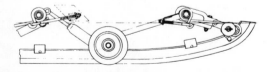

Lynx type spring adjuster

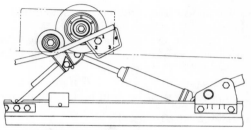

Pantera, El Tigre spring adjuster

Jag, Panther

1. Tip the snowmobile on its side. Use the cardboard to protect against scratching. Using the special spring tool, remove the rear springs from the adjustment blocks.

2. Remove the four cap screws and lock washers securing skid frame to tunnel.

3. Remove the skid frame from the tunnel. Account for the axles and bushings.

CLEANING COMPONENTS

1. Wash entire skid frame with soap and water; then dry thoroughly.

2. Touch up all rusted and chipped paint surfaces; sand affected areas before painting.

3. Remove spacers and bushings. Clean all spacers, bushings, shafts and axles with cleaning solvent. Dry components thoroughly with compressed air.

NOTE: *Clean plastic or rubber bushings and spacers with soap and water only.*

4. Wash remaining metallic components in cleaning solution and dry thoroughly with compressed air.

5. Wash any remaining plastic or rubber components in soap and water only; then dry thoroughly.

NOTE: *Cleaning solvent may damage non-metallic parts.*

INSPECTING COMPONENTS

NOTE: *Whenever a part is worn excessively, cracked, defective or damaged in any way, replacement is necessary.*

1. Inspect all threaded components for stripped threads.

2. Inspect all bushings and corresponding pivot areas for cracks, defects or wear.

3. Inspect wheels for any damage. Bearings must rotate freely. Replace both wheels if damage or wear is evident.

4. Be sure rear axle and inner axles are straight.

5. Inspect all springs for abnormal bends or cracks.

6. Inspect the eyebolts for separation of the eye of abnormal bends.

7. Inspect eyebolt mounting flanges on the chassis or skid frame. Repair if damaged or replace with new parts.

8. Inspect the entire skid frame. No unusual bend is to be evident in the skid frame.

INSTALL SKID FRAME

1. Tip the snowmobile on its side. Use cardboard to protect against scratching.

2. Apply low temperature grease to the skid frame inner axles (Pantera and Lynx only). Insert axles and make sure axles rotate smoothly in the front or rear arms.

3. Pull track away from the tunnel and install skid frame.

4. Move front arm of skid frame into position with front mounting hole in the body tunnel. Slide lock washer onto cap screw and secure front arm to tunnel. DO NOT TIGHTEN CAP SCREW AT THIS TIME.

NOTE: *To aid in centering front arm of skid frame with holes in tunnel, position skid frame and track at a 45° angle to the bottom of the tunnel.*

5. Push skid frame and track into the tunnel.

6. Move rear arm of skid frame into position with rear mounting holes in body tunnel. Slide lock washer onto cap screw and secure rear arm to tunnel. DO NOT TIGHTEN.

NOTE: *Rear of skid frame may not align with mounting holes in tunnel. To obtain proper alignment of rear arm and mounting holes, use a soft mallet and drive the rear arm in the proper direction until alignment is obtained.*

7. Tip snowmobile onto opposite side and use a piece of cardboard to protect against scratching.

8. Secure front arm using directions given in step 4; then secure rear arm using directions given in step 6.

9. On Pantera and Lynx models, align upper axle assembly with mounting holes in tunnel. Secure axle with lock washers and cap screws.

10. On Lynx models, secure rear spring to tunnel brackets with eyebolts. Tighten to desired tension.

11. On all other models, use the special rear spring tool to position rear spring on adjustment blocks. For ease of installation, install springs in the number 2 position.

12. On the Pantera and Lynx models, tighten the upper axle cap screws to 23 ft-lb.

13. Tighten the four cap screws that secure skid frame to 23 ft-lb.

14. Adjust track tension and alignment.

15. Set suspension to the desired tension.

Skid Frame Disassembly

5000, 6000, EL TIGRE

NOTE: *Basic skid frame disassembly is similar for both the 5000 and 6000 series El Tigre. The procedure given is for the 5000 series model*

Remove Hi-Fax

1. Remove the lock nut and machine screw securing the hi-fax to the rails.

2. Using a hammer and a piece of wood, drive the hi-fax toward the rear of the skid frame.

NOTE: *Be sure that the skid frame rails are not accidentally damaged or nicked.*

Wheels and Rear Axle Housing Removal

1. Remove cap screws and flat washers securing idler wheels to rear axle.

2. Slide the rear idler wheels, spacers and hex washers off rear axle.

3. Remove the rear axle from the right and left housings.

4. Remove the two cap screws and lock nuts securing the right and left rear axle housing. Slide the housings off the rails.

Rear Arm Removal

1. Remove the cap screw, nut and bushings securing the stationary end of shock absorber to the front arm bracket.

2. Remove the two cap screws and lock nuts securing the rear arm assembly to the rails; then remove the center cap screw which is threaded into the rear arm pivot axle. Repeat procedure for opposite side. Slide the rear arm assembly, rear arm brackets and washers to the rear of skid frame.

NOTE: *If the shock absorber is to be removed from the rear arm, remove the cap screw and lock nut securing moveable end of shock absorber.*

Front Arm Removal

1. Remove lock nuts securing suspension spring eyebolts; then remove eyebolts.

2. Remove cap screws and lock nuts securing front arm to front arm bracket.

3. Remove the cap screw and lock nut securing front arm stop to front crossbrace.

4. Remove the cap screw, washers and lock nut securing front arm stop to front arm.

5. Remove front arm, front arm stop and spacers from the skid frame. Set these components together.

NOTE: *If further disassembly of the skid frame rails is required, remove the shock pads, front crossbrace and front arm bracket.*

Front Arm Installation

NOTE: *If shock pads, front crossbrace and front arm bracket were removed to service rails, it will be necessary to install them at this time.*

1. Install front arm stop on front arm. Secure using a cap screw, washers and lock nut.

2. Secure front arm stop to front crossbrace using a cap screw and lock nut.

3. Install spacers in front arm; then secure front arm to front arm bracket using cap screws and lock nuts.

NOTE: *Be sure spacers are in position before securing bracket.*

4. Install the front suspension springs. Secure with eyebolts and lock nuts.

Rear Arm Installation

1. If moveable end of shock absorber was removed during disassembly, secure to the rear arm using bushings, cap screw and lock nut.

2. If the rear axle housing was removed, be sure to install housing so that the wide flange weldment is positioned upward. If installed incorrectly, suspension will not work properly.

3. Secure stationary end of shock absorber to front arm bracket using bushings, cap screw and lock nut.

4. Secure the rear arm bracket and tab lock washer to the rails using cap screws and lock nuts.

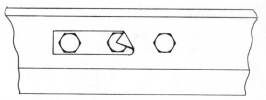

Bend tab washer

5. Secure rear arm to rear arm bracket using nyloc cap screws.

NOTE: *Be sure spacer washer is in position on rear arm axle before installing rear arm.*

6. Bend the tab washer so that the corner of the washer locks the rear arm nyloc cap screw.

Rear Axle and Rear Axle Housing Installation

1. Slide left and right rear housing into position on skid frame rails. Secure to rails using cap screws and lock nuts.

2. Slide rear axle into position in rear housings. In order, place the following on each end of axle: rectangular washer, spacer and idler wheel. Secure wheels to axle using washers and nyloc cap screws.

WEAR STRIP REPLACEMENT
Lynx, Pantera

1. Drive the spring pins out of the wear strip and aluminum wear rail. Pins are positioned in both the front and rear of the wear rail.

2. Using a hammer and a piece of wood, drive the wear strip toward the rear of the skid frame.

NOTE: *Be sure the skid frame rails are not accidentally damaged or nicked.*

3. Inspect the skid frame rail for any damage. Replace if conditions dictate.

4. Apply low temperature grease to both the skid frame rail and the groove of the wear strip.

5. Slide the wear strip onto the back end of the rails. Continue to drive the wear strip with a hammer and wood block until spring pin holes of wear strip are aligned with holes in the rail.

6. Insert the spring pins that secure wear strip.

NOTE: *Make sure front roll pin is positioned through both wear strip and aluminum rail.*

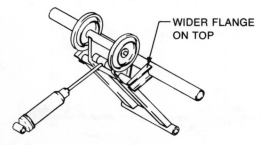

Bolt shock absorber to bracket

WIDER FLANGE ON TOP

Jag, Panther

1. Remove the lock nut and cap screw securing the wear strip to the wear rail.

2. Using a hammer and a piece of wood, drive the wear strip toward the rear of the skid frame.

NOTE: *Be sure the skid frame rails are not accidentally damaged or nicked.*

3. Inspect the skid frame rail for any damage. Replace if conditions dictate.

4. Apply low temperature grease to both the skid frame rail and the groove of the wear strip.

5. Slide the wear strip onto the back end of the rail. Continue to drive the wear strip with a hammer and wood block until bolt hole of wear strip is aligned with hole in the rail.

6. Insert the cap screw and lock nut that secure the wear strip. Tighten securely.

Skid Frame Adjustment

5000, 6000, EL TIGRE

Track Tension

1. Lubricate the rear suspension grease fittings.

2. Check to be sure rear idler wheels are between internal drive lugs.

WARNING: *Shut engine off and make sure ignition switch is in the OFF position. Personal injury could result if this warning is ignored.*

3. Raise the rear of the snowmobile.

4. Press track down at midspan and measure distance between bottom of hi-fax and inside surface of track. Desired distance must be between ¾–1 inch.

5. If measurement is not as specified, loosen idler wheel adjusting bolt jam nut. Back off jam nut until it is approximately ½-inch away from the adjusting bolt head. Perform this step on opposite side jam nut.

6. If measurement obtained in step 4 is more than as specified, tighten adjusting bolts. If measurement obtained is less than

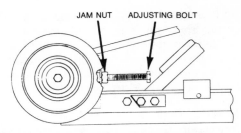

JAM NUT   ADJUSTING BOLT

Lock jam nut after adjusting track tension

specified, loosen adjusting bolt. When measurement is between specifications, lock adjustment by bottoming jam nut against rail housing.

NOTE: *An excellent check at this time would be to slide your hand along the inside of the tunnel and vigorously push the underside of the track up and down. Track must not hit top of tunnel or slap skid frame.*

7. After correct track tension is obtained, check track alignment.

NOTE: *Track tension and track alignment are interrelated; always perform both adjustments even if only one seems necessary. Always establish correct track tension before checking and/or adjusting alignment.*

Track Alignment

Proper track alignment is obtained when rear idler wheels are equidistant from inside edge of internal drive lugs.

WARNING: *Shut engine off and make sure ignition switch is in the OFF position. DO NOT allow anyone to stand in front of or to the rear of the snowmobile when checking track alignment. Personal injury or bystander injury may result if this warning is ignored.*

1. Make sure both rear idler wheels are positioned between internal drive lugs.

2. Using a safety stand, raise rear of snowmobile until track is completely off the shop floor and free to rotate. Skis are to be placed against a wall or other stationary object.

3. Start engine, accelerate slightly to turn

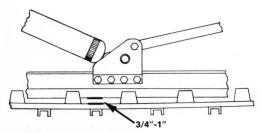

3/4"-1"

Checking track tension

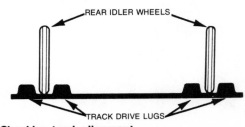

REAR IDLER WHEELS

TRACK DRIVE LUGS

Checking track alignment

the track several revolutions and SHUT
ENGINE OFF (ignition switch is the OFF
position). Note to which side track has run.

NOTE: *Allow track to coast to a stop
when checking alignment. DO NOT apply
brakes as this may produce an inaccurate
alignment condition.*

4. If track ran to left or right, or is rubbing
against inside surface of internal drive lugs,
loosen adjusting bolt jam nut until it is approximately ½-inch away from bolt head.
Perform this step on opposite side jam nut.

5. Rotate adjusting bolts clockwise or
counterclockwise until proper alignment is
established. Bottom jam nuts against skid
frame.

NOTE: *After jam nuts are bottomed
against skid frame, an equal length of bolt
is to extend from the jam nut to the bolt
head.*

6. When adjustment is completed, lower
rear of snowmobile. Start engine and test run
track under actual operating conditions.

7. After test run is completed, recheck
track alignment and adjust if necessary.

NOTE: *Make sure correct track tension is
maintained when alignment is adjusted.*

Suspension Adjustment

The rear springs should be adjusted to suit
the weight and riding preference of the operator. The front spring adjustment primarily
influences the way the snowmobile performs
in snow and the effort required to steer the
snowmobile.

The optimum setting of the rear spring
prevents the suspension from "bottoming
out" on most bumps. The springs should not,
however, be set so stiff to prevent the suspension from working properly under normal
riding conditions.

To determine the optimum suspension adjustment, jump up and down on the rearmost
part of the runnig board. The suspension
should just be able to "bottom."

The optimum setting for the front spring is
when spring tension is sufficiently stiff to
prevent the suspension from collapsing in
deep snow but not so stiff that steering becomes ineffective.

NOTE: *Maintain equal suspension adjustment on both sides of the skid frame.*

FRONT SPRING ADJUSTMENT

The front eyebolts on the El Tigre are
equipped with self-locking nuts. Tighten or

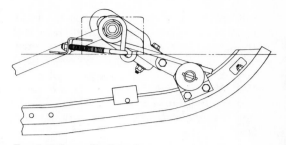

Front spring adjustment

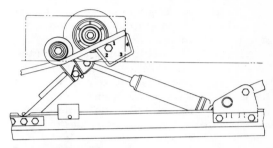

Rear spring adjustment

loosen the spring adjusting nut to obtain the
desired suspension adjustment. Make the
same adjustment on the opposite side eyebolt. Be sure adjustment is equal on both
springs.

REAR SPRING ADJUSTMENT

Rear spring tension is adjusted by a four position cam mounted on the tunnel. Spring tension can be changed by rotating the cam
using the handle from the spark plug wrench.
To increase spring tension, the handle should
be rotated toward the rear of the snowmobile. To decrease spring tension, rotate
the handle toward the front of the machine.
Be sure both cams are adjusted equally.

NOTE: *DO NOT move the adjustment cam
directly from the number "1" to the
number "4" position. Always adjust in numerical sequence.*

PANTERA, JAG, LYNX, PANTHER
Track Tension

Track tension is directly related to the overall
performance of the snowmobile. If the track
is too loose, it may slap against the tunnel
causing wear, or it may ratchet on the track
drive sprockets. An extremely loose track
may allow the track to climb over the drive
lugs causing a locked track.

However, if the track is too tight, accelerated slide wear and rear idler wheel wear will

result. In addition, a track that is too tight will prevent the snowmobile from reaching optimum performance. Track tension must be checked at least once a month and, if necessary, adjusted.

WARNING: *Shut the engine off and make sure the ignition switch is in the OFF position before checking or adjusting the track tension.*

Check Tension

1. Before checking tension, remove excess ice and snow buildup from the track and inside the skid frame.

2. Raise the rear of the snowmobile off the ground. Make sure the track is free to rotate.

3. Exert moderate pressure at midspan of the lower track section. Measure the distance between the bottom of the slide and the inside surface of the track. The desired distance is 19–25 mm (¾–1 inch). If the distance is not as specified, an adjustment must be made.

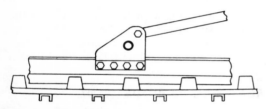

Checking track tension

Adjust Tension

1. Loosen the rear idler wheel adjusting bolt jam nut. Continue to loosen the jam nut until it is approximately 15 mm (½ inch) away from the adjusting bolt.

2. If the distance between the bottom of the slide and the inside surface of the track (See: To Check Tension) is more than 25 mm (1 inch), the adjusting bolt must be tightened. Tightening the adjusting bolt moves the rear idler wheel rearward, thereby taking up excess slack in the track. Conversely, if the distance between the bottom of the slide and the inside surface of the track (See: To Check Tension) is less than 19 mm (¾ inch), the adjusting bolt must be loosened. Loosening the adjusting bolt moves the rear idler wheel forward, thereby increasing the slack in the track. Perform this step on the opposite side adjusting bolt.

3. When specified track tension (19–25 mm) is obtained, lock the adjustment in place by bottoming the adjusting bolt jam nuts

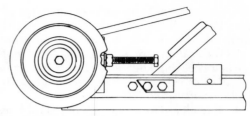

Track tension adjusting bolt

against the rear idler wheel support bracket.

NOTE: *Since track tension and track alignment are interrelated, always check both track tension and track alignment, even if only one particular adjustment seems required.*

WARNING: *If jam nuts are not locked and loosened, there is a possibility that the track may become locked. If the track locks during operation, personal injury may result.*

Track Alignment

Arctic recommends that the track alignment be checked once a month or whenever the track tension is checked or adjusted. Proper track alignment is obtained when the rear idler wheels are centered between the internal drive lugs on the inside surface of the track. The rear idler wheels, internal drive lugs and the track will wear excessively if the track is not aligned properly. Therefore, proper track alignment must be obtained to prevent accelerated wear of critical components.

Check Track Alignment

1. Before checking track alignment, remove excess ice and snow buildup from the track and from the inside of the skid frame.

2. Raise the rear of the snowmobile off the ground using a safety stand. Make sure the track is free to rotate. The tips of the skis must be positioned against a wall or similar object for safety.

3. Start the engine and accelerate slightly. Use only enough throttle to turn the track several revolutions. SHUT ENGINE OFF

NOTE: *Allow the track to coast to a stop. DO NOT apply the brake because it could produce an inaccurate alignment condition.*

4. When the track STOPS rotating, check the relationship of the rear idler wheels and the internal drive lugs. If the track runs to the left or right, or if the rear idler wheels rub against the inside surface of the internal

drive lugs, an adjustment is required. However, if the rear idler wheels are centered between the inside surface of the internal surface of the internal drive lugs, track alignment is acceptable.

Adjust Track Alignment

WARNING: *Make sure the engine is shut OFF and the track is NOT rotating before checking or adjusting track alignment. Personal injury could result if contact is made with the revolving track.*

1. Loosen the rear idler wheel adjusting bolt jam nut until it is approximately 15 mm (½ inch) away from the adjusting bolt head. Perform this step on the other adjusting bolt jam nut.

Adjusting track alignment

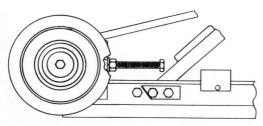

Track alignment screw and locknut

2. Rotate the right-hand adjusting bolt clockwise if track ran to the right. If the track ran to the left, rotate the left-hand adjusting bolt clockwise. Rotate 1 to 1½ turns, then recheck and continue to adjust until proper alignment is obtained.

NOTE: *Make sure correct track tension is maintained whenever the track alignment is adjusted.*

3. Lock the two adjusting bolt jam nuts.

4. Lower the rear of the snowmobile to the ground. Start the engine and test run the track under actual field conditions.

5. After the test run is completed, recheck the track alignment (See: To Check Track Alignment).

Adjust Suspension

The suspension should be adjusted for the operator only. The rear spring should be ad-

justed for the weight and riding preference of the operator. Also, the rear springs should be adjusted to accommodate the weight of an additional passenger when two people are riding. The front spring adjustment primarily influences the way the snowmobile performs in snow and the effort required to steer the snowmobile.

The optimum setting on the rear springs prevents the suspension from "bottoming out" on all but the most severe bumps. The springs should not be adjusted so stiff that the suspension will not work properly under normal conditions.

A good test of a properly adjusted suspension is when the operator should just be able to "bottom" the suspension when jumping up and down on the rearmost part of the running board. The optimum setting for the front spring is when the spring tension is sufficiently stiff to prevent the suspension from collapsing in deep snow but not so stiffly that steering becomes ineffective.

REAR SPRING ADJUSTMENT CAM

Pantera, Jag, Panther

The Jag, Pantera and Panther models are equipped with a rear spring adjustment cam to fit the individual needs of the operator. The cam is numbered 1–4 for easy identification with the high position (4) providing the stiffer ride and position 1 designed for the lighter driver under slow speed trail driving. Positions 2 and 3 are for the average driver under normal conditions with position 3 providing the stiffer ride.

Spring tension can be changed by rotating the cam using the handle from the spark plug wrench. To increase spring tension, the handle should be rotated toward the rear of the snowmobile. To decrease spring tension, rotate the handle toward the front of the ma-

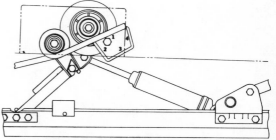

Rear spring adjuster—Pantera, Jag, Panther and El Tigre models

chine. Be sure both cams are adjusted equally.

NOTE: *DO NOT rotate the adjustment cam directly from position 1 to the number 4 position. Always adjust in numerical sequence.*

REAR SPRING ADJUSTMENT

Lynx

Tighten or loosen the spring adjusting nut to obtain the desired suspension adjustment. Perform this step on opposite side adjusting nut. Always maintain equal adjustment on each spring.

NOTE: *When the adjusting nut is tightened, spring tension is increased. If the adjusting nut is loosened, however, spring tension is decreased. Adjust rear spring tension to prevent bottoming out on all but the most severe bumps.*

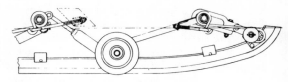

Front and rear spring adjuster (Lynx)

FRONT SPRING ADJUSTMENT

Tighten or loosen the front spring adjusting nut to obtain the desired suspension adjustment. Perform this step on opposite side adjusting nut.

NOTE: *There are two adjustments for the rear and two for the front of the suspension frame. Be sure that the adjustments on the front adjusting bolts are equal. Also, make sure the adjustments are equal on the rear adjusting bolts or adjuster cams.*

4

John Deere

INTRODUCTION

This chapter contains service and maintenance information for the John Deere "Fire" series Snowmobiles.

The text is divided into sections pertaining to a component or operational system.

Emphasis is placed on diagnosing malfunctions, analysis and testing. Diagnosing mal-functions lists possible troubles and their causes. The troubles are analyzed to help you understand the problem, so it can be corrected rather than just replace the parts.

SERIAL NUMBER

An individual serial number is assigned to each snowmobile. This number consists of

A. Engine
B. Fuel system
C. Electrical system
D. Power train
E. Suspension

John Deere components

thirteen letters, numbers, or spaces. The first letter indicates the "family of machine" (snowmobile); the next three numbers or letters, the "model or machine designation"; the letter in the fifth position indicates the "model year". This is followed by a space (for computer purposes) and a six-digit serial number and the letter "M" denoting Horicon as the factory of manufacture. When ordering parts, use only the six-digit number. When writing about or filling out warranty claims, use all thirteen numbers, letters and spaces shown on the snowmobile serial number plate. All parts are identified by the snowmobile serial number rather than the engine serial number.

A. Lower plug   B. Fill plug

Checking oil level in chain case

ROUTINE MAINTENANCE

It is of the utmost importance to keep your snowmobile's mechanical and electrical components in the very best condition possible. By keeping a close watch on parts which have a tendency to wear, or break, serious problems (especially when it is 10° below and you are deep in the woods) can be avoided.

LUBRICANTS

Oil used in the chain case should be a good grade of SAE 90.

Remove plug from the lower part of the chain case. If oil flows from this hole, the oil level is satisfactory. If oil must be added, remove fill plug and add SAE 90 oil until it flows from the lower hole. Remove oil from chain case with a syringe.

CARBURETOR

All John Deere snowmobiles are equipped with Mikuni Carburetors and fuel pumps. They are covered in detail in chapter two (carburetors).

FUEL FILTER

The fuel filter will be found in the gas line between the gas tank and the fuel pump. It is a see through type for easy inspection. If it appears dirty it should be replaced. This is cheap insurance against a stalled engine deep in the woods.

BRAKE SYSTEM

Brakes should be inspected each day before starting the snowmobile and any malfunction must be repaired at that time. The following instructions cover the most common systems used by John Deere.

Mechanical Disk Brake—Early Model

REMOVAL

1. Remove brake cam body, puck and backing plate.
2. Slide brake disk off shaft.
3. Remove brake puck body with puck.
NOTE: *When removing puck from brake puck body it may be necessary to heat the puck with a hand torch to remove it.*

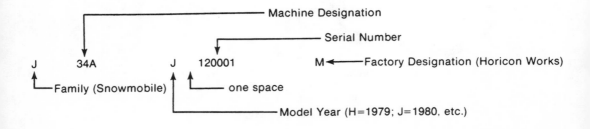

Maintenance Interval Chart

Item	As Needed	Daily	Every 150 Miles	Every 300 Miles	Annually
Clean windshield.	X				
Check condition of skis and steering.		X			
Check track condition and tension.		X			
Check throttle control operation.		X			
Check operation of brakes.		X			
Check emergency stop and key switch.		X			
Check lighting system.		X			
Check chain case oil level.			X		
Check chain tensioner.				X	
Check in-line fuel filter.					X
Check drive belt condition.		X			
Check carburetor adjustments.			X	X	X
Check choke adjustments.			X	X	X
Check fan belt tension.				X	X
Check ski alignment.	X				
Check headlight adjustment.	X				
Check ski wear rods and wear plates.				X	X
Check side suspension wear bars.				X	X
Use Never-Seez on throttle cable end.					X
Check all components for condition and tightness.					X
Service drive and driven sheaves.					X
Store snowmobile properly.					X

Brake cam body, puck and backing plate

Installing brake puck body

Brake puck body and puck

INSPECTION

1. Replace brake pucks if they are contaminated or worn enough to prevent proper brake adjustment.

2. Inspect brake disk, cam, pins and brake cable. Replace worn or damaged parts.

ASSEMBLY

1. Use two-part epoxy glue to secure "thin" puck in the brake puck body.

NOTE: *DO NOT glue the "thick" puck and backing plate in the brake cam body.*

2. Install brake puck body over bolts in tunnel.

Installing brake cam body

3. Use an anti-seize on drive shaft and install key and brake disk.

4. Place backing plate and "thick" puck in brake cam body. Install this assembly and secure with nuts.

ADJUSTMENT

1. Loosen or tighten jam nuts on brake cable until the cam is parallel with the

Installing thin puck

Adjusting brake cable and cam

Brake lever adjustment

Brake puck body

ground (level) and pointing straight ahead.

2. Remove cotter pin and loosen or tighten the adjusting nut on the brake post until 1 to 1-½ inches (25 to 38 mm) clearance exists between the brake lever and handgrip. Install cotter pin.

3. After adjusting brake, check operation of stop light switch.

Mechanical Disk Brake—Late Model

REMOVAL

1. Disconnect brake cable from arm.
2. Screw bottom jam nut off brake cable.

A. Jam nut   B. Brake cable

Removing brake cable

3. Remove arm from brake puck body.
4. Remove muffler.
5. Remove bracket, brake puck body and puck.
6. Remove brake disk and flat spring.
7. Remove retainer with puck.

INSPECTION

1. Replace brake pucks if they are contaminated.

Removing retainer with puck

IMPORTANT: *New pucks are ⅜ inch thick. If either puck is worn to only* ³/₁₆ *inch in thickness, replace both pucks.*

2. Inspect brake disk, arm, adjusting screw and brake cable. Replace worn or damaged parts.

ASSEMBLY

1. Install retainer with puck over bolts in tunnel.
2. Use an anti-seize on drive shaft and install brake disk and flat spring.
3. Install arm with adjusting screw and brake puck in brake puck body.

IMPORTANT: *Be sure metal part of brake puck faces the screw and not the brake disk.*

4. Install brake puck body, arm, brake puck and bracket.
5. Install brake cable through bracket and tighten upper and lower jam nuts.

NOTE: *Threads on brake cable should be approximately at the midpoint of the threads when tightened to the bracket.*

A. Brake disc
B. Flat spring

Installing brake disc

A. Brake cable
B. Bracket
C. Jam nuts

Installing brake cable

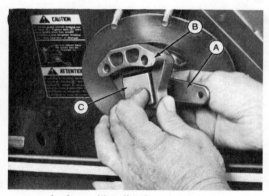

A. Arm with adjusting screw
B. Brake puck body
C. Brake puck

Installing arm and brake puck in brake puck body

Installing brake cable to arm

tighten jam nuts on brake cable until arm is in correct position.
7. Install muffler.

ADJUSTMENT

1. Apply the brake control lever and measure the distance from the lever to the handgrip. It should be 1 to 1-½ inches (25 to 38 mm).

Installing body, arm, puck and bracket

6. Connect brake cable to arm.
NOTE: *Arm should be pointing down approximately 15 degrees from parallel before connecting the brake cable. Loosen or*

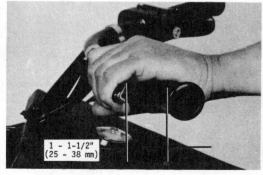

Brake adjustment

A. Jam nut
B. Adjusting screw

Brake adjustment

2. Adjust brake by loosening jam nut and tightening adjusting screw. Tighten jam nut.
3. Check brake tension and readjust if necessary.
NOTE: *Be certain dowel on end of brake cable is seated properly in recess of brake control lever.*
4. After adjustment, check operation of stoplight switch.

DRIVE BELT

The drive belt should be inspected each day before starting the snowmobile. Follow belt inspection and maintenance tips which are covered in chapter one, "General information and maintenance".

SUSPENSION

Inspection and Maintenance

Slide suspensions are covered in chapter one in general terms and one of the more com-

Removing slide suspension

Exploded view of slide suspension

1. Axle
2. Spacer
3. Idler wheel (2 used)
4. Spacer (2 used)
5. Cap screw (6 used)
6. Wheel bracket (2 used)
7. Push nut (4 used)
8. Bumper (4 used)
9. Shaft
10. Bearing (2 used)
11. Cap screw (2 used)
12. Washer (4 used)
13. Cap (2 used)
14. Lock nut (2 used)
15. Slide Rail
16. Bolt (2 used)
17. Rivet (4 used)
18. Cap screw (2 used)
19. Wheel mount (2 used)
20. Cap screw (2 used)
21. Washer (2 used)
22. Spacer (2 used)
23. Bushing (2 used)
24. Washer (2 used)
25. Cap screw
26. Wear bar (2 used)
27. Pad (2 used)
28. Shaft
29. Cap screw (2 used)
30. Washer (2 used)
31. Idler wheel (4 used)
32. Cap screw (2 used)
33. Wear bar stop (2 used)
34. Axle
35. Nut (2 used)
36. Cap screw (2 used)
37. Spacer
38. Lock nut (3 used)

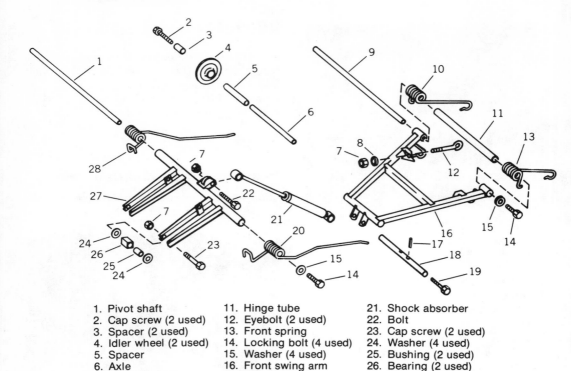

1. Pivot shaft
2. Cap screw (2 used)
3. Spacer (2 used)
4. Idler wheel (2 used)
5. Spacer
6. Axle
7. Locknut (5 used)
8. Washer (2 used)
9. Pivot shaft
10. Front spring
11. Hinge tube
12. Eyebolt (2 used)
13. Front spring
14. Locking bolt (4 used)
15. Washer (4 used)
16. Front swing arm
17. Spring pin (2 used)
18. Shaft
19. Screw (2 used)
20. Rear spring
21. Shock absorber
22. Bolt
23. Cap screw (2 used)
24. Washer (4 used)
25. Bushing (2 used)
26. Bearing (2 used)
27. Rear pivot arm
28. Rear spring

Exploded view of slide suspension

mon slide rail systems used on John Deere snowmobiles is covered in detail in the following section.

Removing Suspension

1. Remove suspension retaining bolts from each side of tunnel. Remove rear bolts first.

2. Turn the snowmobile on its right side and remove the suspension.

IMPORTANT: *Siphon all fuel from the*

Suspension retaining bolts

tank to prevent spillage when snowmobile is on its side.
CAUTION: *Gasoline is dangerous. Avoid fire due to smoking or careless maintenance practices.*

Replacing Slide Suspension Wear Bars

1. Remove suspension.

2. Remove cap (13) from front of suspension.

3. Use a wood block and hammer to remove the wear bar.

4. Lubricate slide rail and wear bar with a liquid soap solution.

5. Install new wear bar from the front and drive it in place with a soft mallet.

6. Install cap.

7. Install suspension.

Replacing Rear Idler Wheels and Axle

1. Remove suspension.

2. Remove cap screws, idler wheels and washers from each end of rear axle shaft.

Removing slide wear bar

Rear axle shaft and wheels

Installing rear axle

3. Loosen both adjusting screws and slide rear axle forward. Remove axle through square hole in slide rail.

4. To reassemble: Place rear axle through slide rail. Be sure grooves in axle fit slide rail correctly.

5. Partially tighten both adjusting screws.

6. Install idler wheel, washer and cap screw on each end of axle.
NOTE: *Use Loctite on each cap screw.*
7. Install suspension.

Adjusting Track Tension

1. Support rear of snowmobile so that track is clear of ground.

2. Tension the track to give ½-inch (12.7 mm) clearance between the inside of track and bottom of the wear bar. Measure below shock absorber mount. Track should be suspended as shown.

3. Adjust both sides equally. Tighten jam nuts.

4. Start engine and idle track slowly until it rotates several times.

5. Shut off engine and allow track to coast to a stop. DO NOT APPLY BRAKE.
Check alignment as follows:

1. Rear idler wheels should run in center of drive lugs.

2. Slide wear bar should be in center of slide rail opening on each side of track.

3. If either Step 1 or Step 2 is off, retention track.
NOTE: *Track will run to the loose side. For example, if the track is too far to the left side, tighten the left side to move the track to the right.*

4. Run track again to recheck.

A. Jam nuts
B. Adjusting screws

Adjusting track tension

Adjusting Suspension Springs

Ride the snowmobile to determine spring adjustments.

FRONT SPRING ADJUSTMENT

1. Turn adjusting nuts counterclockwise to reduce tension or clockwise to increase tension, Fig. 9.

Adjusting front spring tension

A. Bottom position
B. Top position

Adjusting rear spring tension

2. In deep snow (for more lift) increase tension. In light snow (for more steering control) reduce tension.

IMPORTANT: *Never turn adjusting nuts all the way out. At least two threads on each screw must protrude through its respective adjusting nut.*

REAR SPRING ADJUSTMENT

1. If suspension bottoms frequently, increase rear spring preload.

2. Move springs from bottom position (A) to top position (B) to increase spring preload.

TRACK ANALYSIS

Ply Separation

Ply separation is a parting of the rubber from the tensile cords on any of the three belts.

Track Stretch

Track stretch occurs on a used track. Track stretch is first noticed by lack of adjustment on the track-adjusting screws. Remove the track and lay it flat. Measure ten pitches on the track. This distance should not exceed 32.9 inches.

NOTE: *A pitch is the distance (center-to-center) from one drive lug to the other.*

Obstruction Damage

Cuts, slashes or gouges in the track are caused by broken glass, sharp rocks or buried steel. Damage occurs during rapid acceleration or side-skidding over foreign objects.

See Chapter one—"Suspension and Track Systems—for more detailed explanation of track problems and maintenance.

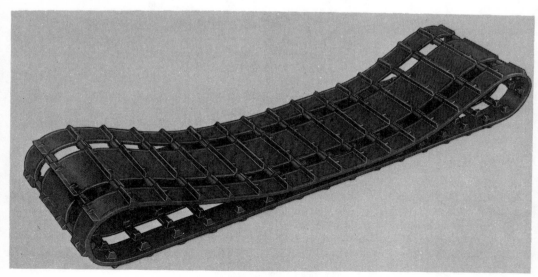

John Deere track

Wear Clips

Wear clips wear from operating on rough, dry terrain, railroads and highway roadsides, gravel roads and other non-approved snowmobile field conditions.

The slide wear bar becomes hot. Sand, dirt, and grit become imbedded in the bar causing wear on the wear clips. The slide wear bars must be replaced when this condition occurs.

Lug Damage

Lug damage to the sides or rear edges of the drive lug is usually caused by lack of snow lubrication. Excessive track tension and dirt or soil (summer operating conditions) in the drive mechanism can also cause lug damage.

Racheting Damage

Racheting damage to the top of the lugs is caused by loose track tension, pulling too great a load, or frequent prolonged periods of rapid acceleration.

Over-Tension Damage

Too much track tension causes excessive friction between the slide wear bars and the wear clips. The wear bars will melt and adhere to the wear clips.

The first indication of this condition is that the track may "stick" or "lock-up", causing loss of engine horsepower.

Loose Track Damage

Operating a track too loose causes the outer edge to flex too much resulting in cracks in the outer belts. Some wear on the driving lugs will also occur. Riding double (excessive weight) can also cause the track to flex and break the edge.

Impact Damage

Impact damage will cause the rubber on the tread side to open up exposing the cords. This may happen in more than one place.

Edge Damage

Edge damage is the operator's fault. The most frequent cause is tipping the snowmobile on it's side to clear the track, allowing the track to come in contact with an abrasive surface.

Disassembly and Repair
REMOVING TRACK

1. Siphon fuel from tank.
2. Remove chain case cover, chain tensioner, sprockets and drive chain.
3. Remove suspension.
4. Remove cap screws securing bearing flangettes to tunnel.
5. Move drive shaft toward chain case side. Lift end with spacer to remove shaft.
6. Remove track.

Removing track driveshaft

REPAIRING TRACK

Any of the following conditions require wear clip or track replacement.

1. Wear clip missing (replace clip).
2. Excessively worn wear clips (replace clips).
3. Wear clip guides missing on more than three successive wear clips (replace clips).
4. Fiber glass rod broken (replace track).

REPLACING WEAR CLIP

1. Break clip off with pliers or saw with hacksaw.

   IMPORTANT: *Use care when using hacksaw so as not to damage rubber or fiber glass rod.*
2. Use Track Wear Clip Installing Tool JDG-46 to install new wear clip.

Installing Track

1. Place track in tunnel.
2. Install the drive shaft, chain case sprocket, drive chain and chain tensioner.

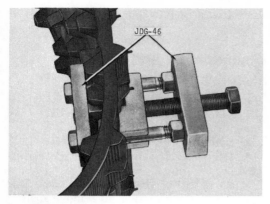

Installing wear clip

3. Adjust track tension.
4. Fill chain case with SAE 90 oil.
5. Fill fuel tank.

Track Stud Patterns

Two stud kits and two track stud patterns are available.
   The stud kits are:
AM 55177—Steel Stud Kit

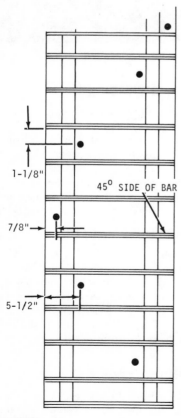

18 stud pattern

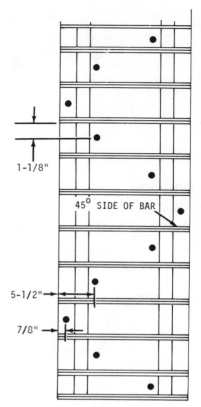

36 stud pattern

AM 55178—Carbide Stud Kit
   Each kit contains 18 studs.
   One track stud pattern consists of 18 studs; the other 36 studs. Use two kits for the 36 stud pattern. DO NOT use steel and carbide together. Use two like kits.
   The 18 stud pattern is used for normal and trail riding. The 36 stud pattern is used for hardpack and lake running.
   NOTE: *Carbide wear rods must be used on the skis when using the 36 stud pattern.*
   IMPORTANT: *Upper tunnel wear strips must be installed whenever the track is studded.*

TUNE UP

All newer John Deere Snowmobiles are equipped with C.D.I. breakerless ignition systems. This means no mechanical breaker points to wear, break, or stick open or closed. C.D.I. ignition systems are very reliable and trouble free. Most C.D.I. systems are covered in the ignition section under general tune up "Chapter one". The specific tune-up specifications for John Deere engines follow in the next section.

Tune Up Specifications

Year	Engine Series	Type Cooling	Spark Plug (Champion)	Plug Gap (Inches)	Ign. Timing at (6000 RPM)	Engine Size (C.C.)	Engine Manufacturer
1976-78	340/22	F.C.	QN-1	.025	−20°	339	Kioritz
	440/22	F.C.	QN-1	.025	−20°	438	Kioritz
	340/23	Liquid	QN-1	.025	−20°	339	Kioritz
	440/23	Liquid	QN-1	.025	−20°	438	Kioritz
1979-80	TA 340 A	F.C.	QN-3	.025	22°	339	Kawasaki
	TA 440 A	F.C.	QN-3	.025	22°	436	Kawasaki
	K340-2FA	F.A.	QN-3	.025	*.085	338	Kohler
1980	TB 340 A	F.A.	N-3	.025	+22°	338	Kawasaki
	TC 440 A	Liquid	N-2	.025	16°	436	Kawasaki

− 3000 RPM
+ 6500 RPM
*inches

ENGINES

John Deere has used many different engines in their snowmobiles starting with C.C.W., Kohler, Kioritz and Kawasaki. From 1976 to 1980 only Kioritz and Kawasaki are used. The 1979 and 1980 models are exclusively Kawasaki engined. They are referred to as John Deere "Fire Burst" engines.

Engine Specifications

Year	Engine Model	No. of Cylinders	Displacement (C.C.)	Bore (M.M.)	Stroke (M.M.)	Comp. Ratio
1976-78	340/22	2	339	58	64	6.9
	440/22	2	438	66	64	7.2
	340/23	2	339	58	64	7.2
	440/23	2	438	66	64	6.7
1978-79	K340-2FA	2	338	62	56	6.9
1980	TB 340 A	2	338	60	60	6.9
1979-80	TA 340 A	2	339	60	60	6.9
	TA 440 A	2	436	68	60	6.5
1980	TC 440 A	2	436	68	60	6.9

DRIVE SYSTEM

Drive Sheave

The John Deere (Comet) clutch (drive sheave) is used on all newer model John Deere snowmobiles and will be the only clutch (sheave) covered in this section.

The centrifugally-operated drive sheave, is both a clutch and variator.

The drive sheave is "matched" to the driven sheave and to the engine to provide smooth operation. It is important to use the proper components for repair.

IMPORTANT: *Never operate the engine with the drive belt removed. The engine could overspeed and cause possible engine and drive sheave failure.*

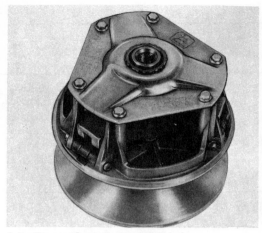

John Deere (Comet) drive clutch

Disassembly and Repair

REMOVING DRIVE SHEAVE

Raise hood and drive blt guard. Remove drive belt and knock-out plug from side of pan.

Use Compressor ring to compress movable face to expose cross hole in hub.

Install a two-piece nut (special tool), around hub. Engage pins on nut in hub cross hole.

Hold nut and remove retaining cap screw, lock washer and pilot washer. Turn the puller

A. Cross hole
B. Compressor ring (special tool)

Compressor ring

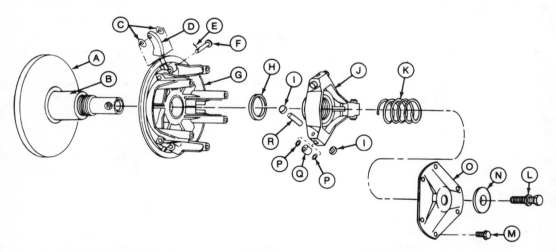

A. Fixed face sheave
B. Bronze bushing
C. Washers (6 used)
D. Roller arm (3 used)
E. Spring pin (3 used)
F. Pivot pin (3 used)
G. Movable face sheave

H. Spacing washer
I. Button (6 used)
J. Spider
K. Spring
L. Retaining cap screw with lockwasher
M. Cap screw (6 used)

N. Pilot washer
O. Cover plate with bushing
P. Washers (6 used)
Q. Roller (3 used)
R. Pin (3 used)

Exploded view of drive clutch

Two piece nut installed

A. Spider tool
B. Hub lock

Spider tool and hub lock tool (installed)

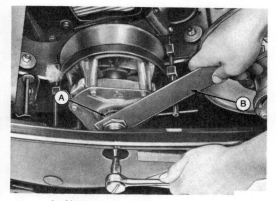

A. Nut
B. Nut wrench

Removing drive clutch

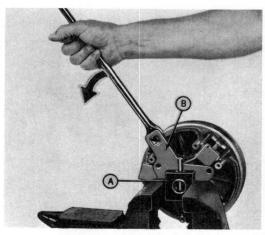

A. Hub lock
B. Spider tool

Removing spider from the hub

into hub, until drive sheave comes loose from the crankshaft.

DISASSEMBLING DRIVE SHEAVE

1. Remove puller from hub.
2. Remove every other screw securing drive sheave cover plate to movable face. Remove the three remaining cap screws equally, a few turns at a time. This allows the cover plate to come off slowly and equally. Remove cover plate and spring.
3. Place puller tool over hub with spring pins on tool engaging spider. Install the hub lock tool over hub with pin of tool through cross hole in hub.
4. Clamp assembly very securely into vise and install a ½-inch drive long handle into the spider tool and turn counterclockwise to loosen spider from the hub.
5. Remove spider tool and hub lock. Turn spider off the hub by hand.

IMPORTANT: *Remove spacer rings and movable face. Take note of the number of spacers for installation later on.*

INSPECTING BUSHINGS

Inspect bushing and cover plate. If bushing is worn or damaged, replace cover plate.

Inspecting the bushing in cover plate

INSPECTING GUIDE BUTTONS AND ROLLERS

Inspect guide buttons and rollers in spider. Replace if necessary. Use pliers to remove guide buttons. Remove pin, roller and two washers. Place roller in spider with a steel washer on each side of the roller. Install pin and guide buttons. Tap buttons gently until they are seated.

NOTE: *1977 Model 440 Snowmobiles have a fiber washer on the thrust side of the spider.*

NOTE: *Small dot on guide buttons must be positioned straight up or straight down. This allows bearing surface of guide button to match bearing surface in movable face.*

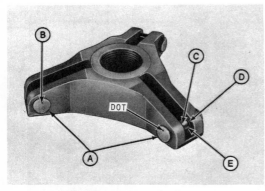

A. Guide button   D. Fiber washer
B. Dot
C. Steel washers   E. Roller

Installing guide buttons

INSPECTING ROLLER ARMS

1. Inspect roller arms for wear and replace as necessary. Use screwdriver to pry spring pin out as far as possible and then use side

A. Spring pin
B. Pivot pin

Removing spring pin from pivot pin

A. Spring pin   C. Pivot pin
B. Steel washers   D. Roller arm

Installing pivot pin

cutters to remove spring pin, from the end of the pivot pin. Remove pivot pin, roller and three steel washers.

2. Install roller arm in movable face with a steel washer on each side of the arm. Install pivot pin from left to right. Install steel washer and a new spring pin through pivot pin.

INSPECTING FIXED AND MOVABLE FACES

1. Check sheave faces for pitting or wear and replace as necessary.

2. Inspect bushing of movable face and hub of fixed face for damage or excessive wear. Measure outside diameter of fixed face hub and inside diameter of movable face bushing. Maximum allowable clearance is 0.030 inch. If clearance is greater than 0.030 inch replace movable face bushing.

3. Use a hacksaw blade and carefully cut through the movable face bushing in several places.

IMPORTANT: *Do not saw into the metal of the movable face. This could weaken and damage the movable face. Remove bushing with a small cold chisel and hammer.*

Cutting movable face bushing

Snap ring position on movable face bushing

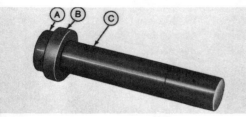

A. 27509 Disc   C. 27488 Handle
B. 27516 Disc

Tool for installing movable face bushing

Installing movable face bushing

4. Install new bushing in movable face with snap-ring of bushing up as shown.

5. To complete installation of bushing, use a bushing, bearing and seal driver set. Install 27516 disk and 27509 disk to 27488 Handle as shown. This combination will install movable face bushing.

6. Use a press and ring compressor to install bushing flush with movable face.

NOTE: *Ring Compressor to compress snap ring when installing movable face bushing.*

LUBRICATING DRIVE SHEAVE

1. Lubricate the drive sheave before assembly. Use anti-seize lubricant or its equivalent on the following:

a. Roller arms and roller pins in the movable face.

b. Guide buttons in the spider and on mating surface of movable face.

NOTE: *Use Loctite® on the spider-to-hub threads. This will prevent spider from loosening while in use.*

ASSEMBLING DRIVE SHEAVE

2. Install movable face over fixed face hub and place required number of spacer rings, on hub.

3. Install spider on movable face. Align identification marks on spider with identification marks on movable face. Proper alignment of these marks is necessary for proper balance of the drive sheave.

4. With one hand, grasp the spider assembly and movable sheave (B). Hold the fixed

Installing spacer rings

Identification marks on spider and movable face

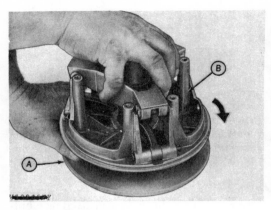

A. Fixed sheave
B. Moveable sheave

Installing spider and movable face

A. Hub lock
B. Spider tool

Tightening spider to the hub

sheave (A) and with the other hand turn the spider and movable sheave clockwise to start the threads of the spider onto the hub post. Continue to tighten the assembly as far as possible by hand.

5. Place spider tool over hub with spring pins on tool engaging spider. Install hub lock over hub. Clamp assembly very securely into vise. Install a ½-inch drive long handle in spider tool and turn clockwise to tighten spider to hub.

6. Remove spider tool and hub lock.

7. Install spring and cover plate. Tighten the six screws evenly and securely.

INSTALLING DRIVE SHEAVE

1. Clean crankshaft tapered surface and place drive sheave on crankshaft.

A. Two-piece nut   C. Nut wrench
B. Compressor ring

Installing drive clutch

2. Use compressor ring and compress movable face to expose cross hole in hub.

3. Install two-piece nut and hold with a wrench.

4. Install the lockwasher and pilot washer onto the retaining cap screw. Install and tighten retaining cap screw to 50 ft-lbs.

IMPORTANT: *Do not torque the retaining cap screw more than 50 ft-lbs because it will "swell" the hub end causing the drive sheave to "stick."*

5. Install drive belt, belt guard and secure hood.

John Deere Driven Sheave

The John Deere Driven Sheave, is used on the 340 and 440 Cyclone and Liquifire Snowmobiles. The driven sheave acts as a take-up for the action of the drive sheave. The driven sheave is also "torque-sensitive."

John Deere driven clutch

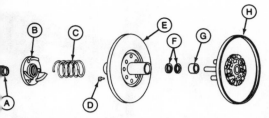

A. Bushing
B. Cam bracket
C. Spring
D. Button

E. Sheave and post
F. Shims
G. Bushing
H. Moveable sheave

Assembly drawing of driven clutch

DRIVEN SHEAVE

Removal

1. Raise the hood and drive belt guard. Remove drive belt.

2. Remove cap screw and washer and slide driven sheave with key off the shaft.

Removing driven clutch

DRIVEN SHEAVE DISASSEMBLY

1. Remove three cap screws securing cam to movable face.

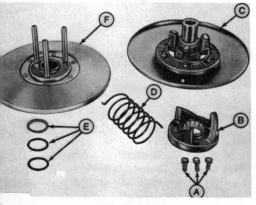

A. Cap screws
B. Cam
C. Fixed face

D. Spring
E. Spacers
F. Moveable face

Disassembling driven clutch

2. Remove cam, spring and fixed face with insert buttons from movable face. Do not lose spacers between movable face and fixed face.

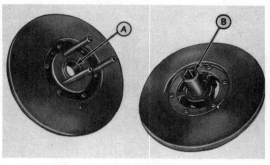

A. Movable face bushing
B. Fixed face hub

Movable face bushing and fixed face hub

DRIVEN SHEAVE INSPECTION

1. Inspect movable face bushing and fixed face hub for wear. Replace parts as necessary. Excessive looseness could cause binding.

2. Replace movable face bushing as follows:

3. To remove and install bushing use bushing, bearing and seal driver set. Install 27507 Disk and 27505 Disk to 27488 Handle as shown in. This combination will remove and install movable face bushing.

4. Use a press and remove old bushing.

5. Use a press and install new bushing flush with the hub of movable face.

6. Inspect spring for cracks or pits. Replace as necessary.

7. Check sheave faces with a straight-edge. Replace if badly worn, grooved, scored or pitted.

8. Inspect bushing in cam and fixed face hub for wear. Replace parts as necessary.

9. Replace bushing in cam as follows:

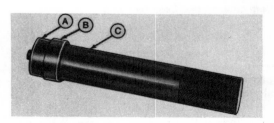

A. 27505 Disc
B. 27507 Disc

C. 27488 Handle

Tool for removing movable face bushing

Removing movable face bushing

Removing cam bushing

Installing movable face bushing

Installing cam bushing

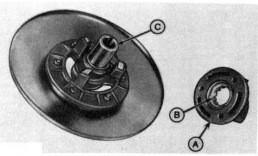

A. Cam   C. Fixed face hub
B. Bushing

Cam bushing and fixed face hub

Inspecting insert button

10. Place cam on two wooden blocks and use a cold chisel to remove bushing.

11. Install new bushing by pushing in place with your thumbs. Be sure bushing is aligned properly when installing.

12. Inspect insert buttons for wear. Buttons and mating surfaces on cam must be smooth. Replace insert buttons as a set if worn. If not replaced as a set, binding and improper sheave operation could result.

13. Replace insert buttons as follows:
a. Use pliers and break off insert button ramp.

b. Use a $^{15}/_{64}$-inch drill and very CAREFULLY drill out the shank of the insert button. DO NOT enlarge the hole or the new insert button will not fit snug.

c. Use two part epoxy glue on the shank of the new insert button and tap it in place very LIGHTLY with a plastic hammer. Be careful not to break the insert button.

Drilling out insert button shank

DRIVEN SHEAVE ASSEMBLY
Pretensioning Driven Sheave

NOTE: *The spring in the driven sheave must be pretensioned differently as altitude and temperature changes occur.*

As temperature or altitude increases, engine horsepower decreases. The drive system now upshifts too rapidly for an engine with less horsepower. In order to counteract this, the drive system must be modified to obtain proper governed speed. Low governed speed results in poor performance.

Engine governed speed should be as follows:

1976 Snowmobiles
(Serial No. 50,001–70,000)

Snowmobile	Governed Speed
340 Cyclone	6500–7000 rpm
440 Cyclone	6500–7000 rpm
340 Liquifire	7000–7500 rpm
440 Liquifire	7250–7750 rpm

1977 Snowmobiles
(Serial No. 70,001- and up)

Snowmobile	Governed Speed
340 and 440 Cyclone	6200–6700 rpm
340 and 440 Liquifire	6800–7300 rpm

IMPORTANT: *Do not adjust the driven sheave to provide engine speeds in excess of the governed speeds listed.*

Additional driven sheave pretension increases engine speed; less pretension decreases speed. The John Deere driven sheave can be pretensioned as shown in the chart.

Pretensioning Chart for Driven Sheave Spring

Insert spring tang in cam hole number.	Place cam and spring over fixed face hub with tang on spring in hole of fixed face. Rotate cam clockwise past the ramp indicated.	Degrees of pretension.	Pounds of spring tension when measured at sheave rim.
1	1 ramp	50°	5 lbs.
2*	1 ramp	80°	6 lbs.
3	1 ramp	110°	8 lbs.
4	2 ramps	140°	10 lbs.

*This is the factory setting for 340 and 440 Cyclone and Liquifire Snowmobiles.

1. Lay movable sheave flat with posts up. Place spacers on hub of movable sheave.

2. Install fixed sheave hub through movable sheave.

3. Install spring in proper hole in cam, as indicated in the chart above. The proper hole for most applications is No. 2.

4. Install cam with spring over with tang of spring in hole in fixed face.

5. Rotate cam past the proper ramp as indicated in the chart. Push down on cam making sure posts of movable face fit in recesses in cam.

6. Install and tighten cap screws securely.

Installing spacer

Spring installed in cam

DRIVEN SHEAVE INSTALLATION

1. Lubricate shaft and inside of driven sheave hub with anti-seize lubricant.

2. Be sure spacers are on shaft.

3. Place key in driven sheave. Place sheave inline with shaft and back key out of sheave slightly. This will help line-up sheave with keyway in shaft.

4. Slide sheave in place and push key in to lock sheave to shaft.

5. Install washer and retaining cap screw. Tighten cap screw to 20 ft-lbs.

Installing spring and cam on fixed face post

Installing driven clutch on shaft

5

Polaris

INTRODUCTION

Polaris was one of the first to adopt the slide rail suspension to most of their production models. Along with a lightweight air-cooled engine, the firm has earned a reputation for making solid dependable machines using their own engines, clutches and other drive line components. Now with the addition of the three cyl 500 cc liquid cooled engine that is used exclusively in the top of the line Centurion they also have one of the fastest production sleds available.

IDENTIFICATION

Both the engine and the chassis serial numbers are easily visible on the Polaris models. The engine serial number is found by lifting the cowling and checking on the exhaust side of the engine for the engine name plate which bears the engine number. The chassis serial number is found on the right-side of the machine (operator's right, in the driving position) at the operator's right foot area. These numbers are most important and should be recorded even before the unit is used for the first time. They must be given when ordering parts or claiming warranty.

ROUTINE MAINTENANCE

This one important aspect of the snowmobile which the average owner is able to do. By consulting his owner's manual he can follow

Maintenance Interval Chart

Service/Inspection	Daily	Weekly	Monthly	Annually
Clean Windshield	X			
Check Skis and Steering	X			
Check Track and Track Tension	X			
Check Throttle Controls	X			
Check Brake Operation	X			
Check Ignition and Kill Switches	X			
Check all Lights	X			
Check Chain Case Oil Level		X		
Check in-line Fuel Filter		X		
Check Drive Belt		X		
Check Carburetor Adjustments			X	

Maintenance Interval Chart (cont.)

Service/Inspection	Daily	Weekly	Monthly	Annually
Check Choke Operation			X	
Check Ski Alignment			X	
Check Fan Belt			X	
Check Ski Wear Rods			X	
Check Suspension Wear Bars			X	
Check All Components for Condition and Tightness				X
Service Drive and Driven				X
Clutches				X

the periodic lubrication chart included and can perform the necessary lubrication. A visual inspection of the vehicle before each usage is a good practice.

Every owner should also have a maintenance rundown chart. If the maintenance is

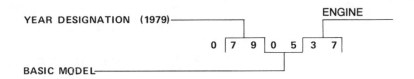

MODEL DESIGNATION	ENGINE DESIGNATION	ENGINE DESIGNATION
05 — TX	23 — EC25PT—07 Twin FA	39 — EC34PL—02 Twin LC
06 — TX-L/Centurion	25 — EC25PS Single FC	43 — EC44PM—01 Twin FC
10 — Gemini	26 — EC25PM—01 Twin FC	45 — EC44PT—05 Twin FA
11 — Apollo 340	37 — EC34PT—05 Twin FA	53 — EC51PL—01 Three LC
18 — Cobra	38 — EC34PM—03/04 Twin FC	

MODEL NUMBER	MACHINE DESCRIPTION	MODEL NUMBER	MACHINE DESCRIPTION
0791025	Gemini 244cc Single FC	0790523	TX 250cc Twin FA
0791026	Gemini 250cc Twin FC	0790537	TX 340cc Twin FA
0791138	Apollo 340cc Twin FC	0790545	TX 440cc Twin FA
0791838	Cobra 340cc Twin FC	0790639	TX-L 340cc Twin LC
0791843	Cobra 440cc Twin FC	0790653	Centurion 500cc Three LC

not done by the owner (e.g., lubrication) it should be done by an authorized dealer's mechanic.

Brake Adjustment

Polaris snowmobiles use a hydraulic disc brake unit. Turn the single, socket-head allen screw inward until the brake pads contact the disc, then back off ¼-turn. The master cylinder is located beneath the rectangular plate beside the brake lever on the handlebar. Remove the screws to lift the cover to check or replenish the brake fluid. The fluid level should be within ⅛ in. of the top of the chamber. Use heavy-duty motor vehicle brake fluid which meets SAE specification J1703. If the brake action is spongy, there may be air trapped in the system. A fitting is mounted just above the stoplight switch to allow brake bleeding. Connect a bit of fuel line to the fitting (or hold a large funnel below it). Pull on the hand lever (on the handlebars) and slowly loosen the bleed fitting's nut until the brake fluid just flows out. Pump the hand lever several times, adding more fluid to the reservoir as needed, until the air bubbles no longer appear in the brake fluid. Hold the hand lever on while you retighten the bleed fitting.

Hydraulic brake bleeding valve

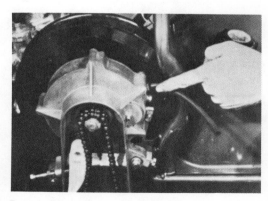

Put a rubber tube on the bleeder valve

Opening the bleeder valve

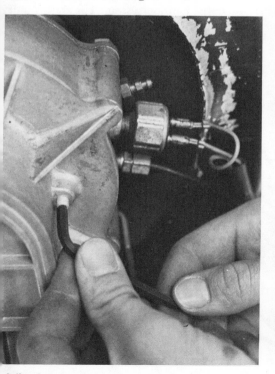

Adjusting the disc brake

Trach Tension and Alignment

The procedure for track adjustments is outlined in Chapter 1. The adjusting nuts are located just in front of the rear idler wheels on most Polaris suspension systems. The track's slack should be measured at the midpoint of the bottom slide rails.

Adjusting track tension

Ski Alignment

Measure the edge-to-edge spacing of the skis at the front spring mount and again at the rear spring mount. The two dimensions should be equal; if not, the tie-rods which lead from the steering column out to the

steering arms must be adjusted. Loosen the locknut on each steering arm and rotate the arm itself clockwise to bring the ski tips closer together (counterclockwise to spread the tips of the skis). When the skis are parallel, the locknuts can be retightened.

Headlight Adjustment

The headlights should be adjusted by turning the adjusting screws on the back of each light so that the high beam is 2 in. below the level of the light units at a point 25 feet from the front of the lights.

TUNE-UP

Ignition System

Polaris engines are fitted with either breaker point (magneto) style ignition systems or with the solid state capacitor discharge (CDI) system. The breaker point gap and timing can be adjusted as outlined in Chapter 1. Polaris does not recommend that the ignition timing be altered on the CDI system although there is a notch around the mounting screws which allows most of the units to be rotated a few degrees back and forth. The cooling fan must be removed from fan-cooled engines to gain access to the ignition system. The starter unit must then be removed so that the flywheel is visible. The ignition can be adjusted through the two slots in the flywheel. If the breaker points must be replaced, the flywheel must be removed with a puller. The ignition timing (and the spark plug gap) is given in the "Tune-Up Specifications" chart.

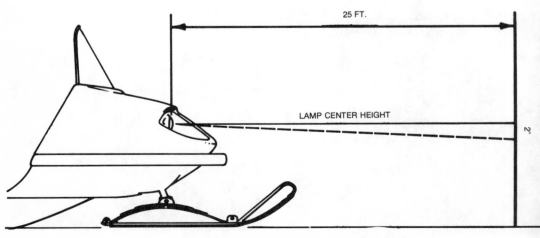

Aim headlight(s) against a wall to adjust the pattern

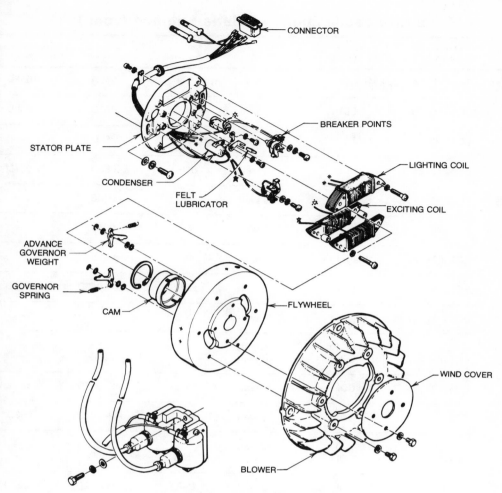

Breaker point type ignition system

Tune-Up Specifications—Polaris Engines

Year	Engine Model	Ignition Type	Alternator Output	Spark Plug Equivalent	Original Timing*	Recommended Timing*
976	EC17PM	Mag. Pt.	55 watt	B7ES	.113D	—
	EC25PS	Mag. Pt.	75 watt	B7ES	.014S	—
	EC25PC	Mag. Pt.	75 watt	B8ES	.005S	—
	EC25PT–06	CDI	75 watt	N-2	.082D	.053D
	EC25PT–05	CDI	75 watt	N-1 or N-57G	.082D	.053D
	EC34PC	Mag. Pt.	75 watt	N-3	.005S	—
	EC34PQ	CDI	140 watt	B7ES	.083D	—

Tune-Up Specifications—Polaris Engines (cont.)

Year	Engine Model	Ignition Type	Alternator Output	Spark Plug Equivalent	Original Timing*	Recommended Timing*
1976	EC34PT–05	CDI	75 watt	N-2	.082D	.053D
	EC34PT–06	CDI	75 watt	B10EV	.082D	.053D
	EC44PQ	CDI	140 watt	B7ES	.083D	—
	EC44PT–05	CDI	75 watt	B8ES	.083D	.057D
1977	EC25PS	Mag. Pt.	75 watt	N-3	.014S	—
	EC25PC	Mag. Pt.	75 watt	N-2	.005S	—
	EC25PM–01	Mag. Pt.	75 watt	N-2	.005S	—
	EC25PT–07	CDI	75 watt	B9ES	.042-.067D	.053D
	EC34PM–03	Mag. Pt.	75 watt	N-3	.005S	—
	EC34PQ	Mag. Pt. CDI	75 watt 140 watt	N-3	.006S .088D	— —
	EC34PT–05	CDI	75 watt	B9ES	.042-.067D	.053D
	EC34PL–01	CDI	75 watt	B9ES	.042-.067D	.053D [4]
	EC44PQ	Mag. Pt. CDI	75 watt 140 watt	N-3	.006S .088D	— —
	EC44PT–05	CDI	75 watt	B9ES	.050-.072D	.057D
	EC44PT–06	CDI	75 watt	B9ES	.050-.072D	.057D

*D—Dynamic timing/5,000 RPM
S—Static timing
4—Reference Racing Bulletin No. 77-2

Year	Machine Model	Engine Model	Ignition Type	Alternator Output	Spark Plug RFI/NGK
1978	Colt	EC25PS	Mag. Pt.	75 watt	BR8ES
	Colt	EC25PC	Mag. Pt.	75 watt	BR9ES
	S/S 340	EC34PM—03/04N	Mag. Pt.	75 watt	BR8ES
	Cobra	EC34PM—04	Mag. Pt.	75 watt	BR9ES

Tune-Up Specifications—Polaris Engines (cont.)

Year	Machine Model	Engine Model	Ignition Type	Alternator Output	Spark Plug RFI/NGK
1978	Cobra	EC44PM—01	Mag. Pt.	75 watt	BR9ES
	TX	EC25PT—07	CDI	75 watt	BR9ES
	TX	EC34PT—05	CDI	75 watt	BR9ES
	TX	EC44PT—05	CDI	90 watt	BR9ES
	TX-L	EC34PL—02	CDI	75 watt	BR9ES

Year	Engine Model	Point Gap		Ignition Timing			
				Static		Running	
		MM	Inches	MM BTDC	Inches BTDC	MM BTDC	Inches BTDC
1978	EC25PS	.35	.014	.360	.014	2.96	.116
	EC25PC	.35	.014	.048	.002	1.69	.067
	EC34PM–03/04N	.35	.014	.048	.002	1.69	.067
	EC34PM–04	.35	.014	.048	.002	1.69	.067
	EC44PM–01	.35	.014	.051	.002	1.83	.072
	EC25PT–07	—	—	—	—	4.31*1	.169*1
	EC34PT–05	—	—	—	—	4.31*1	.169*1
	EC44PT–05	—	—	—	—	4.19*2	.165*2
	EC34PL–02	—	—	—	—	5.05*3	.198*3

Timing specified at 3,000 RPM

1 – EC25PT–07/EC34PT–05
Acceptable Variance
4.02mm–4.59mm BTDC
.158 in.–.180 in. BTDC
28°–30° BTDC

2 – EC44PT–05
Acceptable Variance
3.76mm–4.65mm BTDC
.148 in.–.183 in. BTDC
26°–29° BTDC

3 – EC34PL–02
Acceptable Variance
4.60mm–5.52mm BTDC
.181 in.–.217 in. BTDC
30°–33° BTDC

Year	Machine Model	Engine Model	Ignition Type	Alternator Output	Spark Plug		Plug Gap Inches
					RFI NGK	Champion	
1979	Gemini	EC25PS	Mag. Pt.	75 watt	BR8ES	N-3	.020
	Gemini	EC25PM–01	Mag. Pt.	75 watt	BR8ES	N-3	.020
	Apollo	EC34PM–03	Mag. Pt.	75 watt	BR8ES	N-3	.020

Tune-Up Specifications—Polaris Engines (cont.)

Year	Machine Model	Engine Model	Ignition Type	Alternator Output	Spark Plug RFI NGK	Champion	Plug Gap Inches
1979	Cobra	EC34PM–04	Mag. Pt.	75 watt	BR9ES	N-2	.020
	Cobra	EC44PM–01	Mag. Pt.	75 watt	BR8ES	N-3	.020
	TX	EC25PT–07	CDI	75 watt	BR9ES	N-2	.020
	TX	EC34PT–05	CDI	90 watt	BR9ES	N-2	.020
	TX	EC44PT–05	CDI	90 watt	BR9ES	N-2	.020
	TX-L	EC34PL–02	CDI	90 watt	BR9ES	N-2	.020
	Centurion	EC51PL–01	CDI	120 watt	BR9ES	N-2	.020

Year	Engine Model	Point Gap Inches	Ignition Timing Static MM BTDC	Inches BTDC	Degrees BTDC	Running MM BTDC	Inches BTDC	Degrees BTDC
1979	EC25PS	.014	.3646	.014	8±3	2.958	.116	23 @ 2,000
	EC25PM–01	.014	.0476	.002	3±3	1.690	.067	18 @ 2,000
	EC34PM–03	.014	.0476	.002	3 ± 3	1.690	.067	18 @ 2,000
	EC34PM–04	.014	.0476	.002	3 ±3	1.690	.067	18 @ 2,000
	EC44PM–01	.014	.0513	.002	3±3	1.826	.072	18 @ 2,000
	EC25PT–07	—	—	—	—	4.305*1	.169*1	29 @ 3,000*1
	EC34PT–05	—	—	—	—	4.305*1	.169*1	29 @ 3,000*1
	EC44PT–05	—	—	—	—	4.192*2	.164*2	27.5 @ 3,000*2
	EC34PL–02	—	—	—	—	5.050*3	.198*3	31.5 @ 3,000*3
	EC51PL–01	—	—	—	—	3.748*4	.147*4	27 @ 3,000*4

*Timing specified at 3,000 RPM

1–EC25PT–07/EC34PT–05	2–EC44PT–05	3–EC34PL–02	4–EC51PL–01
Acceptable Variance	Acceptable Variance	Acceptable Variance	Acceptable Variance
4.02mm–4.59mm BTDC	3.76mm–4.65mm BTDC	4.60mm–5.52mm BTDC	3.48mm–4.02mm BTDC
.158 in.–.180 in. BTDC	.148 in.–.183 in. BTDC	.181 in.–.217 in. BTDC	.137 in.–.158 in. BTDC
28°–30° BTDC	26°–29° BTDC	30°–33° BTDC	26°–28° BTDC

Timing Chart

55.6 MM Stroke			60 MM Stroke		
Degrees BTDC	MM	Inches	Degrees BTDC	MM	Inches
1	.0052	.0002	1	.0057	.0002
2	.0211	.0008	2	.0228	.0008
3	.0476	.0018	3	.0513	.0020
4	.0846	.0033	4	.0913	.0035
5	.1321	.0051	5	.1426	.0056
6	.1902	.0074	6	.2053	.0080
7	.2588	.0101	7	.2793	.0109
8	.3378	.0132	8	.3646	.0143
9	.4273	.0167	9	.4611	.0181
10	.5271	.0207	10	.5688	.0223
11	.6373	.0250	11	.6877	.0270
12	.7578	.0297	12	.8177	.0321
13	.8884	.0349	13	.9588	.0376
14	1.0293	.0404	14	1.1108	.0436
15	1.1802	.0463	15	1.2736	.0500
16	1.3412	.0527	16	1.4473	.0568
17	1.5121	.0594	17	1.6318	.0641
18	1.6929	.0665	18	1.8269	.0717

Timing Chart (cont.)

55.6 MM Stroke			60 MM Stroke		
Degrees BTDC	MM	Inches	Degrees BTDC	MM	Inches
19	1.8835	.0740	19	2.0325	.0798
20	2.0837	.0818	20	2.2486	.0883
21	2.2936	.0901	21	2.4751	.0972
22	2.5130	.0987	22	2.7118	.1065
23	2.7417	.1077	23	2.9587	.1162
24	2.9798	.1171	24	3.2156	.1263
25	3.2270	.1268	25	3.4824	.1368
26	3.4833	.1368	26	3.7589	.1477
27	3.7485	.1473	27	4.0452	.1589
28	4.0226	.1580	28	4.3409	.1705
29	4.3053	.1692	29	4.6460	.1825
30	4.5966	.1806	30	4.9604	.1949
31	4.8963	.1924	31	5.2838	.2076
32	5.2044	.2045	32	5.6162	.2207
33	5.5205	.2169	33	5.9574	.2341
34	5.8447	.2296	34	6.3072	.2478
35	6.1767	.2427	35	6.6655	.2619

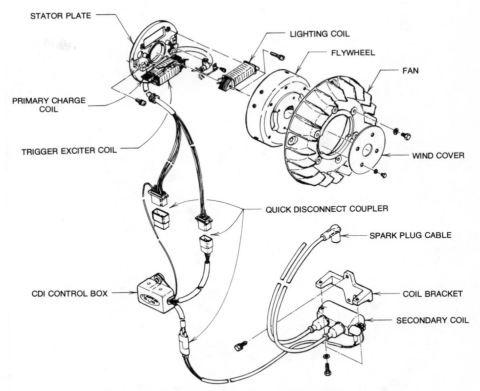

Capacitor discharge type ignition system

1. Carburetor assembly
2. Cap
3. Throttle spring
4. Throttle plate
5. E-ring
6. Jet needle
7. Throttle valve
8. Needle jet
9. Plate
10. Screw
11. Banjo bolt
12. Washer
13. Banjo connector
14. Starter plunger
15. Washer
16. Spring
17. Plunger cap
18. O-ring
19. Throttle stop screw

CARBURETOR

All of the 1976 and later Polaris engines use Mikuni slide-type carburetors. Complete tuning and rebuilding information is included in Chapter 2.

20. Spring
21. Air screw
22. Spring
23. Pilot jet (#35)
24. Needle jet setter
25. Washer
26. O-ring
27. Needle valve
28. Packing
29. Float arm
30. Float pin
31. Packing
32. Bowl
33. Float
34. Cap
35. Main jet (#125)
36. Banjo bolt
37. Washer
38. Screw

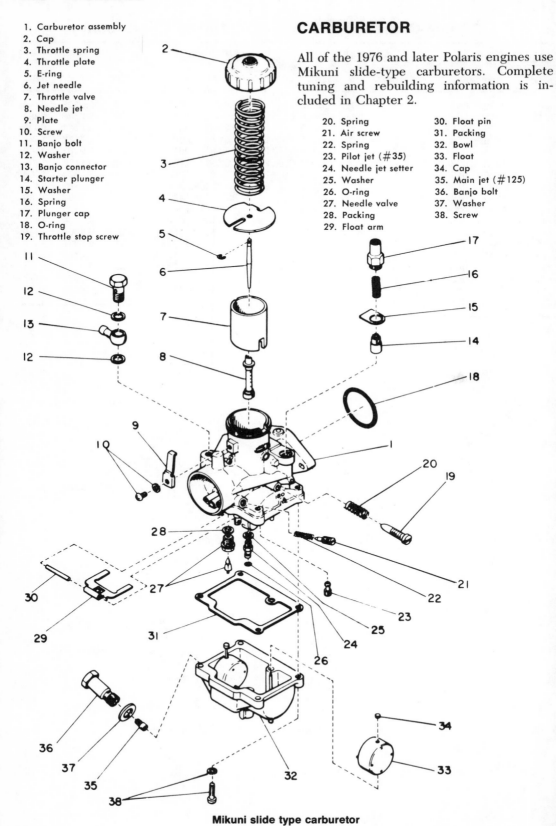

Mikuni slide type carburetor

Carburetor Specifications

Year	Engine Model	No. of Cyl.	Carb. Size Type and Number	Original Jetting		Recommended Jetting/0'–5,000'		Recommended Jetting/5,000'–10,000'	
				Main	Pilot	Main	Pilot	Main	Pilot
1976	EC17PM	1	VM24SH (1)	102.5	35	—	—	—	—
	EC25PS	1	VM30SH (1)	125	35	117.5	—c	115	35 c
	EC25PC	2	VM26SS (2)	112.5	35	—	—c	95	35 c
	EC25PT-06	2	VM32SS (2)	260H	30	—	35 c	190H	30 c
	EC25PT-05	2	VM32SS (2)	230H	35	—	—c	—	—c
	EC34PC	2	VM26SS (2)	107.5	35	—	—c	105	35 c
	EC34PQ	2	VM30SS (2)	122.5	30	117.5	—c	110	30 c
	EC34PT-05	2	VM32SS (2)	270H	30	260H6	—c	230	30 c
	EC34PT-06	2	VM34SS (2)	270H	30	—	—c	—	—c
	EC44PQ	2	VM30SS (2)	125	25	115	—c	115	25 c
	EC44PT-05	2	VM34SS (2)	320H	35	—	—c	270	35 c

cWith air silencer installed   6Lower "E" clip to No. 4 position
HHex head   7Lower "E" clip to No. 4 position

Year	Engine Model	No. of Cyl.	Carb. Size Type and Number	Original Jetting		Recommended Jetting/0'–5,000'		Recommended Jetting/5,000'–10,000'	
				Main	Pilot	Main	Pilot	Main	Pilot
1977	EC25PS	1	VM30SH (1)	117.5	35	—	—c		
	EC25PC	2	VM26SS (2)	112.5	35	—	—c		
	EC25PM-01	2	VM26SS (2)	130H	35	—	—c		
	EC25PT-07	2	VM30SS (2)	220H	35	—	—c		
	EC34PM-03	2	VM26SS (2)	150H	35	130H	—c		
	EC34PQ	2	VM30SS (2)	122.5	30	117.5	—c	Not specified	
	EC34PT-05	2	VM32SS (2)	280H	30	270H	—c		
	EC34PL-01	2	VM38SS (2)	340H	45	320H7	—c		
	EC44PQ	2	VM30SS (2)	115	25	—	—c		
	EC44PT-05	2	VM34SS (2)	320H	35	—	—c		
	EC44PT-06	2	VM34SS (2)	320H	35	—	—c		

Condensed Data (cont.)

Year	Machine Model	Engine Model	Cyl. Disp. CC's	Carburetor Model, Mount Type & No.	Std. Main Jet & Type	Std. Pilot Jet	Air Screw Adjust. (counter-clockwise from seat)
1978	Colt	EC25PS	244	VM30SH (1) Flange	117.5 Round	35	1 turn
	Colt	EC25PC	250	VM26SS (2) Rubber	112.5 Round	35	1 turn
	S/S 340	EC34PM–03 EC34PM–04N	333	VM26SS (2) Rubber	130 Hex	35	1 turn ½ turn
	Cobra	EC34PM–04	333	VM26SS (2) Rubber	130 Hex	35	1 turn
	Cobra	EC44PM–01	432	VM34SS (2) Rubber	200 Hex	35	1 turn
	TX	EC25PT–07	249	VM30SS (2) Rubber	220 Hex	35	1 turn
	TX	EC34PT–05	336	VM32SS (2) Rubber	280 Hex	30	1 turn
	TX	EC44PT–05	432	VM34SS (2) Rubber	370 Hex	45	1 turn
	TX-L	EC34PL–02	333	VM38SS (2) Rubber	310 Hex	45	1 turn

Year	Engine Model	Jet Needle No. "E" Clip Position	Needle Jets	Throttle Valve Cutaway	Valve Seat	Fuel Mixture
1978	EC25PS	5DP7–4	O–8 (171)	3.0		
	EC25PC	5DP–5 or 5DP3–3	O–8 (164)	3.0		
	EC34PM–03 EC34PM–04N	5DP7–2 5EP6–3	O–8 (259) P–2 (259)	2.5 3.0		
	EC34PM–04	5DP7–3	P–2 (259)	3.0	1.5MM	40 : 1
	EC44PM–01	6DP1–3	P–6 (166)	2.5		
	EC25PT–07	5DP7–3	P–2 (171)	2.5		
	EC34PT–05	6DH7–3	P–4 (159)	2.0		
	EC44PT–05	6DH7–3	P–6 (166)	2.5		
	EC34PL–02	6DH4–3	Q–2 (247)	2.5		

Condensed Data (cont.)

Year	Machine Model	Engine Model	Cyl. Disp. CC's	Carburetor Model, Mount Type & No.	Std. Main Jet & Type	Std. Pilot Jet	Air Screw Adjust. (counter-clockwise from seat)
1979	Gemini	EC25PS	244	VM30SH (1) Flange	117.5 Round	35	1 turn
	Gemini	EC25PM−01	244	VM26SS (2) Rubber	120 Hex	35	1 turn
	Apollo	EC34PM−03	333	VM26SS (2) Rubber	130 Hex	35	1 turn
	Cobra	EC34PM−04	333	VM26SS (2) Rubber	130 Hex	35	1 turn
	Cobra	EC44PM−01	432	VM34SS (2) Rubber	200 Hex	35	1 turn
	TX	EC25PT−07	249	VM30SS (2) Rubber	220 Hex	35	1 turn
	TX	EC34PT−05	336	VM32SS (2) Rubber	290 Hex	30	1 turn
	TX	EC44PT−05	432	VM34SS (2) Rubber	320 Hex	30	1 turn
	TX-L	EC34PL−02	333	VM38SS (2) Rubber	260 Hex	45	1 turn
	Centurion	EC51PL−01	500	VM34SS (3) Rubber	210 Hex	35	1½ turn

Year	Engine Model	Jet Needle No. "E" Clip Position	Needle Jets	Throttle Valve Cutaway	Valve Seat	Fuel Mixture
1979	EC25PS	5DP7−4	O−8 (177)	3.0		
	EC25PM−01	5DP7−2	O−8	2.5		
	EC34PM−03	5DP7−2	O−8	2.5		
	EC34PM−04	5DP7−3	P−2 (259)	3.0		
	EC44PM−01	6DP1−3	P−6 (166)	2.5	1.5MM	40 : 1
	EC25PT−07	5DP7−3	P−2 (171)	2.5		
	EC34PT−05	6DH7−2	P−4 (159)	2.0		
	EC44PT−05	6DH7−2	Q−0 (166)	2.5		
	EC34PL−02	6DH4−3	Q−2 (247)	2.5		
	EC51PL−01	6DH7−2	Q−2 (166)	3.0		

FUEL SYSTEM

Fuel Pump

The fuel pumps for all Polaris engines are basically the same. The differences are in the size and location of the pumps. Pumps may be mounted on the crankcase or on the machine using an impulse hose.

In the two cycle engine, the pressure in the crankcase changes with the up and down stroke of the piston. The amplitudes of pressure vary according to the RPM and degree of throttle opening. Whether idling or full throttle, the pressure built up in the crankcase has enough amplitude to operate the pump.

When the piston is on the upstroke, crankcase pressure in that cylinder becomes less positive, the diaphragm in the fuel pump moves toward the engine causing a negative pressure or suction in the pump chamber which causes the inlet valve from the fuel supply to open and permits fuel to enter the chamber; this same suction causes the outlet valve (to the carburetor) to close so fuel cannot return from the carburetor.

When the piston begins its downward stroke, the pressure from the crankcase becomes positive, causing the fuel pump diaphragm to move in the opposite direction, reversing the pressure in the fuel pump chamber. This causes the inlet valve in the pump to close and the outlet valve (to the carburetor) to open, filling the float bowl in the carburetor. When the float level in the

carburetor reaches its standard level the needle valve will close, preventing more fuel from entering the carburetor, even though the fuel pump continues to try to provide the carburetor with fuel.

ENGINE

Removal

It should be noted that because of the critical nature of the alignment of the drive belt, engine removal and installation should be performed only by an authorized Polaris dealer. Failure to align this belt correctly will cause rapid wear and eventual breakage. If an emergency should arise where engine removal is a necessity, follow this removal procedure.

1. Disconnect the fuel line at the fuel pump and clamp it to prevent leakage (e.g., vice grips, clamp).

2. Disconnect the main wire receptacle.

3. Remove the throttle cable from the hand grip by pushing the cable back and out. Thread the throttle cable through the dash, but do not disconnect the linkage from the carburetor(s).

4. Using a half-inch wrench, remove the recoil guide from the steering hoop.

5. Remove the choke from the dash by removing the choke knob and then the retaining nut. The choke may now be threaded through the dash.

6. The muffler is now disconnected by releasing the two exhaust springs and the whole assembly is pulled from the body.

7. The front and rear motor mounts may now be removed. Once this has been accomplished, the engine must be pulled back so that the drive belt can be removed. Then the engine may be lifted from the chassis.

NOTE: *Engine removal is similar on all Polaris models.*

Engine Disassembly and Assembly.

1. Remove the choke assemblies, being careful not to damage the carburetor plunger surfaces. If there are scratches present, use wet, 400 grit sandpaper to remove them.

2. Disconnect the carburetor fuel lines from the fuel pump and, with a half-inch wrench, loosen the carburetor bolts and remove each carburetor.

1. Gasket
2. Diaphragm
3. Valve

Fuel pump (diaphragm type)

Flywheel puller and chain wrench holding the flywheel

Remove cylinder heads then remove base nuts

3. The wires must be removed from the quick-disconnect casing along with the fuel pump and the external ignition coils.

4. Unbolt the fan housing. It is not necessary to remove the recoil starter to accomplish this.

5. Remove all air baffles.

6. Using some means to keep the flywheel from turning (e.g., chain wrench), remove the flywheel nut, rope starter pulley, and the inspection plate.

7. Using a puller and keeping the flywheel stationary, crank the puller drive with a wrench or socket to remove the flywheel.

8. With the flywheel removed, check the timing mechanism. It must work freely.

9. Remove the stator plate by unscrewing the hold-down screws.

10. To release the fan cover, remove the five fastening bolts.

11. Remove the cylinder head bolts, the head, cylinder base nuts, cylinders, and gaskets, in that order.

12. Use needlenose pliers to release the wrist pin keepers. Using a drive pin with the correct inner diameter, or the Polaris piston puller (No. 2870202), remove both pin and piston.

Hold piston while cylinder is being removed

Bend locking tabs back from seal bolts then remove bolts

Tap seal cover with block of wood to loosen

Use an impact screw driver to loosen oil seal plate screws

Tap side of crankcase to break free the gasket seal

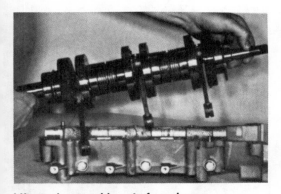

Lift crank assembly out of crankcase

13. Turn the engine to the drive-side end and remove the capscrews from the seal plate. To break the seal loose, tap on one corner of the seal to rotate the seal around the crankshaft. Do not attempt to drive a screwdriver between the seal and the crankcase. Severe damage could result to the aluminum construction.

14. Rotate the casing until the flywheel end of the crankshaft is toward you, and remove the four screws which hold the crankshaft seal. If the seal is to be removed, it will come out when the casing halves are split apart. It is recommended, if the engine is to be totally disassembled, to insert a new seal upon assembly. Once this seal is removed, it should be noted that there is a spacer ring behind it. (This ring is not included on some engines.)

15. Turn the engine block on its side and remove all of the crankcase bolts.

16. With a rubber hammer, tap the fan housing brackets to separate the casing halves. Make sure, in performing this operation, that all the bolts have been removed. Do not attempt to wedge the casing halves apart.

17. Once the halves have been separated, remove the crankshaft from the remaining half. When removing the crankshaft, note the placement of the seal and spacer ring.

Assembly

Before assembling the engine, make a thorough inspection of the crankcase halves for damage or wear. It may be found that the labyrinth seal rings have marked the casing. This is not a cause for worry if the marks are not deep. These marks can be sanded out with fine grit sandpaper used with water. However, if the marks are deeper than $1/16$ in., the case should be replaced. It is important to wash the crankcase halves thoroughly to remove all metal particles before assembly.

1. After cleaning the crankcase halves, apply the appropriate sealer to the crankcase sealing surfaces.

2. Center the crankshaft in the casing half

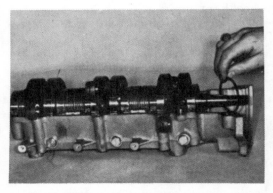

Replacing spacer ring on the magneto end of the crankshaft

Rotate the seal plate while you slip it on the crankshaft

and install the other half of the crankcase. Gently tap the crank on the end to further center it. Once this is done, the cap screws may be installed. The large ones are torqued to 25 ft-lbs and the smaller ones to 18 ft-lbs.

3. To install the drive-side seal, lubricate it, slip it over the crankshaft end, and rotate it into position.

4. After greasing the wrist pin needle bearings, install the assembly into the connecting rod. Put the connecting rod spacer units on either side of the bearing, with the countersunk ends facing the bearing. The piston can now be installed with the "F" mark (found on the top of the piston) facing the fan side of the engine. Install the wrist pin and keepers.

5. The cylinders are installed with a ring compressor or with your fingers if no compressor can be found.

6. The head gasket must be installed with the ridge facing down, toward the cylinder. The head must be rotated so that the "EXH" (exhaust) marking on the head matches with the exhaust side of the cylinder. Cylinder head nuts are torqued to 19 ft-lbs. These must be torqued evenly and gradually. (e.g.,

Installing the seal plate (Magneto end)

Torque all in sequence to 10 ft-lbs, then repeat the torquing sequence and torque to 15 ft-lbs, and then to the torque figure in the "Torque Specifications" chart. The tightening sequence is illustrated in Chapter 1.)

7. The spacer ring on the crankshaft should now be installed—if the engine had one upon disassembly. (Newer models have none.) After lubricating the outer seal, install it slowly over the crankshaft, being careful not to damage the sealing surface.

8. The rear fan cover can be installed by tightening the five mounting bolts. Now the air shroud can be attached.

9. Install the stator plate and fasten it with its own mounting screws. Install the flywheel and the emergency rope starter pulley. To torque the flywheel, hold the flywheel stationary (e.g., using chain wrench) and torque to 35 ft lbs.

10. Install the coils, fuel pump, and carburetors.

11. Wire installation is next. It is important to replace the wires in the correct receptacle position. They must match in color the ones with which they will be joined.

12. The choke mechanism can be installed only after the plunger is thoroughly cleaned. The outer fan housing can now be installed.

The procedure is the same for all Polaris engines. On the 500 cc, three-cylinder engine, the rotor and stator plate removal is different from the others and shall be explained here.

When removing the rotor, extreme care should be taken to not damage the stator wiring. To remove the rotor, place the appropriate puller on the rotor and keep the puller from turning while the puller drive is being turned.

NOTE: *Once the rotor is removed, locate the aligning key which may become lodged in the magnetic coils.*

The stator is removed by loosening the three phillips screws. Do not pry against the coils to remove the stator or irreparable damage will result. Once the stator is removed, pull the grommet wire guide out of the casing.

The assembly is the reverse of the disassembly procedure with the torque on the rotor nut being 66 ft lbs.

RECOIL STARTER

The recoil starter is a self-contained unit which is mounted to the end of the crankcase

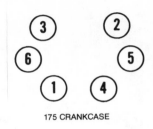

175 CRANKCASE

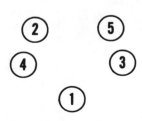

244 CRANKCASE

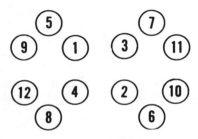

TWIN CRANKCASE

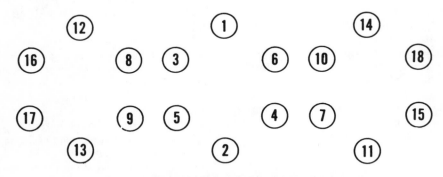

CRANKCASE TORQUE PATTERN 3 CYL.

Crankcase bolt tightening sequence

with six bolts. The complete unit must be removed to gain access to the ignition system or to dissasemble the crankcase. The recoil starter can remain assembled unless there is a need to replace the starter cable or to repair some of the starter's internal working parts.

CAUTION: *You should wear safety glasses for this operation.*

1. Push the starter cable through the

"Tee" handle just enough so that the cable clamp can be removed to free the handle.

2. Pull the cable through the hole in the starter's case and catch the cable in the notch in the cable reel. The reel can then be rotated to release the spring tension.

3. Remove the center retaining nut to disassemble the recoil starter unit, but be certain that *all* of the spring tension has been re-

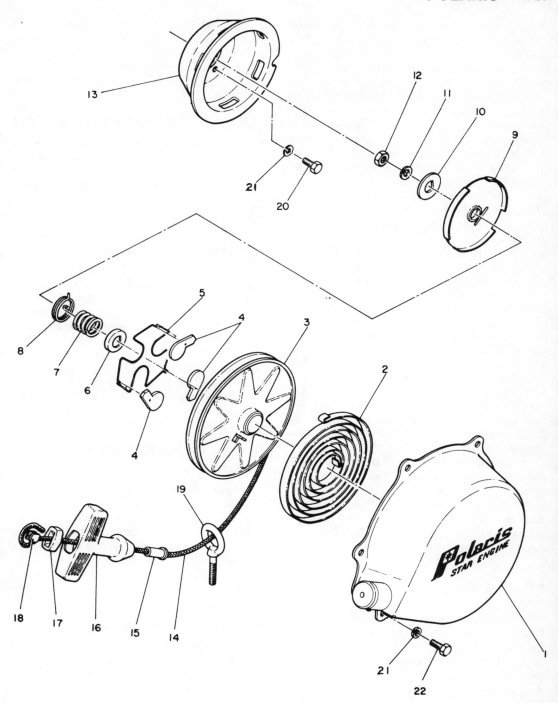

1. Recoil case
2. Power spring
3. Reel
4. Ratchet
5. Return spring
6. Washer (A)
7. Friction spring
8. Return spring
9. Friction plate
10. Washer (B)
11. Spring washer
12. Nut
13. Starting pulley
14. Rope
15. Not used
16. Starter handle
17. Not used
18. Not used
19. Eye bolt
20. Bolt
21. Spring washer
22. Bolt

Recoil starter for engines with nylon rope

leased. The retainer plate, the three ratchets, two small springs and the washer can then be lifted from the back of the unit.

4. The complete cable reel can now be lifted carefully from the starter case. The rewind spring is supposed to be held in a clip in the cover, but it may be free. Lift the cable reel slowly and be prepared to force it back down to catch the rewind spring if the spring is loose. Look through the small hole near the center of the cable reel to see that the rewind spring has disengaged from the catch. The cable can then be removed from the reel if it needs to be replaced.

5. The cable does not have to be removed to replace a broken rewind spring, but the cable reel must be removed as outlined in the previous steps. Use visegrip pliers to grip the rewind spring while you work it free from its catch in the starter cover.

6. Fit the end of the new rewind spring in the notch in the inside of the starter case and wind the spring inward on itself. Wear thick gloves to minimize the chance of the spring cutting your fingers if it does slip free while winding it into place.

7. Align the rewind spring with the catch on the cable reel while you place the cable reel over its shaft. The small window in the cable reel allows you to see that the spring is fitting over the catch.

8. Install the three recoil ratchets and the two small return springs inside the starter reel.

9. The retainer plate, its two washers and hex nut can now be installed and the nut tightened to complete the assembly of the recoil starter unit.

POWER TRAIN

All of the Polaris snowmobiles use a conventional centrifugal clutch, drive belt and torque converter type of automatic transmission system. The clutches vary in detail, but they all are made only for Polaris as are the torque converters. The torque converter's idler shaft drives a sprocket, inside the chaincase, which transfers the power via a roller chain to the sprocket which couples to the end of the track's front drive sprocket. The two chain sprockets and the drive chain are encased in an oil-filled aluminum housing. The centrifugal clutch and torque converter should be greased occasionally and the oil replenished in the chaincase. The drive belt

tension and alignment should be checked, as outlined in Chapter 1, with the gauges shown in this chapter. The only other power train maintenance which should normally be required is an occasional adjustment of the drive chain.

Centrifugal Clutch (Drive Pulley)

A factory notation with regard to drive clutches states that all Polaris drive clutches are "certified balanced and tested" by the factory alone. If any drive clutch is repaired by other than the factory, the warranty is void. Tampering with the mechanism is not recommended.

REMOVAL AND INSTALLATION

The drive belt should be removed before removing the centrifugal clutch. A single bolt and lockwasher retain the clutch to the end of the crankshaft, but a special puller (Polaris No. 2870130) is necessary to remove the clutch *after* the single bolt is removed. Protect the pulley faces with a rubber hose or an old drive belt and hold them with a chain wrench while removing the clutch.

A torque wrench is needed to install the centrifugal clutch. Torque the single bolt to 40–45 ft-lbs (18–20 ft-lbs on 175 cc engines).

Torque Converter (Driven Pulley)

A few very simple pieces are used to perform the rather complex task of sensing when the snowmobile needs a lower or higher drive ratio for hills or acceleration. The two halves of the torque converter pulley move closer together or farther apart to change the effective diameter of the pulley (by forcing the drive belt to ride near the bottom of the pulley or near the top).

REMOVAL AND INSTALLATION

The air intake silencer and one of the fuel lines may have to be removed, on some Polaris snowmobiles, to allow enough clearance for removal of the torque converter. Leave the drive belt in place to hold the pulley faces while you loosen and remove the single retaining nut on the end of the torque converter's idler shaft. The torque converter can then be removed from its shaft.

OVERHAUL

A single snap-ring retains the various components of the torque converter. Use a screw-

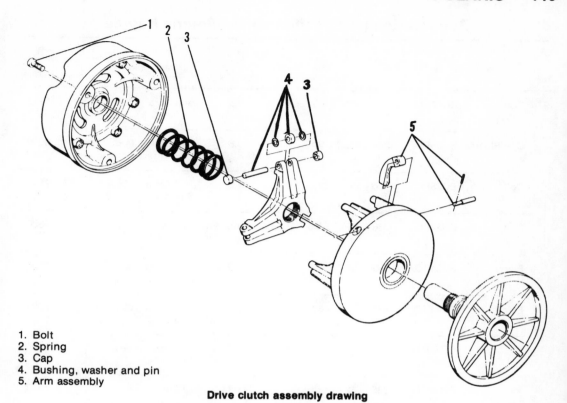

1. Bolt
2. Spring
3. Cap
4. Bushing, washer and pin
5. Arm assembly

Drive clutch assembly drawing

driver to pry the snap-ring away, but cup a rag over the snap-ring so that it doesn't disappear. Note the exact position and number of preload turns on the coil spring while you slide the parts from the outer pulley half's shaft. The only parts which are likely to wear are the faces of the two pulley halves, the cylindrical bearing and the three plastic buttons on the ramp assembly. If any one of these buttons is worn, replace all three—they can be removed or installed by simply pressing them into their mounting holes. The tension spring should have about ⅓ turn (clockwise) of preload on the ramp assembly when the unit is reassembled. It's wise to use a new snap-ring.

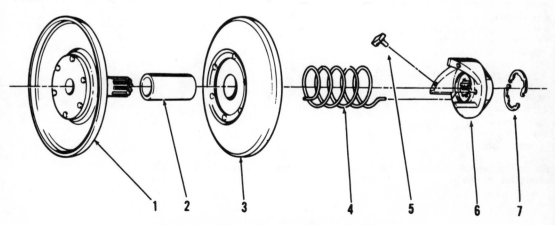

1. Stationary face assembly	5. Ramp button
2. Bearing	6. Ramp assembly
3. Movable face assembly	7. Retaining ring
4. Spring	

Torque converter assembly drawing

General Engine Specifications—Polaris Engine

Year	Machine Model	Engine Model	Cyl. Disp. CC's	Bore MM	Stroke MM	No. of Cyl.	Cyl. Head CC's Uninstalled	Piston Rings	Piston Skirt to Bore ±.002"	Ring End Gap Clearance	Engine Operating RPM ±250 RPM
1976	Colt	EC17PM	175	62	58	1	19.5	Standard 2 Ring	.006		5500
	Colt/Electra	EC25PS	244	72	60	1	26.5	Standard 2 Ring	.006		6000
	Colt	EC25PC	250	53.5	55.6	2	11.0	L + 1.0mm Standard	.006		7500
	Colt	EC34PC	336	62	55.6	2	20.0 Small Fin 20.0 Large Fin	L + 1.0mm Standard	.006		7500
	Electra	EC34PQ	339	60	60	2	15.5	L + 1.0mm Standard	.006		7500
	Electra	EC44PQ	433	67.75	60	2	22.9	L + 1.0mm Standard	.006	.005/.008	7500
	TX	EC25PT–06*	250	53.4	55.6	2	11.3	1.2mm Keystone	—		7500
	TX	EC34PT–05*	336	62	55.6	2	19.7	1.2mm Keystone	—		7500
	TX	EC44PT–05*	433	67.75	60	2	22.8	1.2mm Keystone	—		7000
	Starfire	EC25PT–05*	250	53.4	55.6	2	11.3	1.2mm Keystone	—		8500
	Starfire	EC34PT–06*	336	62	55.6	2	19.7	1.2mm Keystone	—		9500

Engine Model Codes
PM—Standard Fan Cooled
PF—Standard Free Air
PS—High Performance
PC—Free Air Colt Series
PQ—Fan Cooled Silent Star
25PT–06 ⎫
34PT–05 ⎬ TX Free Air
44PT–05 ⎭
25PT–05 ⎫
34PT–06 ⎬ Starfire Free Air
*Chrome Bore

Clearance cannot be changed on TX and Starfire engines; however, de-glazing and refinishing is allowed using fine stones.

General Engine Specifications—Polaris Engine (cont.)

Year	Machine Model	Engine Model	Cyl. Disp. CC's	Bore MM	Bore Inches	Stroke MM	Stroke Inches	No. of Cyl.	Type of Cooling	Cyl. Head CC's Uninstalled	Piston Rings	Piston Skirt to Bore ±.002"	Engine Operating RPM ±250 RPM
1977	Colt/Electra	EC25PS	244	72	2.8346	60	2.362	1	Fan	19.5	(2) 2.0mm Standard	.009	6000
	Colt	EC25PC	250	53.5	2.1063	55.6	2.1886	2	Free Air	11.0	L+1.5mm Standard	.006	7500
	Colt SS	EC25PM–01	244	52.9	2.0824	55.6	2.1886	2	Fan	11.5	(2) 1.5mm Keystone	.005	7000
	TX	EC25PT–07*	249	53.4	2.1017	55.6	2.1886	2	Free Air	11.3	(1) 1.2mm Keystone	—	8000
	Colt SS	EC34PM–03	333	61.78	2.432	55.6	2.1886	2	Fan	21.0	(2) 1.5mm Keystone	.006	6500
	Electra	EC34PQ	339	60	2.362	60	2.362	2	Fan	15.5	L+1.2mm Standard	.0065	7500
	TX	EC34PT–05*	336	62	2.441	55.6	2.1886	2	Free Air	19.7	(1) 1.2mm Keystone	—	7500
	TXL	EC34PL–01	333	61.78	2.432	55.6	2.1886	2	Liquid	17.5	(1) 1.2mm Keystone	.005	8000
	Electra	EC44PQ	432	67.75	2.6673	60	2.362	2	Fan	22.9	L+1.0mm Standard	.008	7500
	TX	EC44PT–05*	432	67.75	2.6673	60	2.362	2	Free Air	22.8	(1) 1.2mm Keystone	—	7000
	TX	EC44PT–06*	432	67.75	2.6673	60	2.362	2	Free Air	22.8	(1) 1.2mm Keystone	—	7000

Engine Model Codes
PM—Standard Fan Cooled
PS—High Performance
PC—Free Air
*Chrome Bore
PQ—Fan Cooled Silent Star
PT—TX Series
PL—Liquid Cooled

Clearance cannot be changed on chrome cylinders; however, they may be de-glazed and refinished using fine stones.

General Engine Specifications—Polaris Engine (cont.)

Year	Machine Model	Engine Model	Cyl. Disp. CC's	Bore MM	Bore Inches	Stroke MM	Stroke Inches	No. of Cyl.	Type of Cooling	Cyl. Head CC's Uninstalled	Piston Rings	Piston/Cylinder Bore Clearance ±.002"	Engine Operating RPM ±250 RPM
1978	Colt	EC25PS	244	72	2.8346	60	2.362	1	Fan	19.5	(2) 2.0mm Standard	.009	6000
	Colt	EC25PC	250	53.5	2.1063	55.6	2.1886	2	Free Air	11.0	L+1.5mm Standard	.006	7500
	TX	EC25PT–07	249	53.4	2.1017	55.6	2.1886	2	Free Air	11.3	(1) 1.2mm Keystone	Dress with fine stone only*	8000
	S/S 340	EC34PM–03 /04N	333	61.78	2.432	55.6	2.1886	2	Fan	21.0	(2) 1.5mm Keystone	.006	6500
	Cobra	EC34PM–04	333	61.78	2.432	55.6	2.1886	2	Fan	21.0	(2) 1.5mm Keystone	.006	6750
	TX	EC34PT–05	336	62	2.441	55.6	2.1886	2	Free Air	19.7	(1) 1.2mm Keystone	Dress with fine stone only*	7500
	TX-L	EC34PL–02	333	61.78	2.432	55.6	2.1886	2	Liquid	18.5	(1) 1.2mm Keystone	.005	8500
	Cobra	EC44PM–01	432	67.72	2.6557	60	2.362	2	Fan	22.9	(2) 1.5mm Keystone	.008	6500
	TX	EC44PT–05	432	67.75	2.6673	60	2.362	2	Free Air	22.8	(1) 1.2mm Keystone	Dress with fine stone only*	7000

*Chrome cylinders may be de-glazed and refinished using fine stones.

General Engine Specifications—Polaris Engine (cont.)

Year	Machine Model	Engine Model	Cyl. Disp. CC's	Bore MM	Bore Inches	Stroke MM	Stroke Inches	No. of Cyl.	Type of Cooling	Cyl. Head CC's Uninstalled	Piston Rings	Piston/ Cylinder Bore Clearance ±.002"	Engine Operating RPM ±250 RPM
1979	Gemini	EC25PS	244	72	2.8346	60	2.362	1	Fan	26.5	(2) 2.0mm Standard	.009	6000
	Gemini	EC25PM–01	244	52.9	2.0824	55.6	2.1886	2	Fan	11.5	(2) 1.5mm Keystone	.005	7000
	Apollo	EC34PM–03	333	61.78	2.432	55.6	2.1886	2	Fan	21.0	(2) 1.5mm Keystone	.006	6500
	Cobra	EC34PM–04	333	61.78	2.432	55.6	2.1886	2	Fan	21.0	(2) 1.5mm Keystone	.006	6750
	Cobra	EC44PM–01	432	67.72	2.6557	60	2.362	2	Fan	22.9	(2) 1.5mm Keystone	.008	6500
	TX	EC25PT–07	249	53.4	2.1017	55.6	2.1886	2	Free Air	11.8	(1) 1.2mm Keystone	Dress with fine stone only*	8000
	TX	EC34PT–05	336	62	2.441	55.6	2.1886	2	Free Air	19.7	(1) 1.2mm Keystone	Dress with fine stone only*	7500
	TX	EC44PT–05	432	67.75	2.6673	60	2.362	2	Free Air	22.8	(1) 1.2mm Keystone	Dress with fine stone only*	6750
	TX-L	EC34PL–02	333	61.78	2.432	55.6	2.1886	2	Liquid	18.5	(1) 1.2mm Keystone	.005	8000
	Cen- turion	EC51PL–01	500	61.78	2.432	55.6	2.1886	3	Liquid	19.5	(1) 1.2mm Keystone	.005	7750

*Chrome cylinders may be de-glazed and refinished using fine stones.

General Engine Specifications—Polaris Engine (cont.)

Year	Machine Model	Engine Model	Cyl. Disp. CC's	Bore MM	Bore Inches	Stroke MM	Stroke Inches	No. of Cyl.	Type of Cooling	Cyl. Head CC's Uninstalled	Cyl. Head CC's Installed	Piston Rings	Piston/Cylinder Bore Clearance ±.002"	Engine Operating RPM ±250 RPM
1980	Gemini	EC25PS	244	72	2.8346	60	2.362	1	Fan	26.5	23.7	(2) 2.0mm Standard	.009	6000
	Gemini	EC25PM–01	244	52.9	2.0824	55.6	2.1886	2	Fan	11.5	11.8	(2) 1.5mm Keystone	.005	7000
	Apollo	EC34PM–03	333	61.78	2.432	55.6	2.1886	2	Fan	21.0	16.8	(2) 1.5mm Keystone	.006	6500
	Galaxy	EC34PM–04	333	61.78	2.432	55.6	2.1886	2	Fan	21.0	16.8	(2) 1.5mm Keystone	.006	6750
	Galaxy	EC44PM–01 /02	432	67.72	2.6557	60	2.362	2	Fan	22.9	21.4	(2) 1.5mm Keystone	.008	6500
	TX/TX-C	EC34PT–07	336	62	2.441	55.6	2.1886	2	Free Air	19.7	15.5	(1) 1.2mm Keystone	Dress with fine stone only*	7500
	TX	EC44PT–05	432	67.75	2.6673	60	2.362	2	Free Air	22.8	21.2	(1) 1.2mm Keystone	Dress with fine stone only*	6750
	TX-L/TX-L Indy	EC34PL–02 /05	333	61.78	2.432	55.6	2.1886	2	Liquid	18.5	15.1	(1) 1.2mm Keystone	.005	8000
	Centurion	EC51PL–02	500	61.78	2.432	55.6	2.1886	3	Liquid	19.5	15.5	(1) 1.2mm Keystone	.005	7750

*Chrome cylinders may be de-glazed and refinished using fine stones.

Engine Bolt Torque (ft./lbs.)

Engine	Cylinder Head	Crankcase		Flywheel	Cylinder Base Studs
		8MM	10MM		
EC25PS	17-18	18-20	23-25	60-65	24-28
All Twin Cylinder	17-18	18-20	23-25	60-65	24-28
EC34PL–02 Liquid Cooled	8MM 16-17	18-20	23-25	60-65	
EC51PL–01 Liquid Cooled	10MM 26-29				

Using clutch aligning tool for correct drive belt alignment

Clutch Alignment and Center Distance

The correct clutch offset is arrived at by the use of the Polaris alignment tool (Part No. 2870161) or a tool with a $^9/_{16}$ in. offset. The motor mounts can be loosened and the engine can be shifted to produce the proper adjustment.

Drive Chain and Sprockets

CHAIN TENSION

To adjust the chain tension, loosen the chain idler locking nut. Turn the adjusting mechanism clockwise until you have ½ in. free-play on the driven clutch.

REMOVAL AND INSTALLATION

1. The complete suspension must be removed to relieve the tension on the drive chain sprockets.

2. Loosen the screws which retain the chaincase cover and remove the cover. Have a container ready to catch the oil.

3. Loosen the locknut on the chain tensioner bolt and turn the bolt coun-

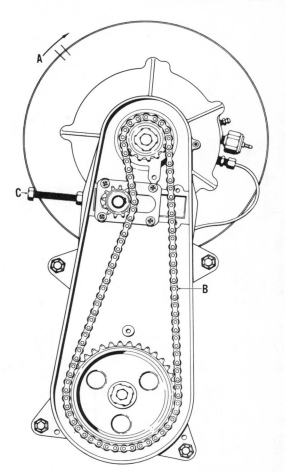

Turn adjusting nut (C) to set drive chain tension

terclockwise to release all of the tension on the drive chain.

4. The drive chain and both sprockets can now be pulled straight out and off their splines. The drive chain has no masterlink. If the chain is worn there is a good chance that both sprockets will have to be replaced as well.

The installation of the drive chain and sprockets is simply the reverse of the disassembly procedure. Be sure to fit a new chaincase gasket and, when the assembly is complete, to readjust the drive chain tension.

SUSPENSION

Track

TENSION AND ALIGNMENT

The following specifications and adjustment procedures must be followed to assure long component life and a comfortable ride.

General Engine Specifications—Polaris Engine (cont.)

Model	Model Number	Suspension Type	Shock	Track Type	Track Width	Track Length (Overall)	Track Length On Ground	Rivet Type	Ice Grousers
Gemini 244	0791025	Stamped Steel Slide Rail	Accessory	Growser Bar	15″	114.44″	42″	Solid	Molded Rubber on Track Belt
Gemini 250	0791026	Stamped Steel Slide Rail	Accessory	Growser Bar	15″	114.44″	42″	Solid	Molded Rubber on Track Belt
Apollo 340	0791138	Stamped Steel Slide Rail	Standard	Molded Rubber	15″	114.85″	42″	—	—
Cobra 340	0791838	Stamped Steel Slide Rail	Standard	Growser Bar	15″	119.5″	48.75″	Solid	Molded Rubber on Track Belt
Cobra 440	0791843	Stamped Steel Slide Rail	Standard	Growser Bar	15″	119.5″	48.75″	Solid	Molded Rubber on Track Belt
TX 250	0790523	Aluminum Extruded Slide Rail	Standard	Growser Bar	15″	114.44″	44.25″	Solid	Molded Rubber on Track Belt
TX 340	0790537	Aluminum Extruded Slide Rail	Standard	Growser Bar	15″	114.44″	44.25″	Solid	Molded Rubber on Track Belt
TX 440	0790545	Aluminum Extruded Slide Rail	Standard	Growser Bar	15″	114.44″	44.25″	Solid	Molded Rubber on Track Belt
TX-L 340	0790639	Aluminum Extruded Slide Rail	Standard	Molded Rubber	15″	120.96″	47.5″	—	—
Centurion	0790653	Aluminum Extruded Slide Rail	Standard	Molded Rubber	15″	120.96″	47.5″	—	Steel Traction Studs

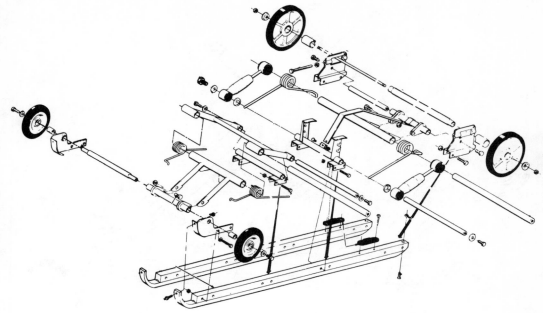

Slide rail suspension

Slide Rail Assembly—Charger, Charger SS, TX, Mustang, and Custom (Glass Rail)

Rear Spring adjustment is basically the only adjustment that can be administered to the suspension. This adjustment is for rider weight only. The highest spring position on the suspension would accommodate a heavy rider or when riding double. The lowest spring position would make a softer ride and would accommodate a lighter rider. Hi-fax should be replaced when no less than ⅛" is remaining at any given point. Failure to do so will result in severe damage to the fiberglass rail.

Type 1 Stamped Steel Slide Rail Assembly

These are stamped steel Type 1 slide suspensions without rider weight adjustment; shock accessory on some applications.

Type II Stamped Steel Slide Rail Assembly (E Slot)

This type suspension was introduced into the Polaris line in 1973 and was continued in the following models and years:
- 1973 TX
- 1974 Electra, Custome II, TX

- 1975 TX, Electra
- 1976 Electra
- 1977 Electra

Type 1 Extruded Aluminum

The locations of suspension mountings in the tunnel as shown are available to owners who wish to tailor their machines for individual riding or handling characteristics.
- A—High ski pressure normally not used.
- B—Less ski pressure than A, but more than C.
- C—Best suited for average conditions.
- D—Most normally used for general riding.
- E—Deep snow running and climbing.

Type I Extruded Aluminum Adjustments

FRONT LIMITER PIVOT ARM

The front limiter pivot arm may be located in either the upper or lower slide rail bracket holes. The upper position (A) provides greater ski lift upon acceleration and is desirable for deep snow running and hill climbing. The lower hole position (B) provides more ski pressure for turning and maneuverability on hard packed surfaces.

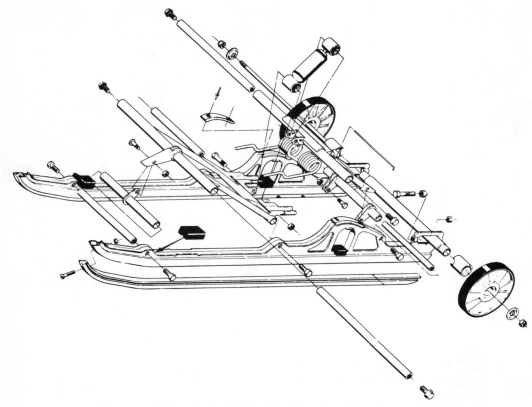

Stamped steel slide rail suspension (Type 1)

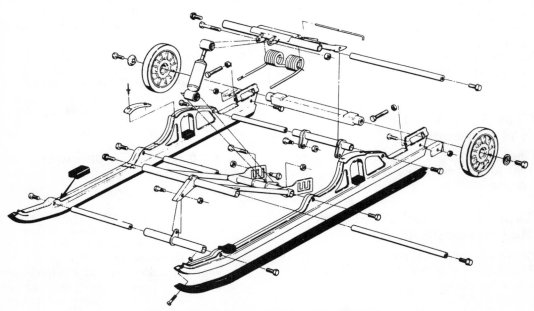

Stamped steel slide rail suspension (Type 2)

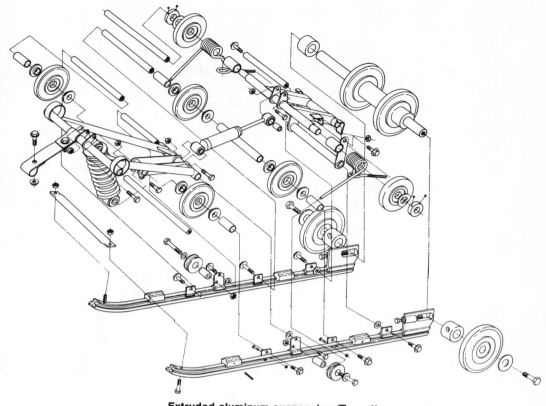

Extruded aluminum suspension (Type 1)

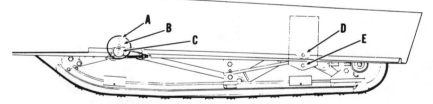

Suspension mounting locations in the tunnel.

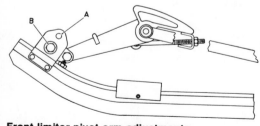

Front limiter pivot arm adjustments

REAR SPRING ADJUSTMENTS

There are two adjustment positions (A) for the rear springs which are located in the center of the suspension on either side. Adjustment is accomplished by moving the spring leg from one shoulder bolt to another.

The lower position is for normal riding qualities, while the upper is reserved for loads in excess of 190 pounds.

Each spring should be located in the same position on either side.

NOTE: *Front suspension torque arm spring adjustment is sufficiently adjusted before machine crating at the factory; increasing spring tension is not necessary.*

The locations of suspension mountings in the tunnel as shown are available to owners who wish to tailor their machine for individual riding or handling characteristics.

A—High ski pressure normally not used.

B—Less ski pressure than A, but more than C.

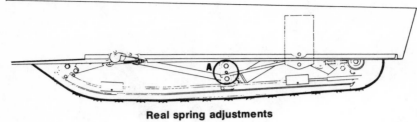

Real spring adjustments

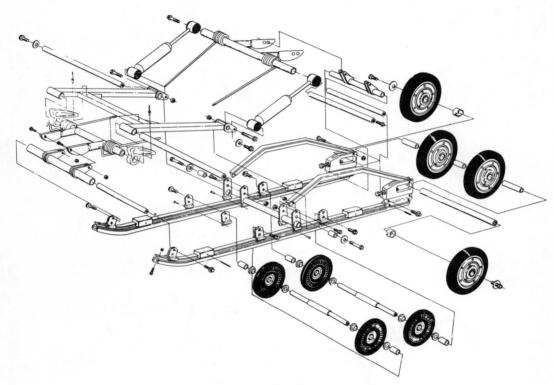

Type II extruded aluminum suspension

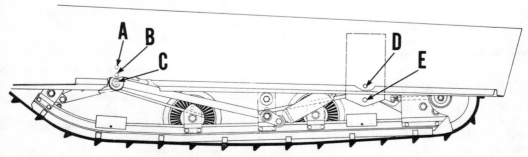

Type II extruded aluminum suspension mountings

C—Best suited for average conditions.

D—Most normally used for general riding.

E—Deep snow running and climbing.

Type I Track Removal

1. Remove the front and rear suspension bolts, then turn the machine on its side to remove the suspension.

2. Remove muffler. Remove three (3) cap screws that hold flangette and bearing in place on the right side of the machine.

3. With the machine on its side, use an Allen wrench to loosen the set screw on the lock collar.

4. To loosen the lock collar, tap with a hammer and punch. Rotate the lock collar with the normal direction of rotation to loosen and against normal rotation to tighten.

5. Remove the chaincase cover. Remove top and bottom sprackets.

6. The driveshaft can now be removed by first pushing the drive sprocket end from the chain case, then pull the shaft from the machine.

7. Reverse procedure for reassembly. When placing suspension into body weld bolt front suspension arm to body first, then rear suspension arm.

Disassembly

Removing sprocket from drive shaft weld. First use a center punch and center punch rivet head as shown. Then use ¼″ drill and drill to a depth of ¼″. If rivet head does not come off, use hammer and chisel lightly.

Replace rivets (9 per sprocket) with bolts (PN 7511967), nuts (PN 7541906) and spacers (PN 5332417).

When replacing sprockets on drive shaft weld, it is very important to index them. On a level surface two of the teeth on each drive sprocket must be resting equally against the surface. Rotate the sprocket assembly, inspecting to insure all teeth are synchronized. If not, it will be necessary to rotate the sprocket in the flanges until tooth alignment is achieved.

Track Tension

Track tension on all models and suspension types can be adjusted using the same procedure for all types and models. Check with a *10 pound* down load on the track at a point approximately 16″ ahead from the center of the rear idler. The tolerances are as follows:

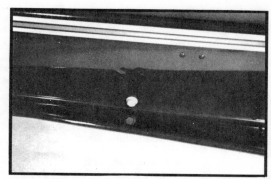

Remove the front and rear suspension bolts and turn the machine on its side

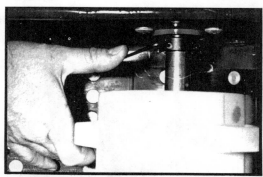

Remove the 3 screws holding the flange and bearing in place

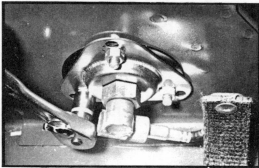

Loosen the set screw on the collar with an Allen wrench

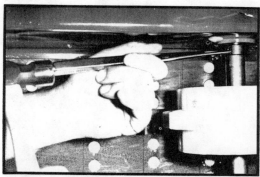

Carefully tap the collar with a hammer and punch to loosen it. Be sure to rotate the collar in the normal direction of rotation

Type	Models	Tolerance
Glass Rail	1972–1973 TX Charger SS, Mustang, Charger Custom	½″ between cleat and hifax
Stamped Steel Types I, II, and III	All	⅛″–⅜″ between cleat and hi-fax
Extruded Aluminum Type I	1976 Starfire, 1976–1979 TX	½″ between cleat and hifax
Extruded Aluminum Type II	1977–1978 TX-L	⅛″–¼″ between track clip and hifax
Extruded Aluminum Type III	1979 TX-L Centurion	⅜″–½″ between track clip and hifax

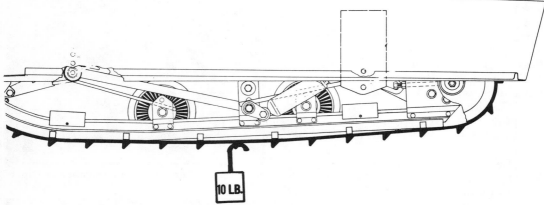

Track tension on all models is adjusted using the same procedure

Remove the chaincase cover and the top and bottom sprockets

Use a ¼ in. drill to break the driveshaft welds and separate the sprocket

Remove the driveshaft

It is very important to index the sprockets on the driveshaft welds when replacing them

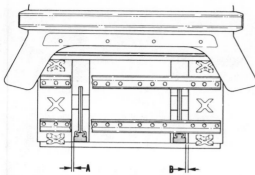

The rear of the machine should be suspended when aligning the track

Track Alignment—All Models

It is necessary to loosen idler shaft nut prior to making adjustments and retighten after adjustments are made.

The rear of the machine should be suspended when aligning the track. Track alignment affects track tension. If the track runs to the left and is not properly tensioned, the left side should be tightened. Use the same procedure for the right side until the track is properly aligned and is correctly tensioned. Tolerances at points (A) and (B) should be as close to the same as possible. Refer to Track Tension on page 19 for proper tension specifications.

CAUTION: *When performing checks or adjustments, stay clear of all moving parts.*

Slide Rail Replacement

1. Remove the single bolt and nut which clamp the plastic slide rail at its curved front end.

2. Hold a block of wood against the front end of the plastic slide rail and tap it with a hammer to drive the worn slide rail from the suspension.

3. Slip the new plastic slide rail onto the suspension from the rear by tapping a block of wood with a hammer to drive the slide rail into place.

4. Drill a new mounting hole in each new slide rail (at the curved front end) and replace the clamp bolt and nut.

Skis and Steering
SKAG REMOVAL

The ski skag can be removed by the removal of the retaining nut and by pushing the bolt down through the ski. Release the rear of the skag from the ski and it will be free to be removed.

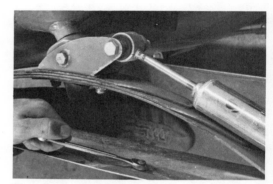

Removing skag retaining nut

STEERING

Ski alignment is attained by the adjustment of the steering rod ends. The skis should be parallel with both each other and with the chassis when the handlebars are in the straight-ahead driving position. If adjustment is needed, it may be made by turning the rod end bearings clockwise or counterclockwise, whichever is needed.

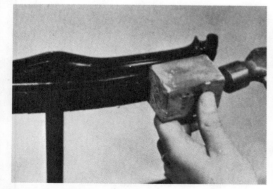

Tapping slide rail to remove

Removing the steering arm clamp bolt

To remove the steering arm, remove both nut and bolt. Both arm and spindle should be marked. After the steering arm is removed, the spindle can be removed from the chassis. The factory recommends that it be lubricated annually.

BRAKE SYSTEM

The brake system on the Polaris is a typical hydraulic system. The system includes a cylinder mounted on the steering bar, a plunger assembly mounted in the chaincase, an adjustable brake pad, and a brake disc.

The principle of operation is that the force applied to the brake lever compresses the fluid which in turn actuates the plunger assembly in the chain case. In this type of pressure chamber, a coil spring pressure holds the piston assembly against the face of the brake lever.

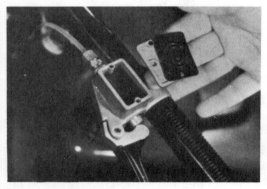

Removing brake reservoir cover

Overhaul

To disassemble the system, remove the brake fluid reservoir cover and the internal diaphragm. After loosening the set screw, turn over the assembly and pump the hand lever to drain the fluid.

NOTE: *Do not spill fluid as it will damage paint.*

Separate the brake lever from the master cylinder by removing the spring pin. After removing the piston and spring from the master cylinder unit, replace the old piston, U-cup, O-ring, and spring with the new units found in the rebuilding kit.

Before assembling the unit, clean all parts in brake fluid—including the master cylinder bore. Install all the new kit parts, giving special attention to the proper seating of the

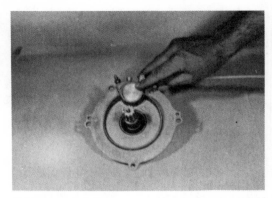

Installing new o-ring

spring. When installing the piston, take care not to damage the seal. Install the brake handle by inserting the spring pin. Place the hand prop back to the original position on the handle bars and tighten the set screws.

Prior to working on the chaincase portion of the brake system, the case must be removed from the engine and cleaned thoroughly. Before this is done, disconnect the flexible hose and the brake light connections (if so equipped). The cover can be removed after unscrewing the five capscrews and the snap-ring. Discard the washer, spring, and plunger once they have been removed because the new kit includes all these parts. Before installation, dip all internal parts in brake fluid and wipe the cylinder bore with the fluid also. Put the new O-rings on the plunger and insert it into the rear cover. Install both the spring and retaining washer and, applying pressure to compress the spring, install the retaining ring. When replacing the brake pads in the rear chain case cover, replace the stationary pad also. Install the rear cover, flexible hose, and brake light wire harness (if so equipped). If

Replacing stationary brake pad

there is excessive pad clearance, adjust the set screw until the pads are tight against the disc and then back off the screw ¼ turn.

NOTE: *The hand brake lever should not be allowed to decrease past ½ in. travel between the handle grip and the lever. Brake pads should not be allowed to wear to the point where the chaincase contacts the brake disc. Brake pads should be replaced in pairs.*

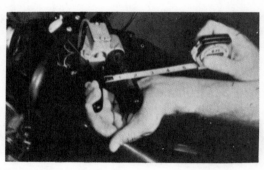

Brake lever adjustment

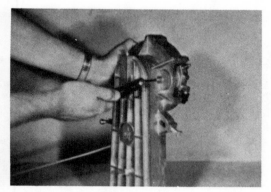

Adjusting brake pad clearance

A spongy action of the brake lever indicates air in the system. The system must be bled. First, fill the master cylinder and then slip a small hose over the ball of the bleeder to direct the fluid away from painted surfaces. Slowly squeeze the brake lever until it bottoms on the handle and hold it in that position. Open the bleeder valve to release the air, close the bleeder, then release the brake lever. Repeat the procedure until a solid stream of fluid is released when the bleeder is opened.

6

Ski-Doo

INTRODUCTION

There are over a million Ski-Doo snow-mobiles. If you own one, you have the most popular snow vehicle ever made. The snow-mobiles, produced by Bombardier Corporation, were among the very first to be offered to the public and the firm has maintained their sales lead from that beginning.

Ski-Doo snowmobiles were once considered rather utilitarian and the firm still makes everyday economy machines and the workhorse twin-track Alpine. The introduction of the free air-cooled line of T'NT F/A machines in 1973 and a new sliderail suspension for the 1974 T'NT, T'NT Everest, and 1975 Olympique and T'NT machines introduced a far more sporting series of machines and features to the line. That was about the time that Ski-Doo broke with tradition and offered colors other then their long-standard yellow.

The engines used in the various Ski-Doo models are generaly standardized so that one basic design, with various didsplacement choices, powers a number of different snowmobile models. The engines are all made by a Bombardier, Limited subsidiary, Rotax, in Austria. With the exception of the F/A air-cooled series. And the new liquid cooled engines which are fast becoming the industry

standard for the faster models. Regardless of the manufacturer the liquid cooled engines develop more horsepower per cc than the fan cooled or free air engines. All of the Ski-Doo engines are fan-cooled have a cast aluminum cooling shroud over the cylinder barrel and cylinder head. Some of the smaller machines are powered by single-cylinder Rotax engines, but most, from the 294 cc through the 640 cc models, are twin-cylinder power-plants.

SERIAL NUMBER IDENTIFICATION

Vehicle

The vehicle serial number and the date of manufacture usually appears on a small metal plate on the right-side of the frame near the back of the machine.

Engine

A small metal plate is mounted on the right-side of the engine's air-cooling shroud with the engine serial number, engine type, bore, stroke, and displacement. Ski-Doo has a rather complex number code to match the serial number to the engine number. On

The engine serial number is on a plate mounted on the fan housing

most engines, the first digit of the serial number indicates the last digit of the model year for that particular engine.

ROUTINE MAINTENANCE

Lubrication

The oil which lubricates the engine must be mixed with the fuel before filling the tank on the various Ski-Doo models.

The drive chain runs in an oil bath inside its case. There is a sight glass or a filler plug on the outside of the drive chaincase on most models, usually about in line with the end of the track driveshaft. On the Alpine and Nordic models with 440 engines, the oil level should be 2¼ in. above the bottom of the drive chaincase and the level should be 3¼ in. above the bottom of the chaincase on the Alpine and Nordic models with 640 engines. Insert a piece of wire through the drive chain adjusting hole to serve as an oil dipstick to measure the oil level on the Alpine and Nordic models. Refill the chaincase, as required, with Ski-Doo Chaincase Oil.

The drive (primary) clutch sliding shafts and internal cams should be lubricated with Ski-Doo High Performance Drive Pulley Lubricant or the equivalent. The clutch on the F/A models can be lubricated through an inspection hole and by compressing the pulley halves. The outer pulley half must be removed, on most other models, to lubricate the internal cams (flyweights) and, on reassembly, the center bolt tightened with a torque wrench to the figure shown in the "Torque Specifications" chart. Do NOT lubricate the drive (primary) clutch.

The driven clutch (torque converter) requires lubrication on most Ski-Doo models. Lubricate the sliding areas down near the base of the pulley, but be extremely careful to avoid using too much grease or smearing it on the faces of either the drive or driven pulleys. The driven clutch on the 1976 and later Ski-Doo twin-cylinder models should NOT be lubricated; the lubricant will destroy the material used in the bushings.

Use a low-pressure grease gun to insert the lubricant into the grease fittings on the steering pivots and, on most models, into the grease fittings on the bogie or idler wheel bearings. Pump the grease gun until a bit of grease appears at the joints and carefully wipe away that excess lubricant. Engine oil

in a standard spout style oil can should be used to lubricate the spring mounting points, the steering column bushings, the brake and throttle cables, and the various linkage pivot points.

The engine oil is mixed with the fuel every time the fuel tank is refilled. The other lubrication should be repeated every 40 hours of snowmobile operation under normal conditions and more often if most driving is done in wet snow or slush.

Maintenance Intervals

Service/Inspection	Daily	Weekly	Monthly	Annually
Clean windshield	X			
Check skis and steering	X			
Check track and tension	X			
Check throttle controls	X			
Check brake operation	X			
Check kill and ign. switch	X			
Check all lights	X			
Check chain case oil level		X		
Check in line fuel filter		X		
Check drive belt		X		
Check carb adjustments			X	
Check choke operation			X	
Check ski alignment			X	
Check fan belt			X	
Check ski wear rods			X	
Check suspension wear bars			X	
Check all components for condition and tightness				X
Service drive and driven clutches				X

Bogie Wheel Suspension System

Brake Adjustment

Most Ski-Doo models are fitted with one of two types of disc brake, a style which requires an occasional adjustment on the brake caliper and a self-adjusting type. A single adjusting nut is located directly in back of the inboard brake puck on the caliper assembly. Tighten the adjusting nut until you can just feel the brake lining drag on the brake disc then back off the nut about $1/6$ turn. A spring steel lever and pawl automatically moves the brake puck closer to the disc on the self-adjusting style.

Track adjusting bolts are located on the chassis corners on some models

Some of the Elan models and the older Ski-Doo machines have a drum or pivot type of brake where the inner surface of the driven pulley (torque converter) serves as the brake drum. The major adjusting point on these style brakes is at the end of the brake cable. Set the brake cable adjusting nuts at their middle position on the adjusting threads, then loosen the nut which retains the inner cable to the brake actuating arm. Pull the inner cable taut and retighten its locknut. The brake cable can then be adjusted to provide proper hand lever movement.

The brake cable must be adjusted, on most Ski-Doo snowmobiles, so that the hand brake lever is never closer then one in. from the handlebar grip when the brake is fully applied. Loosen the locknuts on the brake cable adjuster and turn the adjuster to provide that one in. of lever-to-handlebar clearance, then retighten the locknuts.

Track Tensioning and Alignment

The track tensioning and alignment bolts are located near the right and left rear edges of the chassis. The complete track tensioning and adjusting procedure outlined in Chapter 1 should be followed on Ski-Doo snowmobiles.

Ski Alignment

The skis on Ski-Doo snowmobiles should be adjusted so that their tips are between ⅛ and ¼ in. farther apart than the rear of the skis (toe-out). Turn the handlebars into the straight-ahead position and measure the edge-to-edge distance between the front spring mounts and repeat the measurement at the rear spring mounts; the front distance should be ⅛–¼ in. greater than the rear with

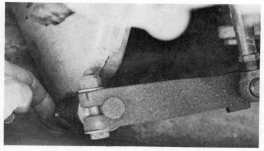

Steering arm, grease fitting, and ball joint

the skis pointed straight-ahead. Loosen the locknuts on the ends of each of the rods which connect the steering column to the steering arms (the tie-rods) above the skis. Turn the tie-rods clockwise to bring the ski tips closer together or counterclockwise to spread the ski tips. Recheck the alignment measurements and retighten the locknuts.

TUNE-UP

Ignition Timing

Some Ski-Doo snowmobile engines are fitted with a capacitive discharge ignition (CDI) system with no breaker points or breaker point adjustment. All of the other Ski-Doo engines have breaker point ignition systems. Most of these ignition systems can be checked for proper timing with a strobe light aimed through a timing hole in the ignition end of the crankcase. If the timing or the breaker point gap must be adjusted, the manual starter and cooling fan assembly must be removed from the end of the engine. If the breaker points must be replaced, the flywheel must be removed, but simple adjustments can be accomplished through small slots in the flywheel. Check the ignition timing before removing the fan assembly; if the timing is correct, then the fan assembly can remain in place.

REMOVAL AND INSTALLATION

It is possible, on some models, to remove the breaker points without first removing the engine from the chassis, but the cramped working area makes the job difficult. The engine should be removed and placed on the workbench. The removal sequence is described in the section of this chapter which deals with engine rebuilding.

1. Remove the bolts which retain the manual starter and carefully lift the complete unit from the end of the engine.

2. Remove the round fan protector shroud from the engine.

3. Remove the three bolts and washers which retain the fan belt's drive pulley and lift the drive pulley and the fan belt from the engine.

4. Use a chisel and hammer to flatten the retaining tabs around the crankshaft end nut.

5. Attach a crankshaft hold-down support tool to the flywheel with the three screws which held the fan belt pulley. The ring gear

A retaining ring secures the fan guard

Removing the fly wheel nut

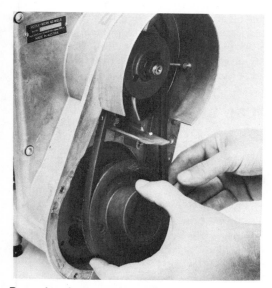

Removing the fan belt and fan belt drive pulley

breaker points and lift the complete breaker point assemblies from the ignition plate.

9. Check the operation of the spark advance cam inside the flywheel and adjust the breaker point gap before installing the flywheel.

10. Assembly is the reverse of the disassembly sequence. Be sure that the spark advance cam engages its slot. Tighten the flywheel nut to 50 ft-lbs and bend the lockwasher's tabs around two sides of the flywheel nut. It is best to use a new lockwasher on the flywheel nut. Install the engine in the chassis and adjust the ignition timing.

must be removed from engines with electric starters before mounting the crankshaft holding tool.

6. The crankshaft holding tool will prevent crankshaft rotation while you loosen and remove the flywheel nut.

7. Use a Ski-Doo flywheel puller tool to remove the flywheel from the end of the crankshaft. Look through the notches in the flywheel, as you remove it, to see where the lever on the ignition advance cam engages the cam notch on the crankshaft.

8. Remove the screws which retain the

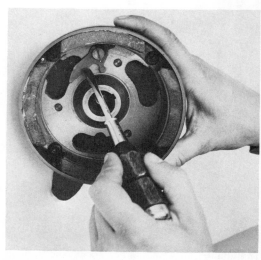

The ignition advance lever is inside the fly wheel

BREAKER POINT ADJUSTMENT

The manual starter and the fan drive pulley must be removed for access to the breaker point adjusting screws. The adjusting screws are located so that they can be turned through the slots in the flywheel. The complete adjusting procedure is described in Chapter 1.

Ignition Timing

The procedures for adjusting the timing on the breaker point ignition systems on most Ski-Doo snowmobiles are described in Chapter 1. The timing on the Ski-Doo capacitive discharge ignition (CDI) systems fitted to some Ski-Doo models can be adjusted by loosening the screws which retain the ignition system to the end of the crankcase. The ignition mounting screws can be turned by reaching through the notches in the flywheel.

Use a self-powered strobe light to check the ignition timing on the CDI systems. Check with the manufacturer to find out which lights work with CDI systems.

1. The ignition timing is given with the system in the fully-advanced position. Do not rev the engine with the drive belt off. Point the skis at a solid wall and support the rear of the machine so that the track can turn without hitting the support you use or the ground.

2. Connect the strobe light's wires as described in the instructions furnished with the particular brand of strobe light. Connect the wires to the ignition wires leading to the cylinder nearest the ignition system (on two-cylinder engines). Remove the plug which covers the ignition timing hole in the top of the crankcase.

3. Start the engine and rev it to a constant 5,000 rpm with the beam from the strobe light aimed through the timing hole in the crankcase to illuminate the timing marks on the flywheel and crankcase. If the timing marks do not coincide, then the screws which retain the ignition system will have to be loosened (with the engine off) so that the complete ignition system can be rotated slightly until the timing marks align with the engine running at 5,000 rpm.

4. Connect the strobe light to the wires for the cylinder on the drive side of the engine and repeat the timing sequence used on the other cylinder. The two cylinders should fire within 0.060–0.080 in. (before top dead center) of one another.

FUEL SYSTEM

Carburetor

The 1976 through 1980 Ski-Doo Snowmobiles were equipped with either a Tillotson (only a few early models) or Mikuni(s). The Mikuni carburetor because of its trouble free operation and simplistic design is fast becoming the universal Snowmobile carburetor. They are covered in detail in section two along with the Mikuni remote fuel pumps, which are used on Ski-Doo Snowmobiles.

Fuel Tank

Use one of the accessory types of hand pump and hose units to siphon the fuel from the fuel tank into a clean container before removing the fuel tank. Drain any fuel which remains in the fuel lines into a separate tank. When replacing the fuel tank connector nut on late model Ski-Doo snowmobiles, the flexible fuel lines should be replaced with new lengths of fuel line cut to match the originals. Use pipe thread compound on the threads of the nut which connects the fuel lines to the tank.

The ignition adjustments are accessible through the flywheel slots

Tune Up Specs

Year	Engine Type	Spark Plug Number[+]	Spark Plug Gap (In.)	Ign. Timing In. B.T.D.C.[x]	Breaker Point Gap	Ign. Type
1978–79–80	247	M175T1	.020	.157	.016 [−]	Breaker
1978–79	248	W240T1	.020	.087	.016	Breaker
1980	277	W275T2	.020	.102	.014	Breaker
1978–79	294	W280MZ1	.020	.094	.016	Breaker
1978	305	W280MZ1	.020	.083	.016	Breaker
1978–79	343	W280MZ1	.020	.083	.016	Breaker
1978	345	W280MZ2	.020	.054	NA	C-D
	346	W260MZ2	.020	.100	.016	Breaker
1978–79–80	354	W340S22	.020	.055	NA	C-D
1978–79	402	W280MZ1	.020	.083	.016	Breaker
	440	M260T1	.020	.121	.016	Breaker
1978–79–80	444	W280MZ2*	.020	.092	.016 [(−)]	Breaker
1979–80	454	W300T2	.020	.055	NA	C-D
	503	W275T2	.020	.081	.016 [(−)]	Breaker
1978–79–80	640	M240T1	.020	.156	.016 [(−)]	Breaker

[+]Bosch spark plugs
*2 Gaskets
[−]1980 models .014 (+ −.002)
[x]Ign. timing is checked at piston travel B.T.D.C. when using these timing specs

Carburetor Specifications—Ski-Doo

Year	Model	Engine Type	Carb. and (No. Used)	Lo Speed Gas Adj. (Turns Out)	Idle Speed (R.P.M.)
1978–79	Elan	247	(1) Tillotson	1	1500–1800
	Spirit	247	(1) Tillotson	1	1500–1800
	Alpine	640	(1) Tillotson	1⅛	1500–1800
	Olympic	343	(1) Mikuni	1½	1500–1800
	Nuvik	343	(1) Mikuni	1½	1500–1800

Carburetor Specifications—Ski-Doo (cont.)

Year	Model	Engine Type	Carb. and (No. Used)	Lo Speed Gas Adj. (Turns Out)	Idle Speed (R.P.M.)
1978–79	Citation	294	(1) Mikuni	1½	1800–2200
1978	TNT	346	(1) Mikuni	1	1800–2000
1978–79	Everest	440	(1) Mikuni	2	1500–1800
	Futura	444 L/C	(1) Mikuni	1½	1500–1800
1978	RV	345	(2) Mikuni	1	3000–3200
	Sonic	345	(2) Mikuni	1	3000–3200
1978–79	Blizzard	354	(2) Mikuni	*1½	2800–3200
	Elite	444	(1) Mikuni	N.A.	N.A.
1979	Blizzard	503	(2) Mikuni	1½	1500–2000
1980	Elan	247	(1) Mikuni	1½	1100–1300
	Spirit	247	(1) Mikuni	1½	1100–1300
	Citation 3500	277	(1) Mikuni	1½	1100–1300
	Citation 4500	377	(1) Mikuni	1	2000
	Citation SS	377	(1) Mikuni	1½	1800–2000
	Everest	503	(1) Mikuni	1	1800–2000
	Futura L/C	464	(1) Mikuni	1½	2000
	Blizzard 5500	503	(2) Mikuni	1½	1800–2000
	Blizzard 7500	354	(1) Mikuni	1½	1800–2000
	Blizzard 9500	454	(1) Mikuni	1	1800–2000
	Alpine	640	(1) Mikuni	1½	1800–2000
	Elite	444	(1) Mikuni	1	1800–2000

*Hi speed 1¼ turns

ENGINE

Removal and Installation

Clean the exterior of the engine thoroughly with solvent or steam and air dry it before removing it from the chassis. The instrument console must be removed from most models to provide sufficnet working room around the engine mounting areas.

1. Remove the throttle and brake levers from the handlebar levers by pulling the

Pull the cable down and slide it out to release inner cable

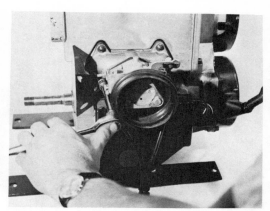

Removing the carburetor with engine on work bench

inner wire down so that the cable drum can be pulled from the lever.

2. Disconnect all of the wiring at the socket and plug connectors and remove the kill button from the handlebars.

3. Remove the negative cable from the battery, on engines with electric starters, and remove the wires leading to the starter.

4. Remove the safety shield from the drive belt and then remove the drive belt as described in Chapter 1.

5. Remove the bolts and brackets which mount the steering column.

6. Remove the complete air silencer unit from the carburetor and disconnect the fuel lines at the carburetor.

7. Remove the bolts which retain the muffler assembly and unhook the springs which connect the muffler to the exhaust manifold.

8. Mark the position of the engine mounting plate in the chassis then remove the four bolts which hold the plate to the chassis.

9. When installing the engine, check the drive belt alignment then torque the engine mounting bolts to the torque figures shown in the "Torque Specifications" chart.

OVERHAUL

Remove the manual starter, fan guard, lower fan pulley, and the flywheel as described in the section of this chapter on ignition repair and replacement.

1. Remove the pulse line from the crankcase to the carburetor and unbolt the carburetor from the engine. Remove the spark plug lead wires and the spark plugs.

2. Remove all of the bolts and screws which hold the front and rear cooling shrouds to the engine. Remove the screws which attach these shrouds to the fan cover.

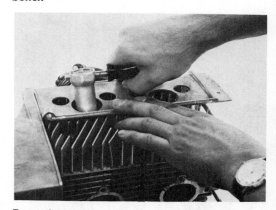

Removing spark plugs with tool kit wrench

Removing the exhaust side cooling shroud

3. Remove the exhaust side cooling shroud so that the exhaust manifold can be removed—the screws which retain the exhaust manifold on some models are hidden beneath the cooling shroud.

4. Remove the nuts which retain the intake manifold and pull the manifold from its

Removing the shroud screws from the fan housing side

Removing the intake manifold attaching nuts

The exhaust side shroud covers the exhaust manifold

Shrouds lower tabs fit below the intake manifold

Loosen the Allen screws on the exhaust manifold

Removing the intake manifold heat block

studs so that the intake side cooling shroud can be lifted from the engine. Engines with twin carburetors have two separate manifolds with pulse lines to the crankcase—remove the pulse lines and the manifolds.

5. Remove the intake manifold heat block piece(s) and the joining manifold from twin-cylinder engines with single carburetors.

6. Loosen the cylinder head hold-down

The twin cylinder intake joining manifold

Removing the cylinder barrel

nuts in the order shown in Chapter 1. Unscrew the exhaust manifold stubs from engines with that type of exhaust manifold before loosening the cylinder head nuts. The cylinder heads can now be lifted from the cylinder barrels.

7. Lift each cylinder barrel from the crankcase.

Use a rag to protect cylinder and crankcase

Removing the cylinder heads

Prying the piston pin retainers out

8. Tuck a rag around the piston the moment the barrel is removed so that no dirt can fall into the crankcase.

9. Pry the piston pin retainers from the pistons and gently tap the piston pins from the piston. Hold the piston firmly so that the shock loads are absorbed by your hand rather than the connecting rod while tapping the pins out.

10. Inspect the piston pin bearings for any signs of wear, pits, or roughness.

11. Lay the crankcase on its side while removing the nuts and washers which hold the two crankcase halves together. Remove the top half of the crankcase. Tap the sides of the crankcase gently with a plastic-headed hammer to free the seal.

12. Lift the crankshaft and connecting rod assembly from the crankcase and note the positions of the grease seals, spacer rings,

Piston pin needle bearing

Test fitting the crankshaft and seals

Cylinder barrel to crankcase gasket

bearings, and O-rings. Use a bearing puller to remove the bearings from the crankshaft.

Assembly

1. Clean all of the internal parts thoroughly and remove any traces of old gaskets or sealer. Use new gaskets, seals, and O-rings in every location.

2. Heat the crankshaft bearings in a container filled with oil. Support the bearings above the bottom of the container in a screen basket and let them warm to 180°–190° F, then slide the bearings, retainer washers, seals, and O-rings into place on the crankshaft.

3. The crankshaft end-play tolerances are achieved by removing or adding shim discs on the ignition and drive ends of the crankshaft. Measure the amount of end-play on the magneto end and insert half that thickness of

shims on the drive end and half that thickness on the ignition end of the crankshaft. The shims fit between the crankshaft retaining disc and the bearings. Determine the number and location of the shims with a test-fitting of the crankshaft assembly and install them on the crankshaft.

4. Heat the crankcase to 180°–200° F and slip the complete crankshaft into place in the bottom half. Apply Ski-Doo L 700 adhesive to the sealing surface of the lower half and slide the heater upper crankcase half into place.

5. Tighten the crankcase nuts to 10 ft-lbs of torque working in a criss-cross pattern to equalize the pressure over all areas at once. When all nuts are tight, repeat the criss-cross tightening (see Chapter 1) to torque the nuts to 16 ft-lbs.

6. Install the electric starter (if fitted) and the engine mounting plate to the crankcase.

7. Spread the piston rings and slide them into place in their proper grooves. Rotate the piston rings so that their endgaps are butted against the tiny pin in each piston ring groove.

8. Install the piston pin needle bearings, the piston pins, and the piston pin retaining rings. The letters "AUS" on the pistons should be toward the exhaust side of the engine. There is a left and a right piston in most twin-cylinder engines; the cutouts in the piston skirts should line up with the transfer ports in the crankcase and cylinder barrel.

9. Tighten two cylinder head hold-down nuts together on one of the cylinder head studs so that the stud can be screwed firmly

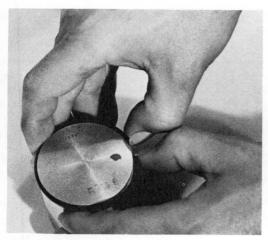

Piston ring installation

Cooling shroud installation

into the crankcase. Remove the nuts and repeat the process to be sure that all of the cylinder studs are tight in the crankcase.

10. Install new cylinder base gaskets and slide the cylinder barrels into place. Be sure that the piston rings are butted against their stop pins in the piston ring grooves. Test-fit the intake manifold.

11. Spread a teaspoon of engine oil over the cylinder walls and rotate the engine a few times to distribute the oil evenly. The cylinder heads and new cylinder head gaskets can then be installed. Torque the nuts to the torque settings indicated for your engine and tighten them gradually in the pattern shown in Chapter 1.

12. Replace the intake and exhaust manifolds, the cooling shrouds, and the carburetor. Install the flywheel, cooling fan, and manual starter as described in the section on ignition repair.

Exhaust manifold installation

RECOIL STARTER

Removal and Installation

Three or four bolts hold the recoil starter to the ignition end of the engine. The starter must be removed or replaced as a complete unit.

Overhaul

1. Pry the circlip from its retaining slot inside the starter cover and remove the circlip, washer, friction spring and washer, and pivoting arm from the center stud. Wear protective goggles and gloves.

2. Pull the starter handle out and pry the rubber buffer from the handle so that the rope knot can be untied or cut to allow removal of the handle, buffer, and rope.

3. Remove the D-shaped washer and the rope pulley from the starter housing.

4. Loosen and remove the two screws which retain the starter rope stop on the outside of the case. Remove the stop and unwind the starter rope. The rope can then be unwound from its pulley. A small pin retains the rope on one style starter and a clip on the second style starter. Remove the pin or clip to fit a new starter rope. Rope installation is the reverse of this procedure except that the nylon rope ends should be sealed so that they don't fray by heating them with a match or candle flame.

5. The starter rewind spring is held inside a two-piece, can-style casing. If the spring must be replaced, pry open the case with a screwdriver tip. Rewind the new spring into the smaller half of the casing so that the O-shaped opening in the end of the spring

Engine Specifications

Year	Model	Type Engine	No. of Cylinders	Carburetor	Displacement C.C.
1980	Elan 250	Rotax	1	Mikuni	250
	Citation 3500	Rotax	1	Mikuni	269
	Citation 4500	Rotax	2	Mikuni	368
	Citation SS	Rotax	2	Mikuni	368
	Everest 500	Rotax	2	Mikuni	497
	Everest L.C.	Rotax	2 L/C	Mikuni	463
	Blizzard 5500	Rotax	2	Mikuni	497
	Blizzard 7500	Rotax	2 L/C	Mikuni	339
	Blizzard 9500	Rotax	2 L/C	Mikuni	437
	Elite	Rotax	2 L/C	Mikuni	437
1976 through 1979	Information not available from Ski-Doo				

points counterclockwise. Hold the pieces with gloves to avoid cutting your hands. Apply a thin coating of low temperature grease to the spring. Press the spring case cover in place and tap it lightly to seal the cover. Check the action of the individual pieces before completing the assembly. The pivoting arm must rotate in a clockwise direction.

ELECTRIC STARTER

Removal and Installation

The muffler must be removed from most engines to allow access to the electric starter. Remove the ground wire from the battery then disconnect the wires which lead to the starter's solenoid switch. The nuts and bolts which hold the starter to the engine can then be removed and the mounting bracket unbolted from the starter. Starter service and repair requires special tools and jigs and should, therefore, be entrusted to your dealer. Reverse the procedure to install the

starter and be sure to connect the ground wire to the battery as the final step.

DRIVE SYSTEM

Description

All of the Ski-Doo snowmobiles use the drive pulley/drive belt/driven pulley series of components which function as an automatic transmission as described in Chapter 1. The drive belt maintenance and removal steps described in that chapter must be used, then, on Ski-Doo snowmobiles. The drive pulley which mounts on the end of the engine's crankshaft has been modified internally to suit the demands of the various Ski-Doo machines, but the basic belt-gripping principles are similar. The later model driven clutch (torque converter) has been changed so that no lubrication is required.

The driven clutch drives an enclosed chain to drive the track in the manner used on virtually every snowmobile. The reversing gear transmission, when fitted, is incorporated

General Torque Specifications —Ski-Doo

M10 crankcase bolts—18–23 ft lbs
M12 crankcase bolts—21–30 ft lbs
18 mm spark plugs—30 ft lbs
14 mm spark plugs—20 ft lbs

into the drive chaincase. The drive chain should be adjusted periodically and the oil level checked and replenished as indicated in the lubrication section of this chapter. The shift linkage to the reversing gear transmission can be adjusted as needed and its oil level should be maintained. Any major fault in the reversing gearbox should be corrected by a Ski-Door dealer with the correct tools and assembly fixtures.

Drive Pulley
REMOVAL AND INSTALLATION

The drive pulley (also called a "centrifugal clutch") on the Ski-Doo engines is a specially balanced unit which should be repaired by an authorized Ski-Doo dealer. The center nut retains the complete clutch. Remove the nut, after bending back the washer tabs, and use a puller to remove the clutch. Tighten the center nut to the figure shown in the "Torque Specifications" chart, when installing the unit, and bend the washer tabs over the sides of the nut.

The removal of the drive pulley center nut on all other Ski-Doo models will expose the working of the unit. Only the outer half of the drive pulley can be removed when that center nut is removed; a special puller is necessary to remove the inner half of the drive pulley from the engine's crankshaft. Many of the late model Ski-Doo drive pulleys have

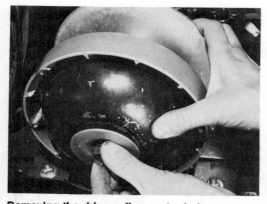

Removing the drive pulley center bolt

Cam lever engagement slots

been designed so that their internal working components (the centrifugal clutch) require no lubrication. Consult the lubrication section and your owner's manual to determine if your machine has this type of clutch; it should only need to be removed or replaced if it fails to function properly. An authorized Ski-Doo repair shop should perform any repairs or adjustments on any Ski-Doo drive pulley. Bend the washer tabs back before loosening the center nut in the drive pulley. Hold the pulley halves together against any internal spring pressure while loosening the nut.

The cover which rests inside the outer half of the drive pulley can be lifted free to expose the actuating cam levers of the centrifugal clutch. The cam levers engage slots in the outer pulley half when the engine speed reaches "engagement" rpm for that particular clutch. The cam levers should pivot freely. Lubricate the lever pivot points and slot and the sliding shaft (except on those late model units where no lubrication is permitted) and see that the outer pulley slides smoothly on the shaft. Wipe away any traces of grease or dirt from the pulley face which grips the drive belt. Use a new lockwasher when installing the unit. Torque the center nut to the figure shown in the "Torque Specifications" chart and bend the lockwasher tabs over two of the flats on the nut.

Driven Pulley
REMOVAL AND INSTALLATION

1. Remove the safety shield from the drive belt, the drive belt, and the muffler. The

The cam levers pivot inside the cover

Wipe excess grease from pulley faces

Align marks on pulley halves

steering column must also be removed from most Elan and Olympique models.

2. If a disc brake is fitted, the bolts which attach the brake caliper assembly must be removed so that the caliper can be removed.

3. Release the drive chain tension by loosening the adjusting nut or by removing the chaincase cover (on models with an automatic chain adjuster) and insert a special Ski-Doo chain tension release tool.

4. Remove the cotter key and the nut which hold the upper drive chain sprocket to the end of the driven clutch (idler) shaft.

5. Pull the driven pulley and its shaft from the chaincase bearing. Tie the upper drive chain sprocket to the chaincase with a piece of wire so that the sprocket and chain remain in position.

6. Reverse the above sequence to install the drive pulley. Fit a new cotter key to the driven shaft's end nut, refill the chaincase with oil, and check the drive chain tension.

The drive clutch shaft is an integral part of the transmission on models with a reverse gear. An authorized Ski-Doo service dealer should repair or replace the driven pulley on these models.

Drive Chain and Sprockets

CHAIN TENSION

Ski-Doo machines have an automatic drive chain adjuster. The amount of free-play in the drive chain must be measured at the driven pulley. The total amount of movement at the rim of the driven pulley should be no more than ½ in. before resistance can be felt. Loosen the locknut on the drive chain adjuster bolt and turn the adjuster bolt until the driven pulley will move only that ½ in. Tighten the locknut.

REMOVAL AND INSTALLATION

The procedures outlined for removal and installation of the driven pulley will allow the removal of the drive cahin's upper sprocket. The drive chain can then be removed. The drive chain is of the endless type so that the sprocket must be removed to remove the chain. If the chain is worn so that the adjuster travel fails to remove the slack, then the chain must be replaced. If the chain is worn, check the sprocket teeth for signs of severe wear on their sides and for a hooked shape on the teeth faces which can result from contact with worn drive chain rollers.

Spring tension bolts for Bogie suspension

SUSPENSION

Track

TENSION AND ALIGNMENT

Bogie Wheel Suspension

The procedures for adjusting the track tension and alignment are outlined in Chapter 1. The track tension on Ski-Doo snowmobiles with bogie wheel suspensions should be measured from the *top* of the track to the *bottom* of the footboard. That dimension should be between 1¼–1½ in. on most Elan models and between 2⅛–2⅜ in. on most other models.

Slide Rail Suspension

Ski-Doo has used a number of different slide rail suspension systems on their various models in different years. The track tensioning and alignment steps in Chapter 1 apply to any of the models.

The track tension on the 1976 and newer slide rail suspensions is measured from the inside of the *bottom* run of the track to the bottom of the slide rail rubbing surface. Pull the track downward, with the rear of the machine supported, so that all of the slack is at the bottom of the track. Take the tension measurement midway between the rear axle and the rearmost guide (bogie) wheel. That slack distance should be between ½ and ¾".

REMOVAL AND INSTALLATION

The tracks on Ski-Doo snowmobiles are endless. The suspension assembly and drive axle must, then, be removed from the chassis to remove or replace the track. The procedures outlined for drive axle, bogie wheel, and rear idler axle service describe the removal of these components. The section on slide rail service describes the removal of these units.

Bogie Wheels

SERVICE

The rear of the snowmobile must be supported and all track and suspension tension released before removing any of the suspension components. A bolt in each end of the bogie wheel units' center shaft holds the units to the chassis. Hold the bogie wheel shaft with vise-grip type pliers while loosening and removing the bolt from each end of the shaft. The bogie wheel unit can then be removed from the chassis. The springs are held by metal straps and the wheels and bearings by a riveted-on outer wheel half. It is best to have a Ski-Doo service dealer replace any worn or broken bogie wheels, bearings, or springs. Make a sketch and notes of the exact position of each of the bogie wheel units so that they can be reassembled in their proper positions beneath the chassis.

Rear Idler Axle
REMOVAL AND INSTALLATION

The rear (idler) axle is mounted on the slide rail itself on that type of suspension system. The procedures outlined here apply to the bogie wheel suspension systems only.

1. Support the rear of the snowmobile and release both track and spring tension.

2. Remove the bolts and nuts which hold the rear axle's two link plates to the sides of the chassis. The complete rear axle and link plate assembly can then be lifted from the chassis. Note the locations of the spacers, springs, bolts and nuts so that they can be reassembled in the proper positions.

Slide Rail
REMOVAL AND INSTALLATION

1. Support the rear of the snowmobile and loosen the track tensioning bolts and the spring tension bolts, but do not remove them.

2. The slide rail pivot arms are held to the sides of the chassis with bolts and nuts. Remove all of these bolts and nuts and the complete slide rail suspension including the rear idler axle can be lifted from the machine.

3. The slide rail plastic surface bearings are held in place with a bolt and nut at the front and a series of pop rivets. A tiny sleeve covers the small shaft of each pop rivet. Remove the attaching bolts, pop rivets, and sleeves to replace the slide rail plastic bearings.

Drive Axle
REMOVAL AND INSTALLATION

The rear axle and the bogie wheel units or slide rail assembly must be removed from the chassis before removing the drive axle.

1. Drain the drive chaincase and release the drive chain tension by backing off on the adjusting bolt or by inserting the Ski-Doo chain tension release tool (in self-adjusting type drive chaincases).

2. Pry the drive axle seal from its retainer on the inside wall of the chassis near the axle's track drive sprocket.

3. Remove the speedometer drive from the end of the drive axle.

4. Remove the three bolts which retain the drive axle bearing housing to the outside of the chassis. Use two or three screwdrivers to gently pry the bearing housing from the chassis and from the end of the drive axle.

5. Remove the cotter pin and the spacer washer from the chaincase end of the drive axle. The complete chaincase assembly must be removed from most Olympic and T'NT models.

6. Pull the track away from the teeth on the drive sprocket so that the drive axle can be pulled away from the lower drive chain sprocket. The drive axle can then be removed from the chassis. The track is now free from the chassis for repair or replacement.

7. Installation is the reverse of the removal procedure. Use new seals and cotter pins and be sure to include the axle spacers. The drive chaincase must be refilled with the correct amount of oil and the drive chain tension checked and adjusted.

Skis and Steering
REMOVAL AND INSTALLATION

The skis are bolted to the front leaf springs with a pivot bolt and the front and a retaining bolt at the rear on some models; others use a simple steel pin with a cotter pin and washer to mount the skis. There is a replaceable spring slider cushion at the rear mount which should be removed and replaced if worn. The runner (skag) bars beneath each ski are attached with nuts and they, too, should be replaced if worn.

The steering pivot arms can be removed by loosening and removing their top mounting bolts to replace the pivot bushings. Each of the ball joints on the ends of the tie-rods should be checked for wear and to be sure that the face of the ball joint is exactly parallel with the face of the steering arm.

ALIGNMENT

The steps required to align the skis and steering are described in Chapter 1 and in the "Routine Maintenance" section of this chapter.

BRAKE SYSTEM

Five different types of brake systems have been used on Ski-Doo snowmobiles during the last few years: a pivot-type which rubs against the face of the driven pulley; a drum-type which rubs against an extension flange on the back of the driven pulley; an adjustable type of cable-operated disc brake; a self-adjusting cable-operated disc brake; and a hydraulically-actuated disc brake.

REMOVAL AND INSTALLATION

Drum-Type Brake

1. Remove the drive belt and cable clamp.
2. Remove the bolt and nut which mount the brake lever to the chaincase and remove the entire brake assembly.
3. If the linings are worn so that the heads of the rivets are near the rubbing surface, the rivets must be drilled out with a $^{11}/_{64}$ in. drill bit and new linings riveted in place.
4. Assemble the components in the reverse order of disassembly. Adjust the brake cable so that the lever on the handlebars moves to within one in. of the handlebar grip with the brake fully applied.

Adjustable Disc Brake

1. Remove the bolt, nut, and inner cable clamp which attach the cable to the brake arm.
2. Remove the outer cable mounting nuts and bracket from the brake mechanism.
3. Remove the stoplight switch.
4. Remove the two bolts and nuts which attach the brake mechanism to the chain case and remove the mechanism.
5. Remove the bolts and push pins which retain the two halves of the caliper.
6. Remove the lining. If worn to less than $^3/_{16}$ in., install new linings.
7. Assemble the components in the reverse order of their disassembly. Adjust the brake and cable as outlined in the "Routine Maintenance" section of this chapter. Adjust the stoplight switch.

Self-Adjusting Disc Brake

1. Remove the bolt, nut, and clamp which attach the inner cable to the brake mechanism.
2. Remove the outer cable mounting nuts and the cable from the brake bracket.
3. Remove the stoplight switch.
4. Remove the bolts and nuts which attach

the brake mechanism to the chaincase and remove the complete mechanism.
5. Use a pair of pliers to pull the wire return spring from the brake bracket mounting tab.
6. Depress the thin steel spring plate with a screwdriver so that the adjusting wheel can be rotated counterclockwise to spread the brake pads apart.
7. Remove the cotter pin and pivot pin from the brake bracket so that the pivoting brake pad and its mounting bracket can be removed.

Removing the wire return spring

Turning the adjusting wheel

8. If the brake lining pads are worn to less than ⅛ in., replace both pads by bending back their mounting tabs.
9. Assemble the components in the reverse order of disassembly, but check the one-way action of the self-adjusting geared wheel and the thin steel ratchet spring before adjusting the brake cable. Adjust the brake cable to allow the brake lever on the handlebars to move to within ½ in. of the handlebar grip with the brake fully applied.

7
Yamaha

INTRODUCTION

Yamaha snowmobiles, produced by Yamaha International Corporation, have long been a part of the snowmobile market. The unique feature of the Yamaha line is the oil injection system which alleviates the need of mixing the oil and gasoline. This system injects the oil into the gas mixture prior to entering the combustion chamber. This is done automatically, at the proper ratio, if it is adjusted correctly.

Yamaha offers a variable-drive ratio which can be altered from 3.5:1 to 1:1 to give maximum acceleration and climbing ability.

IDENTIFICATION NUMBERS— ENGINE AND CHASSIS

The engine serial number is found on the right-side (driver's right) of the carburetor. It

is adjacent to the point where the fan shroud bolts to the engine.

The chassis serial number is on the rear of the machine on the driver's left. The number is located next to the rubber flap which covers the rear of the track.

ROUTINE MAINTENANCE

It is important to note from the first day that routine care and frequent light maintenance can alleviate later costly expenditures. Most frequent checks are necessary if the unit is

Maintenance and Inspection Intervals

Description	20 hours	40 hours	80 hours	Seasonally
Tighten bolts/nuts	X			
Cracks or breakage	X			
Oil leakage	X			
Ignition timing	X			
Abnormal noise	X			
Lights and wiring	X			
Brake functioning	X			
Chassis reinforcements	X			
Power train	X			
Chain housing lubricant	X			
Chain tension		X		
Track tension		X		
Bolts/nuts retightening		X		
Ski alignment		X		
Removal of carbon (complete)				
Spark plug	X			
Cylinder head and			X	
Piston dome		X		
Cleaning/inspection of carburetor			X	
Lubrication		X		

used for great lengths of time over rough or moderately rough terrain.

The information listed in the following chart is recommended by Yamaha as a maximum time guide to general maintenance and lubrication. Terrain, geographical location, and variety of individual use vary from owner to owner. Each owner should, therefore, alter the schedule according to these factors.

Brake Adjustment

1976 AND LATER TWIN-CYLINDER MODELS

Insert a 0.006 in. thick feeler gauge between the disc brake pad's lining and the face of the brake disc (rotor). Loosen the locknut on the adjusting screw and turn the screw in until the brake pad just begins to grip the feeler

Lubrication Chart

Check Point	400 km 20 hrs.	800 km 40 hrs.	1,600 km 80 hrs.	When necessary	Seasonally	Oil/Grease Brand Name
ENGINE:						
Starter case					X	Aeroshell grease #7A or Beacon 325
Oil pump control box		X				Aeroshell grease #7A or Beacon 325
Pump drive cover		X				Aeroshell grease #7A or Beacon 325
Tachometer drive housing		X				Aeroshell grease #7A or Beacon 325
Oil in the oil tank				X		YAMALUBE 2-stroke oil
DRIVE:						
Primary sheave weight	X					Motor oil
Primary shaft and sliding sheave	X					Molybdenum disulfide Snowmobile grease
Front axle housing	X					Shell RETINAX A or General MULTEMP Special #2
Shaft 1 and shaft 2 (Slide rail)			X			Shell RETINAX A or General MULTEMP Special #2
Pivot arm 2 and slider	X					Shell RETINAX A or General MULTEMP Special #2
Drive chain oil replacement					X	SAE 10W/30 motor oil or SE detergent oil
BODY:						
Steering column	X					Shell RETINAX A or General MULTEMP Special #2

Lubrication Chart (cont.)

Check Point	400 km 20 hrs.	800 km 40 hrs.	1,600 km 80 hrs.	When necessary	Seasonally	Oil/Grease Brand Name
Steering links		X				Shell RETINAX A or General MULTEMP Special #2
Ski column		X				Shell RETINAX A or General MULTEMPS Special #2
Ski wear plate		X				Shell RETINAX A or General MULTEMPS Special #2
Ski retaining pin		X				Shell RETINAX A or General MULTEMPS Special #2

gauge. Tighten the locknut and remove the feeler gauge. Adjust the brake cable so that there is 0.021 in. of free-play at the hand lever.

SINGLE-CYLINDER MODELS

Follow the adjusting procedure for the 1976 and later twins to adjust the fixed brake pad, but substitute a 0.040 in. feeler gauge. Adjust the pivoting brake pad at the cable end to give 0.040 in. clearance between the brake and pad face and the brake disc (rotor).

Track Tension and Alignment

The procedures outlined in Chapter 1 should be used to adjust the track tension and the track alignment on Yamaha bogie wheel and slide rail suspension systems. The adjusting bolts are located near the rear corners of the suspension just ahead of the rear (idler) axle.

Ski Alignment

The adjustment of the skis is such that the skis in running position must be perfectly parallel. The parallelism of the skis is checked by measuring from center to center. (The outside of one ski to the inside of the other.) Adjustment of parallelism is accomplished by adjusting the relay rod length.

NOTE: *Measure the distance between the skis (center to center) at the front ends and*

Adjusting track tension on a slide rail type suspension

Checking ski parallelism

at the rear ends respectively. If the difference of the value which is measured exceeds 10 mm, plus or minus, an adjustment is necessary.

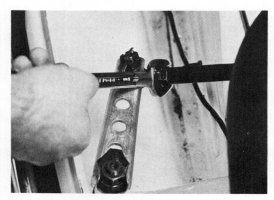

Loosening the tie rod end locknut

TUNE-UP

Spark Plugs

Remove the spark plugs to check and adjust their gaps to the dimensions shown in the "Tune-Up Specifications" chart. When installing the spark plugs, torque them to the value given in the "Torque Specifications" chart.

Breaker Points

REMOVAL AND INSTALLATION

The manual starter, fan shroud, and flywheel must be removed, as outlined in Chapter 1, to remove or replace the breaker points. Adjust the breaker point gap and ignition timing to the figures shown on the "Tune-Up Specifications" chart and install the flywheel fan shroud, and manual starter.

Ignition Timing

CAPACITIVE DISCHARGE IGNITION (CDI)

Follow the sequence described in Chapter 1 to adjust the ignition timing on Yamaha engines equipped with capacitive discharge ignition systems. The correct timing figure is given in the "Tune-Up Specifications" chart in this chapter.

Breaker Point Ignition

Yamaha recommends that the timing on all models be set with a point checker and a dial indicator.

1. Clean the points thoroughly by letting the points snap closed on a piece of business card which has been dipped in lacquer thinner. The card should be drawn from between

the points to remove any residue. Repeat this procedure until the card is thoroughly clean when it is removed. The cleanliness of the points is of great importance.

2. Remove the spark plugs and install the dial indicator (or timing gauge) and adaptor into the right-hand cylinder head.

3. Remove the connector from the four lead wires (gray, orange, black, and green) of the flywheel magneto. Connect the point checker's red lead or one lead from a continuity tester to the flywheel magneto's gray lead wire. Ground the remaining lead of both the point checker and the continuity tester to a suitable ground.

The timing gauge and the continuity tester can be purchased, as a set, at any of the leading snowmobile outlets.

4. Rotate the crankshaft until top dead center is found. This is the point where the needle on the gauge hesitates before it reverses direction. Set the zero reading on the face so that it corresponds with the needle position at this point.

5. With the piston at top dead center, rotate the crankshaft backward until the indicator reads the correct setting (e.g., 1.8 mm. before top dead center).

NOTE: *On units with centrifugal advances, the advance mechanism must be held in the full-advance position before adjusting the breaker points.*

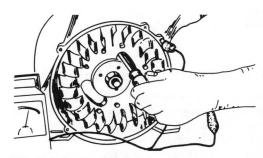

Adjusting the breaker points

6. Point adjustment is performed by loosening the point securing screws and by moving the point set with a slotted screwdriver. Set the points so that they just open (the light just goes out or the gauge registers point opening). This will take a great amount of time at first, but do not get impatient; the performance of your machine is at stake.

7. Tighten the securing screws slowly, as this may affect the timing greatly. The torque of the screws may move the points set position.

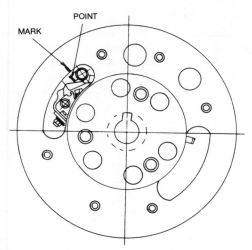

WHEN THE MARK ON THE FLYWHEEL MAGNETO ALIGNS WITH THE POINTER ON THE DINAMO STATOR, A SPARK TAKES PLACE (WITH THE ADVANCED IGNITION TIMING).

POINT

MARK

Breaker point ignition visible through flywheel slots

8. Repeat the above procedure for the left-hand cylinder and the left-hand set of points. The left-hand primary ignition wire is orange.

When the mark on the flywheel magneto aligns with each of both right and left timing marks on the stator (twins), the tops of the pistons are positioned 1.8 mm BTDC respectively.

FUEL SYSTEM

Carburetor

The removal and installation, overhaul, and adjustment of the Mikuni and Keihin carburetors is described in Chapter 2. The initial low and high-speed settings and fuel level for each Yamaha engine are given in the following "Carburetor Specifications" chart. The Autolube oil injection pump is linked to the carburetor so be sure to adjust the oil pump linkage whenever tuning the carburetors or when the carburetor is removed and replaced.

Fuel Pump

The fuel pump on most Yamaha snowmobile engines is an integral part of the carburetor. Consult Chapter 2 for repair or replacement of the fuel pump portion of the Keihin or Mikuni diaphragm-type carburetors.

Fuel Tank

Pump all of the fuel from the tank with a hand held siphon pump. Some Yamahas have a priming pump which can be used for this

Tune-Up Specifications

| Year | Engine Model | Spark Plug | | Point Gap m.m. | (mm B.T.D.C.) Ign. Timing | Idle Speed | Fuel Oil Ratio |
		Number	Gap (in.)				
1976–80	SS338	B9EV	.020–.024	NA	1.6	2000	Auto lube
	SS433	B9EV	.020–.024	NA	1.6	1500	Auto lube
All	E338	BR9EV	.028–.031	NA	1.6	1700	Auto lube
	Y338D	BR7HS	.020–.024	.35 M.M.	1.5	1800	Auto lube
	S433D	BR8EV	.020–.024	.35 M.M.	1.6	1500	Auto lube
1979–80	SA535	BR9ES	.028–.031	NA	1.5	1500	Auto lube
	E294	BR9EV	.028–.031	NA	1.4	1600	Auto lube
1976–80	S246	B8HS	.020–.024	NA	1.2	1300	Auto lube

Carburetor Specifications

Year	Engine Model	Size	No. Used	Carb. Type	Low Speed Set-Turns Off Seat	Hi Speed Set-Turns Off Seat	Fuel Level
1976–80	SS338	PW42X38	1	Keihin	1.0	NA	NA
	SS433	PW42X38	1	Keihin	1¼	NA	NA
All	E338	B38–34	1	Mikuni	1.0	NA	NA
	Y338D	CDX42–38	1	Keihin	1¼	NA	NA
	S433D	CDX42–38	1	Keihin	1.0	NA	NA
1979–80	SA535	BD44–38	1	Keihin	2¼	NA	NA
	E294	B38–32	1	Mikuni	1¼	NA	NA
1976–80	S246	CDX38–32	1	Keihin	2.0	NA	5 MM

purpose or you can buy inexpensive siphon pumps from most snowmobile dealers.

Oil Injection Pump

The lubrication system on Yamaha snow-mobiles is known as the "Autolube Oil Injection System." This system is composed of an oil pump and a separate oil tank. The oil pump is driven by a gear off the crankshaft and it meters the amount of lubricant needed by the engine in all its various load conditions. This variation is accomplished by the connection of the oil pump with the carburetor by means of an actuating rod. The mixture is determined by throttle position. (See

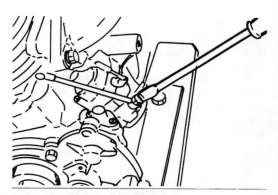

Tightening the oil delivery tube

the "Autolube" section for the correct adjustment procedure).

ENGINE

Removal and Installation

If only the engine is to be removed it is not necessary to remove the magneto assembly. If crankshaft maintenance is to be performed, it is necessary to remove both of these. Maintenance to the magneto assembly and the primary sheaves can be performed with the engine in the snowmobile.

1. Disconnect the taillight connector, which is located at the front of the rider's seat.

2. Loosen the two bolts (with a 10 mm

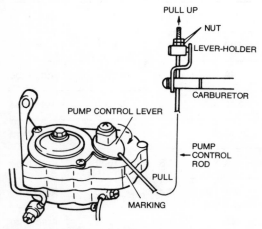

Adjusting points on the autolube system

wrench) which hold the seat. Pull the seat back and raise the rear part.

3. Remove the six screws which hold the air cleaner in position (three exterior and three interior).

4. Remove throttle cable and fuel line from the carburetor. Remove the drive belt shroud on the left-side of the engine. This can be done by loosening the knob at the forward end and then lifting the latch at the rear. Raise the guard a few inches, then pull it toward you.

5. Disconnect the fuel line, the oil line decompressor wire, and the spark plug wire. When removing either oil or gasoline lines, it is advisable to clamp the lines, as neither the oil nor the gasoline tanks have shut-off valves.

6. Disconnect the wire harness from the magneto.

7. Remove the muffler by unfastening the two springs. It may be necessary to raise the muffler slightly when removing the engine.

8. Remove the drive belt by gripping it in the middle and pulling it up. This will provide sufficient slack in the belt to allow it to be slipped off from first the secondary sheave and then the primary sheave.

9. Remove the four engine bolts. It is advisable to remove these bolts so that the lower engine brackets come out with the engine.

10. The engine is now ready for removal. Grasp the engine firmly at each end, slide the assembly back, and lift it out. Place the engine on a level, clean bench for further work.

The removal procedure for all other models are similar to that of the 292, so use this procedure to remove all others.

Top End Disassembly

During disassembly, keep matching parts together (e.g., right piston with right cylinder).

1. Remove the cylinder heads. Each head is held in place by four nuts. Break each of the nuts loose before loosening them all the way.

NOTE: *Upon reassembly, the head bolts are torqued gradually, and in pattern, to 16.5–19.5 ft-lbs.*

2. Remove the cylinders. When lifting off the cylinders, it is best to insert a clean rag around the rod to prevent any carbon or broken parts from falling into the crankcase.

3. The piston assembly can now be removed using needlenose pliers to remove the piston pin retainers. With a soft drift pin, push the piston pin out far enough to allow the piston to be removed from the rod. Be sure to remove the needle bearings in the upper rod end so as not to lose them when the engine is moved.

Removing the exhaust manifold bolts

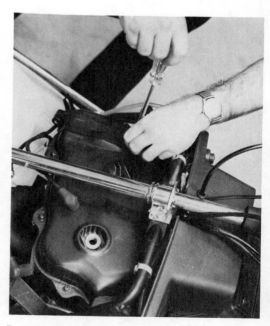

Remove the cooling shroud for access to the cylinders

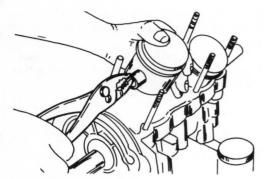

Removing piston pin retainer clip

Installing piston rings

Piston ring stop pins

Top End Assembly

1. Measure the piston-to-cylinder bore wear as outlined in Chapter 1 and check the piston ring end-gap.

2. Fit the piston rings to the piston with the ring ends butted against the tiny pin in each piston ring groove.

3. Install the cylinder barrels and the cylinder heads and torque the nuts in the pattern shown in Chapter 1 to the torque values shown in this chapter.

4. Replace the cooling shroud (if fitted), the exhaust manifold, and the carburetor.

Crankcase

DISASSEMBLY AND ASSEMBLY

The illustration shows the proper sequence for removing the crankcase bolts. This sequence must be followed in order to avoid distortion of the two halves.

After the bolts have been removed, use a soft hammer to tap around the edge of the case. The case should be split by hand. The cases have locating pins. It is imperative that these pins be gathered and kept in a safe location until the cases are reassembled again.

After removal of the crankshaft from the

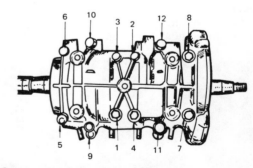

Crankcase bolt tightening sequence

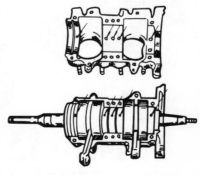

Aligning pin locations

case, the wear of the connecting rod (big end), the crank pin, bearing should be checked. Excessive wear of the connecting rod is checked by measuring the axial play of the connecting rod (small end) when it is moved from side to side with your fingers. The axial play of the connecting rod (small end) when it is moved from side to side with your fingers. The axial play should not exceed 0.08 in. (2 mm). After the crank pin and bearing have been put in their normal positions, maximum axial play should not exceed 0.032–0.040 in.

Use a feeler gauge to measure free-play. Free-play should not be confused with axial play. Free-play is the clearance between the rod and the crankshaft shims. The correct play should be 0.010–0.029 in.

The assembly of the crankshaft into the crankcase should be done with great care. Each of the crankshaft bearings has a lockpin hole in the outer race and two aligning marks offset 90° from the lockpin hole. The aligning marks should be matched with the sealing surface of the upper crankcase half to ensure correct matching of the knock pin in the knock pin hole. Should the crankshaft be assembled in the crankcase halves with the bearings misaligned, the knock pin will be pushed into the body of the crankcase and the bearing will not be properly secured once the crankcase halves are sealed. Damage to

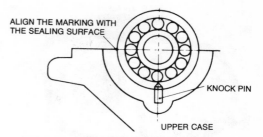

ALIGN THE MARKING WITH THE SEALING SURFACE

KNOCK PIN

UPPER CASE

Cross section of bearing and aligning pin

both the crankshaft and the crankcase can, consequently, occur.

The bottom half of the crankcase can be fitted onto the other half and the crankcase bolts can be inserted. Be sure that the proper torque setting and torque pattern is followed. The correct torque for the crankcase bolts is 7.5 ft-lbs for the initial tightening and 18 ft-lbs for the final torquing. The torque tightening pattern is the same as the loosening pattern shown in disassembly.

Oil Pump

REMOVAL AND DISASSEMBLY

1. Loosen the oil delivery pipe set screw and the oil pump drive gear cover. The cover can be removed by loosening four bolts with a 10 mm box wrench.

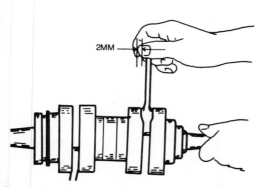

2MM

Connecting rod axial play

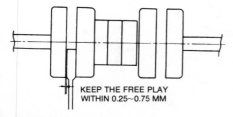

KEEP THE FREE PLAY WITHIN 0.25~0.75 MM

Connecting rod free play

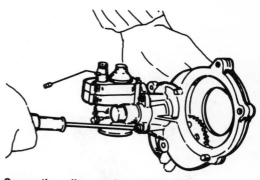

Separating oil pump from drive cover

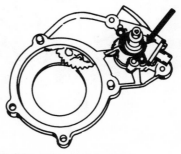

Autolube oil pump gasket

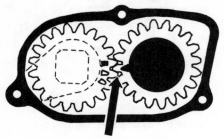

AUTOLUBE GEAR ALIGNMENT
AT IDLE POSITION

ALIGN TIMING MARKS AS SHOWN

Align timing marks

2. The oil pump can be removed with the oil pump drive gear cover.

3. Loosen the two screws which separate the oil pump drive cover from the oil pump.

4. As illustrated, the gasket for the pump case is seen inside the case. It is important that it be reinstalled upon assembly.

5. Remove the three phillips screws from the drive gear cover.

The assembly and installation is the reverse of the removal and disassembly procedure.

AUTOLUBE

The care of the Autolube is very important. It ensures the correct amount of oil injection with the gasoline. The autolube tanks should be supplied with Yamalube oil. With every addition of lubricant, check the rubber hose from the tank to the oil pump for obstructions or pinching.

PUMP ADJUSTMENT

1. Fully open the carburetor throttle valve.

2. Turn the pump control lever so that it matches the mark on the oil pump housing. (Adjustment can be made by turning the pump control rod nuts.)

3. After adjusting, fully tighten the locknuts. This is done by holding the bottom nut while tightening the top nut.

Make a check after each adjustment. Remember, this adjustment is critical. With the throttle completely open, the lever must exactly match the mark on the oil pump casing.

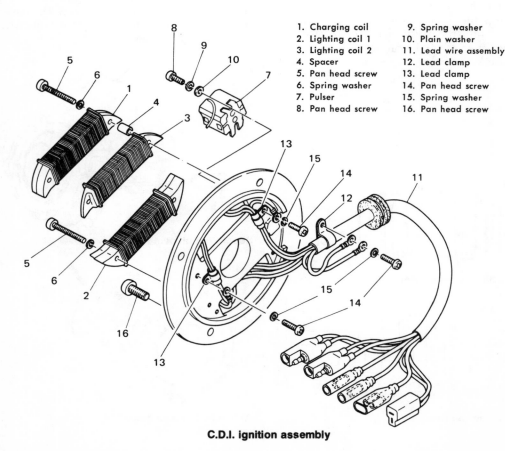

1. Charging coil
2. Lighting coil 1
3. Lighting coil 2
4. Spacer
5. Pan head screw
6. Spring washer
7. Pulser
8. Pan head screw
9. Spring washer
10. Plain washer
11. Lead wire assembly
12. Lead clamp
13. Lead clamp
14. Pan head screw
15. Spring washer
16. Pan head screw

C.D.I. ignition assembly

Flywheel Magneto
REMOVAL

After removing the starter assembly, the magneto assembly may be removed.

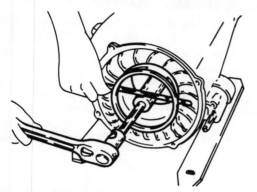

Loosening flywheel center bolt

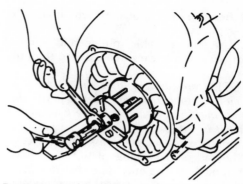

Removing flywheel with puller

1. Using a 26 mm socket, loosen the flywheel securing nut. In order to loosen the nut it is necessary to insert a bar through a hole in the pulley, to steady the flywheel.

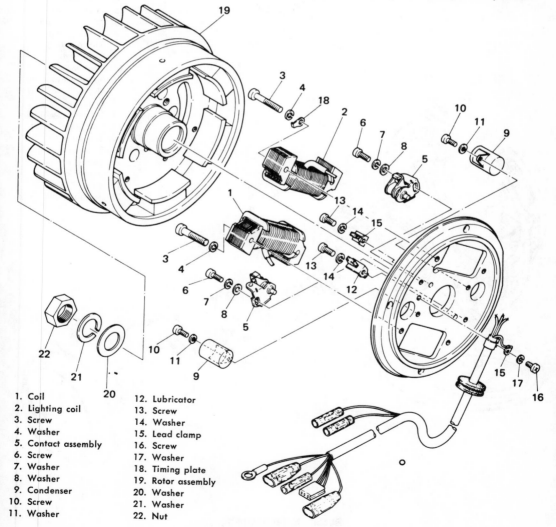

1. Coil
2. Lighting coil
3. Screw
4. Washer
5. Contact assembly
6. Screw
7. Washer
8. Washer
9. Condenser
10. Screw
11. Washer
12. Lubricator
13. Screw
14. Washer
15. Lead clamp
16. Screw
17. Washer
18. Timing plate
19. Rotor assembly
20. Washer
21. Washer
22. Nut

Breaker point ignition assembly

2. Remove the bolts which hold the starter pulley.

3. Use the suitable puller and screws (short ones which are threaded into the pulley).

NOTE: *Immediately after the flywheel is removed, take the woodruff key off the crankshaft and attach it to the flywheel so that it is not lost.*

All parts of the magneto assembly, except for the magneto backing plate, must have been removed. The only time that this plate needs to be removed is in the case of complete engine teardown. The backing plate has to be removed in order to split the cases.

This is done by removing the four hold-down screws.

Starter

REMOVAL AND DISASSEMBLY

1. Remove the four bolts that hold the starter assembly to the engine. The starter mechanism will slide off. Wear protective goggles and gloves.

2. Placing the starter on a level surface, turn it over so that the center nut is facing up. Remove the nut and the washers.

3. The exploded view of the starter assembly is shown. Complete disassembly should

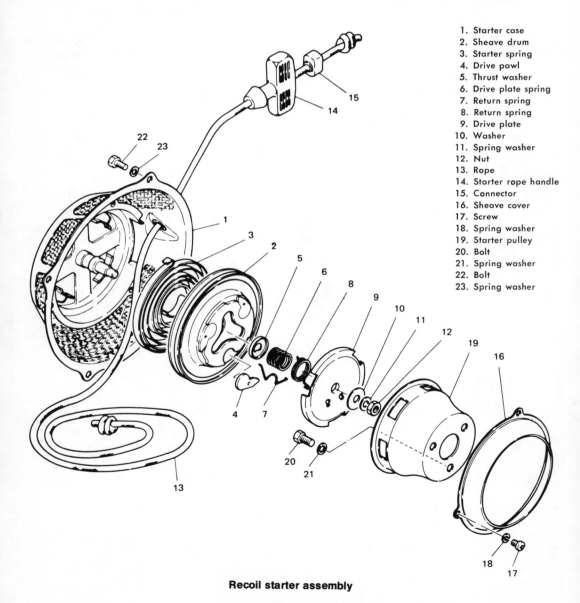

1. Starter case
2. Sheave drum
3. Starter spring
4. Drive pawl
5. Thrust washer
6. Drive plate spring
7. Return spring
8. Return spring
9. Drive plate
10. Washer
11. Spring washer
12. Nut
13. Rope
14. Starter rope handle
15. Connector
16. Sheave cover
17. Screw
18. Spring washer
19. Starter pulley
20. Bolt
21. Spring washer
22. Bolt
23. Spring washer

Recoil starter assembly

only be followed if the starter rope or the return spring has to be replaced.

It is important, when assembling the main return spring, that the spring be installed in the correct position and coiled in the proper direction. The spring is hooked to the center shaft and wound outward in a clockwise direction. The spring must be wound in the correct direction or the starter mechanism will not function. The main spring must be preloaded ⅓–⅔ of a turn for positive return.

Before reinstalling the unit, pull the starter rope out 3–5 in. to see if the starter pawls extend. If this was attached to the engine, these pawls would engage the starter drive. If the pawls do not extend out, then the whole assembly must be disassembled to find the trouble.

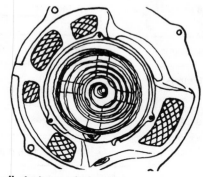

Recoil starter rewind spring

POWER TRAIN

Drive System
SHEAVE ADJUSTMENT

Use the sheave gauge to check the following:
1. Center to center distance between the primary and secondary sheaves.

General Engine Specifications

Year	Engine Model	No. of Cyls.	Displacement (CC)	Bore (MM)	Stroke (MM)	Comp. Ratio
1976–80	SS338	2	338	60	59.6	6.4
	SS433	2	433	68	59.6	7.0
All	E338	2	338	60	59.6	6.5
	Y338D	2	338	60	59.6	6.6
	S433D	2	433	68	59.6	6.7
1979–80	SA535	2	535	73	64	6.0
	E294	2	294	56	59.6	6.5
1976–80	S246	1	246	73	59	6.6

Engine Rebuilding Specifications

Engine Model (cc)	New Piston-to-Cylinder Clearance (in.)	Maximum Piston-to-Cylinder Clearance (in.)	Piston Ring End-Gap (in.)
246	0.0018–0.0020	NA	0.012–0.020
292	0.0018–0.0020	0.0040	0.012–0.020
338	0.0018–0.0020	0.0040	0.012–0.020
433	0.0018–0.0020	0.0040	0.012–0.020

Torque Specifications

ENGINE

Parts	Size	Torque
Spark plug	0.55 in. (14 mm)	18–22 ft lbs
Cylinder head mounting nut	0.3 in. (8 mm)	First: 14 ft lbs Final: 16.6–19.5 ft lbs
CDI rotor mounting nut	0.6 in. (16 mm)	50.6–54.2 ft lbs
Crankcase mounting bolt	0.3 in. (8 mm)	First: 7.2 ft lbs Final: 14.4 ft lbs
Starter pulley mounting bolt	0.3 in. (8 mm)	7.2–8.6 ft lbs
Engine mounting nut	0.4 in. (10 mm)	21.6 ft lbs

DRIVE

Parts	Size	Torque
Primary sheave mounting bolt	0.47 in. (12 mm)	Initial: 43.3 ft lbs Loosen once and retighten to: 28.9 ft lbs
Secondary sheave mounting nut	0.4 in. (10 mm)	21.6–32.5 ft lbs
Bearing housing mounting nut	0.4 in. (10 mm)	36.1–43.3 ft lbs
Chain drive sprocket mounting nut	0.55 in. (14 mm)	36.1–43.3 ft lbs
Chain driven sprocket mounting bolt	0.4 in. (10 mm)	36.1–43.3 ft lbs
Chain housing cap mounting bolt	0.24 in. (6 mm)	2.8–5.0 ft lbs
Chain housing mounting nut	0.3 in. (8 mm)	7.2–11.5 ft lbs
Brake caliper body mounting bolt	0.4 in. (10 mm)	36.1–43.3 ft lbs
Front axle mounting nut	0.87 in. (22 mm)	50.6–52.8 ft lbs
Front axle housing mounting nut	0.3 in. (8 mm)	7.2–11.5 ft lbs
Suspension shaft mounting bolt	0.3 in. (8 mm)	18.0–21.6 ft lbs
Suspension pivot shaft mounting nut	0.4 in. (10 mm)	36.1–43.3 ft lbs
Rear axle mounting bolt	0.4 in. (10 mm)	36.1–43.3 ft lbs

CHASSIS

Parts	Size	Torque
Bumper end bracket mounting bolt	0.3 in. (8 mm)	10.8 ft lbs

Torque Specifications (cont.)

CHASSIS

Parts	Size	Torque
Engine mounting bolt	0.4 in. (10 mm)	21.7 ft lbs
Level gauge holding bolt	0.24 in. (6 mm)	3.6 ft lbs
Ski runner mounting bolt	0.3 in. (8 mm)	10.8 ft lbs
Steering column mounting bolt	0.24 in. (6 mm)	7.2 ft lbs
Bolt securing steering column to gate	0.24 in. (6 mm)	3.6 ft lbs
Steering lower bracket bolt	0.24 in. (6 mm)	7.2 ft lbs
Steering relay rod adjusting nut	0.4 in. (10 mm)	18 ft lbs
Universal joint mounting nut	0.4 in. (10 mm)	18 ft lbs
Outside arm mounting nut	0.4 in. (10 mm)	21.7 ft lbs
Tank fitting band bolt	0.24 in. (6 mm)	1.4–1.8 ft lbs
Double seat rear holding nut	0.3 in. (8 mm)	13.7 ft lbs
Brake lever holding screw and nut	0.2 in. (5 mm)	2.9 ft lbs
Throttle lever holding screw and nut	0.24 in. (6 mm)	5.0 ft lbs
Double seat front holding screw	0.24 in. (6 mm)	2.9 ft lbs

ELECTRICAL

Parts	Size	Torque
CDI unit mounting bolt	0.2 in. (5 mm)	2.9 ft lbs
Taillight unit mounting nut	0.24 in. (6 mm)	3.6 ft lbs
Headlight body mounting nut	0.2 in. (5 mm)	2.5 ft lbs

FITTINGS

Parts	Size	Torque
Latch mounting nut	0.24 in. (6 mm)	5.1 ft lbs
Back-up plate (hinge) mounting nut	0.24 in. (6 mm)	5.1 ft lbs
Lower trim mounting nut	0.2 in. (5 mm)	1–1.4 ft lbs
Windshield mounting screw	0.2 in. (5 mm)	1–1.4 ft lbs

Torque Specifications (cont.)

FITTINGS

Parts	Size	Torque
Front bumper complete (front) mounting nut	0.3 in. (8 mm)	10 ft lbs
Front bumper complete (side) mounting nut	0.3 in. (8 mm)	10 ft lbs
Bumper end mounting bolt	0.2 in. (5 mm)	2.9 ft lbs
Panel instrument mounting bolt	0.24 in. (6 mm)	3.6 ft lbs
Panel instrument rear mounting nut	0.3 in. (8 mm)	13.7 ft lbs

NOTE: *Tightening torque tolerance is: +20%*
−10%

Standard Torque Specifications

Nut	Bolt	Torque	
		ft lbs	in. lbs
10 mm	6 mm	7.0	85
13 mm	8 mm	15	175
14 mm	8 mm	15	175
17 mm	10 mm	25–30	300–350
19 mm	12 mm	30–35	350–400
22 mm	14 mm	30–35	400–400
26 mm	17 mm	40–50	500–600
27 mm	18 mm	40–50	500–600
30 mm	20 mm	50–60	600–700
14 mm spark plug		20–22	230–250
12 mm spark plug		11–15	130–175
10 mm spark plug		7–9	85–100

2. Off set between the inside edges of the sheaves.

3. Alignment of the sheaves.

If any of these is incorrect, proceed as follows:

NOTE: *The main purpose of this adjustment is to bring the sheaves in alignment and also to align the center of the carburetor with that of the silencer.*

1. Incorrect distance. Loosen the engine mounting bolts and move the engine back and forth.

2. Incorrect off-set. By moving the engine sideways, align the center of the carburetor with that of the silencer, and tighten the engine mounting bolts. Next, place the sheave gauge over the sheaves, and adjust

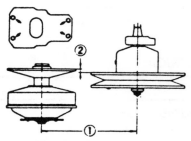

1. Sheave distance:
   270^{+0}_{-3} mm ($10.6^{+0}_{-0.11}$ in)
2. Sheave off-set:
   5.5 ± 0.5 mm (0.217 ± 0.020 in)

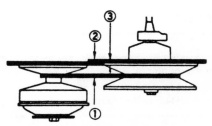

1. Sheave gauge 1
2. Sheave gauge 2
3. 5.5 mm (0.217 in)

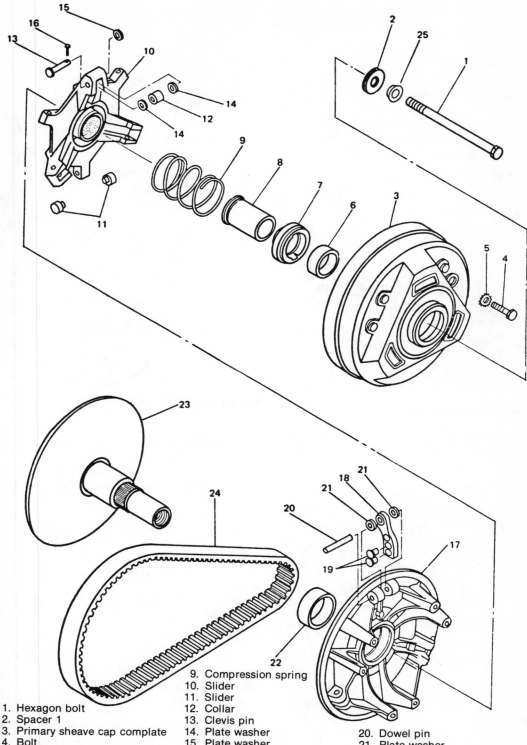

1. Hexagon bolt
2. Spacer 1
3. Primary sheave cap complate
4. Bolt
5. Toth washer
6. Bushing (90387-41017)
7. Spring sheath
8. Collar
9. Compression spring
10. Slider
11. Slider
12. Collar
13. Clevis pin
14. Plate washer
15. Plate washer
16. Cotter pin
17. Primary sliding sheave
18. Weight
19. Counter sunk rivet
20. Dowel pin
21. Plate washer
22. Bushing
23. Primary fixed sheave complete
24. V-belt
25. Conical spring washer

Drive clutch assembly

the sheave off-set correctly by changing spacer position from right to left or vice versa.

REMOVAL

1. Remove the V-belt.
2. Remove the primary sheave mounting bolt.
3. Using the primary fixed sheave puller, remove the primary fixed sheave from the crankshaft.

DISASSEMBLY

1. Install the sheave subassembly tool on the primary sheave.

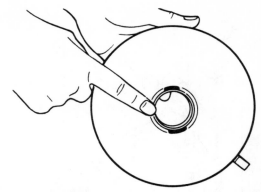

Inspect bushing for wear

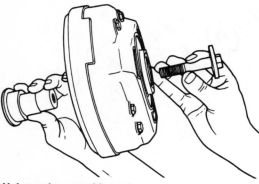

Using sub assembly tool

2. Loosen the six bolts securing the primary sheave cap and sliding sheave.

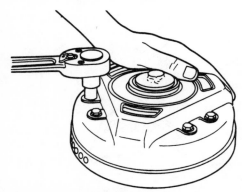

Remove six bolts from cover

3. Remove the sheave subassembly tool. The primary sheave cap and sliding sheave can now be disassembled.
4. Remove the sliding sheave and cap bushing.

INSPECTION

1. Check the tapered ends of the crankshaft and primary fixed sheave for scratches.

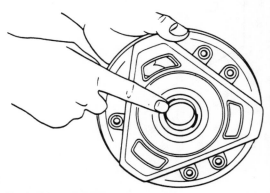

Inspect bushing for wear

If scratched unduly, replace. If scratches are minor, burnish with crocus cloth.

2. If the cap bushing is worn more than specified below, it should be replaced with a new one.
3. Check the compression spring for free length. If excessively fatigued, replace.
4. Check the spider for smooth movement.
5. Check both sheaves for warping. If warped replace.
6. Check the tightness of sliding sheave and cap bushing.

REASSEMBLY

1. Oil the points shown. Do not apply the grease on the portion of X marks. For other parts, oiling is unnecessary.
2. Install the component parts to the sliding sheave and the sheave cap.
NOTE: *When installing the spider in the primary sliding sheave, be sure to align the X mark on the spider with that on the sheave.*
3. Install the sheave subassembly tool and tighten the cap.

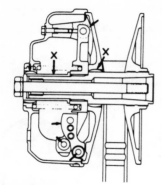

Align X alignment marks

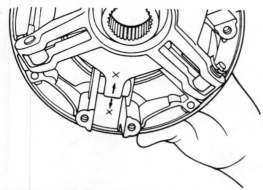

Align X marks on spider and sheave

4. Tighten the six primary sheave cap bolts and remove the subassembly tool.

5. Install the sliding sheave and cap bushing.

6. Clean the tapered portions of crankshaft and fixed sheave.

7. Fit the fixed sheave to the tapered portion of crankshaft, and fit the sliding sheave to the fixed sheave.

8. Tighten the primary sheave bolt.
Tightening torque:
Initial: 6 m-kg

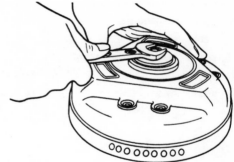

Installing sub assembly tool

Loosen once and retighten: 4~4.5 m-kg

Secondary Sheave

SECONDARY SHEAVE SETTING

It is advisable to change the secondary sheave setting to correspond to the race course and snow conditions. This is done by changing the secondary spring preload.

The spring seat (See illustration) has 4 spring holes. The spring tension (preload) can be adjusted by selecting a spring in the seat and twisting the seat to engage the sheave ramps. In this way the preload can be adjusted in 30° steps.

NOTE: *That spring should be used.*

BELT ADJUSTMENT

The torque converter drive belt alignment and tension are adjusted by moving the engine. A pair of adjusting bolts and locknuts are located at the rear of the engine for fore-and-aft alignment. The forward engine mounting bolts must be loosened before the engine can be moved. Use a metal straight-edge to see that the sides of the two pulleys are exactly parallel. The drive belt should

SNOW CONDITION:	PACKED SNOW OR ICY SNOW	
MODEL:	440A	
SPRING COLOR CODE AND PART NO.:	YELLOW / 90508-54286	
	SPRING POSITION (SPRING SEAT 8A7-17684-00)	TWIST (SPRING) 120°
SECONDARY SPRING SETTING:		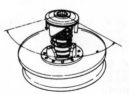

SNOW CONDITIONS:	PACKED SNOW OR ICY SNOW
MODEL:	340A
SPRING COLOR CODE AND PART NO.:	BLUE / 90508-45287

SPRING POSITION (SPRING SEAT 8A5-17684-01)   TWIST (SPRING) 150°

SECONDARY SPRING SETTING:

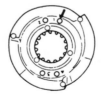   

SNOW CONDITION:	WET SNOW
MODEL:	440A
SPRING COLOR CODE AND PART NO.:	YELLOW / 90508-54286

SPRING POSITION (SPRING SEAT 8A7-17684-00)   TWIST (SPRING) 180°

SECONDARY SPRING SETTING:

SNOW CONDITION:	WET SNOW
MODEL:	340A
SPRING COLOR CODE AND PART NO.:	BLUE / 90508-45287

SPRING POSITION (SPRING SEAT 8A5-17684-01)   TWIST (SPRING) 210°

SECONDARY SPRING SETTING:

deflect 0.40 in. with firm hand-pressure at a point midway between the two pulleys.

Drive Chain and Sprockets
ADJUSTMENT

Adjust the chain tension by loosening the locknut on chain adjuster bolt, then turn adjusting bolt either in or out to obtain the proper tension, retighten lock nut.

SUSPENSION

Track
TENSION AND ALIGNMENT

The steps described in Chapter 1 should be used to align the track and to adjust the track tension. The track tension is measured by pulling down the center of the lower run of the track with a special tension-checking

---

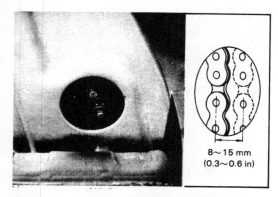

8~15 mm
(0.3~0.6 in)

1. Lock nut   2. Adjusting bolt

Loosen lock nut and turn bolt to adjust chain tension

scale. With a 22 lb downward pull, the 15 in. wide track should move one in. from the slide rail or bogie wheels on all, but the GPX-series Yamahas; the 18 in. wide track should move ⅝ in. with a 22 lb pull. The GPX 338F and GPX 433F track should move 0.69 in. with a 22 lb pull and the track on the GPX 338G and GPX 433G machines should move 0.60–0.80 in. from the slide rails' rubbing surface. Check the track tension on both sides of the track.

REMOVAL AND INSTALLATION

The complete slide rail or bogie wheel suspension and the track drive axle must be re-

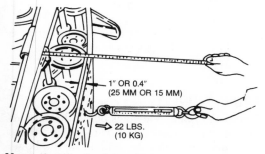

1" OR 0.4"
(25 MM OR 15 MM)

22 LBS.
(10 KG)

Measuring the track tension

moved to replace the track on most Yamaha snowmobiles. The machine can be placed on its side to remove and replace the track or suspension. Track tension and alignment adjustments must be performed with the snowmobile upright as outlined in Chapter 1.

If the center link plate of the drive track comes off the sprocket, the drive track will be quickly worn due to the contact between the rubber center pieces and the sprocket. The drive track should therefore, be checked frequently.

Front Axle

REMOVAL

1. Loosen both track adjusters at the rear of the snowmobile. In order to do this, the locktabs must be bent away from the adjusting bolts as this will make the removal of the chaincase and front axle easier.

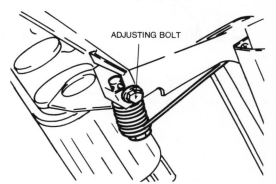

ADJUSTING BOLT

Track adjusting bolts

2. Move to the front, left-side of the vehicle (driver's left) and you will locate the bottom chaincase cover.

3. Remove the six retaining bolts and remove the chaincase cover. An oil drip pan should be placed beneath the snowmobile as oil will drain out of the chaincase when the cover is removed.

NOTE: *This cover need only be removed if the driven sprocket is to be changed.*

4. Moving to the right-side of the snowmobile, pry off the rubber cap in the center of the axle housing.

5. Remove the axle nut and spring washer with a 26 mm socket wrench.

6. Loosen the three bolts (10 mm) which hold the axle housing and remove the housing.

7. Reach in with your hand, grasp the axle, and pull it out as far as possible (about one in.).

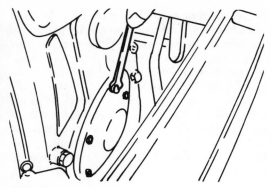

Chaincase cover

Remove axle brg. retainer bolts

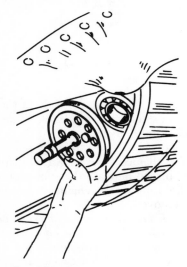

Front axle removal

8. It is now possible to work the sprocket off the end of the axle and lift it out of the snowmobile. The sprocket is a spline-fit to the axle.

9. It is necessary, before going further, to either raise the rear of the vehicle or to tip it onto its side.

10. Once this is done, reach underneath the snowmobile and lift the axle as far as possible so the tip of the axle will extend out the chaincase hole.

11. This should allow enough room to take hold of the right end of the axle and pull it free of its housing on the right-side.

12. Pull the right end of the shaft backward and downward, pulling the shaft free.

13. When the front axle is removed, the track will drop out. This completes the removal of the front axle.

Rear Axle
REMOVAL

1. Prop up the rear of the snowmobile.

2. Disconnect the torsion springs. The strength of the rear spring can be adjusted to two different positions according to snow and running conditions.

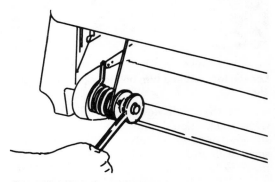

Removing bolt through chassis

3. To make the steering more positive, the rear spring should be hung on the front hook to raise the rear of the machine. To increase traction, the rear spring should be hung on the rear hook to lower the rear of the machine.

4. Once the springs are disconnected, remove the rear pivot bolts which run through the middle of the rear torsion springs (one on each side).

5. The rear axle will drop free of the frame once these two bolts are removed.

Bogie Wheels

Each set of bogie wheels is bolted to the bottom of the chassis. The removal of these bolts, one on each side, will allow the bogie wheel assembly to be removed from the

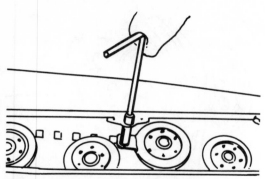

Adjusting the bogie wheel suspension

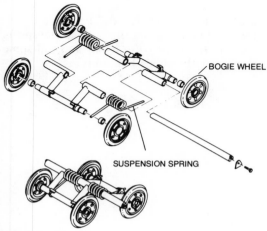

BOGIE WHEEL

SUSPENSION SPRING

Bogie components

chassis. It should be noted that the bolts are secured with lockwashers. These must be replaced.

The individual bogie wheels are riveted together and cannot be disassembled. The bearings are of the sealed type and do not require lubrication.

NOTE: *If the snowmobile is immobile or stored for more than a week, the rear of the machine should be raised and placed on blocks. This will prevent the rubber bogie wheels from flattening under the weight of the machine.*

Slide Rail Suspension
REMOVAL AND INSTALLATION

1. Remove the pivot arm bolts from the outside faces of the chassis on both the right and left-sides. The complete slide rail suspension unit can then be removed from inside the track.

2. A single phillips head screw retains the

plastic slide rail bearing to each slide rail. Remove the screws, slide the worn bearings off, and slide the new bearings into position to replace the screws.

3. The eye bolts must be loosened to replace any broken springs.

4. Reverse the removal sequence to install the slide rail unit.

Steering and Skis

It is important that the steering column support, relay rod, outside arms, and ski columns all be checked for tightness as often as possible. Loosening and excessive wear of any of these components can cause poor handling. The steering column support on the steering gate should be disassembled and lubricated periodically. The ski columns should be lubricated with grease every 20 hours. Lubrication of all other steering linkage should be done every 40 hours.

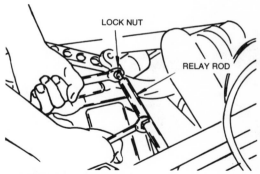

LOCK NUT

RELAY ROD

Adjusting the tie rod

SKIS

Tightness of the steeering column to the steering linkage system is very important in controlling parallelism of the skis while the snowmobile is in forward movement. The skis are supported on five leaf springs which are pivoted at the rear of the ski and are free to expand and contract on the wear plate. This wear plate should be greased often to reduce the friction between the spring and the wear plate.

BRAKE SYSTEM

The brake pads are located on the left-side of the snowmobile (driver in riding position)

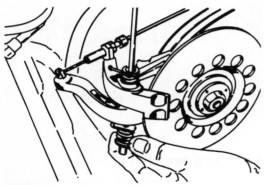

Brake pad removal

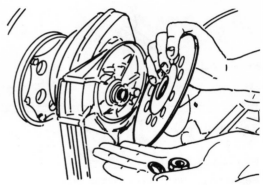

Brake disc removal

and on the outside of the chaincase. The brake pads are removed by pulling the single pivot pin. Once the pin is pulled, the brake pads can be pulled out of the way to allow the

brake disc to be removed. The brake disc is removed by removing the nut and the spring washer, the brake disc itself, and, on some machines, the shims behind it.

Appendix

General Conversion Table

Multiply by	To convert	To	
2.54	Inches	Centimeters	.3937
30.48	Feet	Centimeters	.0328
.914	Yards	Meters	1.094
1.609	Miles	Kilometers	.621
.645	Square inches	Square cm.	.155
.836	Square yards	Square meters	1.196
16.39	Cubic inches	Cubic cm.	.061
28.3	Cubic feet	Liters	.0353
.4536	Pounds	Kilograms	2.2045
4.226	Gallons	Liters	.264
.068	Lbs./sq. in. (psi)	Atmospheres	14.7
.138	Foot pounds	Kg. m.	7.23
1.014	H.P. (DIN)	H.P. (SAE)	.9861
——	To obtain	From	Multiply by

Note: 1 cm. equals 10 mm.; 1 mm. equals .0394″.

Conversion—Common Fractions to Decimals and Millimeters

INCHES			INCHES			INCHES		
Common Fractions	Decimal Fractions	Millimeters (approx.)	Common Fractions	Decimal Fractions	Millimeters (approx.)	Common Fractions	Decimal Fractions	Millimeters (approx.)
1/128	.008	0.20	11/32	.344	8.73	43/64	.672	17.07
1/64	.016	0.40	23/64	.359	9.13	11/16	.688	17.46
1/32	.031	0.79	3/8	.375	9.53	45/64	.703	17.86
3/64	.047	1.19	25/64	.391	9.92	23/32	.719	18.26
1/16	.063	1.59	13/32	.406	10.32	47/64	.734	18.65
5/64	.078	1.98	27/64	.422	10.72	3/4	.750	19.05
3/32	.094	2.38	7/16	.438	11.11	49/64	.766	19.45
7/64	.109	2.78	29/64	.453	11.51	25/32	.781	19.84
1/8	.125	3.18	15/32	.469	11.91	51/64	.797	20.24
9/64	.141	3.57	31/64	.484	12.30	13/16	.813	20.64
5/32	.156	3.97	1/2	.500	12.70	53/64	.828	21.03
11/64	.172	4.37	33/64	.516	13.10	27/32	.844	21.43
3/16	.188	4.76	17/32	.531	13.49	55/64	.859	21.83
13/64	.203	5.16	35/64	.547	13.89	7/8	.875	22.23
7/32	.219	5.56	9/16	.563	14.29	57/64	.891	22.62
15/64	.234	5.95	37/64	.578	14.68	29/32	.906	23.02
1/4	.250	6.35	19/32	.594	15.08	59/64	.922	23.42
17/64	.266	6.75	39/64	.609	15.48	15/16	.938	23.81
9/32	.281	7.14	5/8	.625	15.88	61/64	.953	24.21
19/64	.297	7.54	41/64	.641	16.27	31/32	.969	24.61
5/16	.313	7.94	21/32	.656	16.67	63/64	.984	25.00
21/64	.328	8.33						

Conversion—Millimeters to Decimal Inches

mm	inches	mm	inches	mm	inches	mm	inches	mm	inches
1	.039 370	31	1.220 470	61	2.401 570	91	3.582 670	210	8.267 700
2	.078 740	32	1.259 840	62	2.440 940	92	3.622 040	220	8.661 400
3	.118 110	33	1.299 210	63	2.480 310	93	3.661 410	230	9.055 100
4	.157 480	34	1.338 580	64	2.519 680	94	3.700 780	240	9.448 800
5	.196 850	35	1.377 949	65	2.559 050	95	3.740 150	250	9.842 500
6	.236 220	36	1.417 319	66	2.598 420	96	3.779 520	260	10.236 200
7	.275 590	37	1.456 689	67	2.637 790	97	3.818 890	270	10.629 900
8	.314 960	38	1.496 050	68	2.677 160	98	3.858 260	280	11.032 600
9	.354 330	39	1.535 430	69	2.716 530	99	3.897 630	290	11.417 300
10	.393 700	40	1.574 800	70	2.755 900	100	3.937 000	300	11.811 000
11	.433 070	41	1.614 170	71	2.795 270	105	4.133 848	310	12.204 700
12	.472 440	42	1.653 540	72	2.834 640	110	4.330 700	320	12.598 400
13	.511 810	43	1.692 910	73	2.874 010	115	4.527 550	330	12.992 100
14	.551 180	44	1.732 280	74	2.913 380	120	4.724 400	340	13.385 800
15	.590 550	45	1.771 650	75	2.952 750	125	4.921 250	350	13.779 500
16	.629 920	46	1.811 020	76	2.992 120	130	5.118 100	360	14.173 200
17	.669 290	47	1.850 390	77	3.031 490	135	5.314 950	370	14.566 900
18	.708 660	48	1.889 760	78	3.070 860	140	5.511 800	380	14.960 600
19	.748 030	49	1.929 130	79	3.110 230	145	5.708 650	390	15.354 300
20	.787 400	50	1.968 500	80	3.149 600	150	5.905 500	400	15.748 000
21	.826 770	51	2.007 870	81	3.188 970	155	6.102 350	500	19.685 000
22	.866 140	52	2.047 240	82	3.228 340	160	6.299 200	600	23.622 000
23	.905 510	53	2.086 610	83	3.267 710	165	6.496 050	700	27.559 000
24	.944 880	54	2.125 980	84	3.307 080	170	6.692 900	800	31.496 000
25	.984 250	55	2.165 350	85	3.346 450	175	6.889 750	900	35.433 000
26	1.023 620	56	2.204 720	86	3.385 820	180	7.086 600	1000	39.370 000
27	1.062 990	57	2.244 090	87	3.425 190	185	7.283 450	2000	78.740 000
28	1.102 360	58	2.283 460	88	3.464 560	190	7.480 300	3000	118.110 000
29	1.141 730	59	2.322 830	89	3.503 903	195	7.677 150	4000	157.480 000
30	1.181 100	60	2.362 200	90	3.543 300	200	7.874 000	5000	196.850 000

To change decimal millimeters to decimal inches, position the decimal point where desired on either side of the millimeter measurement shown and reset the inches decimal by the same number of digits in the same direction. For example, to convert 0.001 mm into decimal inches, reset the decimal behind the 1 mm (shown on the chart) to 0.001; change the decimal inch equivalent (0.039″ shown) to 0.000039″.

Decimal Equivalent Size of the Letter Drills

Letter Drill	Decimal Equivalent	Letter Drill	Decimal Equivalent	Letter Drill	Decimal Equivalent
A	.234	J	.277	S	.348
B	.238	K	.281	T	.358
C	.242	L	.290	U	.368
D	.246	M	.295	V	.377
E	.250	N	.302	W	.386
F	.257	O	.316	X	.397
G	.261	P	.323	Y	.404
H	.266	Q	.332	Z	.413
I	.272	R	.339		

Tap Drill Sizes

Screw & Tap Size	National Fine or S.A.E. Threads Per Inch	Use Drill Number
No. 5	44	37
No. 6	40	33
No. 8	36	29
No. 10	32	21
No. 12	28	15
$\frac{1}{4}$	28	3
$\frac{5}{16}$	24	1
$\frac{3}{8}$	24	Q
$\frac{7}{16}$	20	W
$\frac{1}{2}$	20	$\frac{29}{64}$
$\frac{9}{16}$	18	$\frac{33}{64}$
$\frac{5}{8}$	18	$\frac{37}{64}$
$\frac{3}{4}$	16	$\frac{11}{16}$
$\frac{7}{8}$	14	$\frac{13}{16}$
$1\frac{1}{8}$	12	$1\frac{3}{64}$
$1\frac{1}{4}$	12	$1\frac{11}{64}$
$1\frac{1}{2}$	12	$1\frac{27}{64}$

Screw & Tap Size	National Coarse or U.S.S. Threads Per Inch	Use Drill Number
No. 5	40	39
No. 6	32	36
No. 8	32	29
No. 10	24	25
No. 12	24	17
$\frac{1}{4}$	20	8
$\frac{5}{16}$	18	F
$\frac{3}{8}$	16	$\frac{5}{16}$
$\frac{7}{16}$	14	U
$\frac{1}{2}$	13	$\frac{27}{64}$
$\frac{9}{16}$	12	$\frac{31}{64}$
$\frac{5}{8}$	11	$\frac{17}{32}$
$\frac{3}{4}$	10	$\frac{21}{32}$
$\frac{7}{8}$	9	$\frac{49}{64}$
1	8	$\frac{7}{8}$
$1\frac{1}{8}$	7	$\frac{63}{64}$
$1\frac{1}{4}$	7	$1\frac{7}{64}$
$1\frac{1}{2}$	6	$1\frac{11}{32}$

Decimal Equivalent Size of the Number Drills

Drill No.	Decimal Equivalent	Drill No.	Decimal Equivalent	Drill No.	Decimal Equivalent
80	.0135	53	.0595	26	.1470
79	.0145	52	.0635	25	.1495
78	.0160	51	.0670	24	.1520
77	.0180	50	.0700	23	.1540
76	.0200	49	.0730	22	.1570
75	.0210	48	.0760	21	.1590
74	.0225	47	.0785	20	.1610
73	.0240	46	.0810	19	.1660
72	.0250	45	.0820	18	.1695
71	.0260	44	.0860	17	.1730
70	.0280	43	.0890	16	.1770
69	.0292	42	.0935	15	.1800
68	.0310	41	.0960	14	.1820
67	.0320	40	.0980	13	.1850
66	.0330	39	.0995	12	.1890
65	.0350	38	.1015	11	.1910
64	.0360	37	.1040	10	.1935
63	.0370	36	.1065	9	.1960
62	.0380	35	.1100	8	.1990
61	.0390	34	.1110	7	.2010
60	.0400	33	.1130	6	.2040
59	.0410	32	.1160	5	.2055
58	.0420	31	.1200	4	.2090
57	.0430	30	.1285	3	.2130
56	.0465	29	.1360	2	.2210
55	.0520	28	.1405	1	.2280
54	.0550	27	.1440		

Wind Chill Index

TEMP. F°	35	30	25	20	15	10	5	0	-5	-10	-15	-20	-25	-30	-35	-40	-45
MPH* ⬇	(EQUIVALENT TEMPERATURE)																
	Equivalent in cooling power on exposed flesh under calm conditions																
CALM	35	30	25	20	15	10	5	0	-5	-10	-15	-20	-25	-30	-35	-40	-45
5	33	27	21	16	12	7	1	-6	-11	-15	-20	-26	-31	-35	-41	-47	-54
10	21	16	9	2	-2	-9	-15	-22	-27	-31	-38	-45	-52	-58	-64	-70	-77
15	16	11	1	-6	-11	-18	-25	-33	-40	-45	-51	-60	-65	-70	-78	-85	-90
20	12	3	-4	-9	-17	-24	-32	-40	-46	-52	-60	-68	-76	-81	-88	-96	-103
25	7	0	-7	-15	-22	-29	-37	-45	-52	-58	-67	-75	-83	-89	-96	-104	-112
30	5	-2	-11	-18	-26	-33	-41	-49	-56	-63	-70	-78	-87	-94	-101	-109	-117
35	3	-4	-13	-20	-27	-35	-43	-52	-60	-67	-72	-83	-90	-98	-105	-113	-123
40	1	-4	-15	-22	-29	-36	-45	-54	-62	-69	-76	-87	-94	-101	-107	-116	-128
45	1	-6	-17	-24	-31	-38	-46	-54	-63	-70	-78	-87	-94	-101	-108	-118	-128
50	0	-7	-17	-24	-31	-38	-47	-56	-63	-70	-79	-88	-96	-103	-110	-120	-128

MPH* Wind or Snowmobile MPH

Increased Danger of Freezing Exposed Flesh ☐   Great Danger of Freezing Exposed Flesh ▨